JANE AUSTEN

THE PARSON'S DAUGHTER

A familiar sight to Jane Austen: her father's
bookplate. (*British Museum*)

A

FATHER's INSTRUCTIONS

TO HIS

CHILDREN:

CONSISTING OF

TALES, FABLES,

AND REFLECTIONS;

DESIGNED TO PROMOTE

THE LOVE OF VIRTUE,

A TASTE FOR KNOWLEDGE,

AND

AN EARLY ACQUAINTANCE WITH

THE WORKS OF NATURE.

LONDON:

PRINTED FOR J. JOHNSON, ST. PAUL'S CHURCH-YARD,
MDCCLXXVI.

Title page to *A Father's Instructions to his Children* (1776).
(*John Rylands University Library of Manchester*)

Jane Austen

The Parson's Daughter

Irene Collins

hambledon
continuum

Hambledon Continuum
A Continuum imprint

The Tower Building
11 York Road
London, SE1 7NX

80 Maiden Lane
Suite 704
New York, NY 10038

First Published 1998 in hardback
This edition published 2007 in paperback

ISBN 1 85285 172 4 (hardback)
ISBN 1 85285 562 2 (paperback)

A description of this book is available from
the British Library and from the Library of Congress

Typeset by Carnegie Book Production, Lancaster
Printed by Biddles Ltd, King's Lynn, Norfolk

Contents

Illustrations

Between Pages 74 and 75

1   The Revd George Austen, Jane's father, as a young man
    (*Jane Austen Memorial Trust*)

2   The Revd George Austen in 1801, the year of his
    retirement (*Jane Austen Memorial Trust*)

3   St John's College, Oxford, where George Austen and,
    later, his sons James and Henry were Fellows
    (*Cambridge University Library*)

4   Jane Austen: steel engraving (1869) from Cassandra
    Austen's sketch

5   The only known image of Mrs George Austen, Jane's
    mother. A silhouette, *c.* 1800 (*Jane Austen Memorial Trust*)

6   Eliza Hancock, Jane's cousin, a few years before her
    marriage to the Comte de Feuillide (*Jane Austen Memorial
    Trust*)

7   Cassandra Austen, after her sister Jane's death. Undated
    silhouette (*Private Collection*)

8   The Revd James Austen, Jane's eldest brother.
    A miniature, *c.* 1790 (*Jane Austen Memorial Trust*)

9   Jane's fourth brother, Henry, in preaching bands.
    A miniature, *c.* 1820 (*Jane Austen Memorial Trust*)

10 Jane's brother, Francis William (Frank). A miniature, 1796
    (*Jane Austen Memorial Trust*)

Text Illustrations

Preface

An unprecedented number of biographies of Jane Austen, each with a distinctive view of her life and character, has appeared in recent years. Despite their virtues, they have failed to recognise a central fact about Jane Austen: she was a deeply religious woman. Her Christian convictions have either been ignored or mentioned briefly and with apparent reluctance, as though they formed an embarrassing topic likely to make Jane Austen unapproachable to present-day readers. They need not do so, for her religion was of a lively and practical kind which added greatly to her happiness and to her understanding of human nature. To neglect an influence which she encountered every day is to misinterpret her background and give a distorted view of her personality and outlook.

To understand fully the depth and spontaneity of her religious commitment, it is necessary to give more attention to her early life than recent biographers have done. No lover of Jane Austen would wish to underestimate the importance of the tranquillity she enjoyed during her later years at Chawton or of the fulfilment she achieved there: the cottage she lived in with her mother and sister is a centre of interest, affection and inspiration for thousands. It was as the parson's daughter at Steventon, however, that Jane Austen learnt to live and work in a religious environment, to take life seriously and enjoy it fully. It was there that she practised the art of writing, produced early versions of two of her six novels and wrote a third which had received only minor additions when it emerged in its final form. Her nephew, James Edward Austen-Leigh, described the twenty-five years that Jane Austen spent in her father's parsonage as the formative period of her life, and referred to Steventon as 'the cradle of her genius'.

My previous book, *Jane Austen and the Clergy*, used Jane Austen's life and writings to illuminate the contemporary church and in doing so to explain the significance of the clerical characters in her novels. The present book focuses on Jane Austen herself and seeks to explain what it was like to be a parson's daughter in the last decades of the eighteenth century. Other writers have mentioned external factors such as the likely number of rooms at Steventon parsonage and the mediocre level of the rector's income, which are by no means unimportant but cannot be regarded as the heart of the matter.

Admittedly there are problems involved in trying to look closer. Jane's father, the Revd George Austen, in spite of his manifest influence is a somewhat shadowy figure. Research by Deirdre La Faye, Maggie Lane and George Holbert Tucker has produced important information regarding his origins, career and family connections, but his ideas and beliefs are scantily recorded. From his own hand we have merely a few letters to near relatives and a memorandum which he wrote when his son Francis was about to go to sea. The letters are printed in *Austen Papers*; the memorandum has been published only in part, by J. H. and E. C. Hubback in their study of *Jane Austen's Sailor Brothers*. Through the good offices of Deirdre Le Faye, I have been privileged to read a transcript of the memorandum, whose original is in the possession of the great grandson of Admiral Sir Francis Austen. The unpublished part of the document gives a fascinating insight into George Austen's method of teaching religion, and makes one wish that more of his compositions had survived. One of his sermons, which was extant when Emma Austen-Leigh published a short account of *Jane Austen and Steventon* in 1937, has since disappeared.

The collection of Jane Austen's letters to her sister Cassandra, which is the major source regarding her adult life, does not cover her childhood and adolescence: the first letter is dated 9–10 January 1796, when the writer was twenty. There are hints of earlier experiences in her juvenile stories and in her novels – particularly *Northanger Abbey*, whose heroine is also a parson's daughter; but Jane Austen was not fond of writing about children. She was reticent about religion. Her brother Henry published a biographical notice of her shortly after her death, and her niece Anna joined her nephew James Edward in recalling memories of the parsonage in George Austen's time and in gathering as much information as they could about Jane Austen's life there, but Henry's essay is brief and James Edward's memoir sparse, and both are coloured to some extent by changes in attitude during the period of time which intervened.

This book is an attempt to interpret the available evidence in the light of its historical context and thereby to give greater substance to the reader's knowledge of Jane Austen's early life, of the influences which formed her outlook and of the beliefs which permeate her novels.

Writing it has been an enjoyable task, because the Steventon years were for the most part a hopeful time in Jane Austen's life. Like all her admirers, I must be for ever grateful for her continuing presence.

Acknowledgements

I would like to thank Deirdre le Faye for providing a transcript of George Austen's 'Memorandum' to his son Frank; and the great grandson of Admiral Sir Francis Austen for allowing me to cite it. Tom Carpenter of the Jane Austen Memorial Trust, Chawton, assisted with the illustrations. Martin Sheppard of Hambledon Press has made many helpful suggestions at all stages of the book.

The author and the publisher are grateful to the following for permission to reproduce illustrations: the Jane Austen Memorial Trust, Chawton, pls 1, 2, 5, 6, 8, 9, 10, 11, 16; Bath City Library, p. 189, pls 20, 21; the British Library, pp. 67, 91; the British Museum, p. i; Cambridge University Library, pl. 3; Hampshire Record Office, p. 55; the John Rylands University Library of Manchester, pp. ii, xxii, 25; the President and Fellows of St John's College, Oxford, p. 157.

Introduction

Jane Austen was born in her father's parsonage at Steventon in Hampshire in 1775, the seventh child in a family of eight. Her nephew, James Edward Austen-Leigh, was afterwards of the opinion that Jane was fortunate in being the daughter of a clergyman, for it meant that she grew up in a more cultured environment than she would have found in a gentry household at the time. He was referring, he said, not to 'that higher section of country gentlemen who went into Parliament and mixed in London society and took the lead in several counties' but to the large number of smaller landed proprietors who also counted as gentlemen but who 'seldom went further from home than their county town'. The majority of landowners in Hampshire were in this category when the Austens arrived at Steventon: such was their lack of manners and refinement that the squire of the neighbourhood, 'a man of broad acres', was obliged to ask the parson whether Paris was in France or France in Paris, his wife having been 'disputing with him about it'.

> In those days a rector who chanced to be a gentleman and a scholar found himself superior to his chief parishioners in information and manner, and became a sort of centre of politeness and refinement.[1]

During the ensuing decades the standard of culture among the gentry improved to the extent that Jane Austen, in her novel *Emma*, could describe a country squire who provided 'books of engravings', 'drawers of medals' and other scholarly collections to entertain an honoured guest, whilst even a tenant farmer read selections of poetry and sang ballads to his sisters and their school friend in the evenings. Her nephew did not hesitate to attribute such improvement to the influence of the clergy.[2] Jane nevertheless found herself better educated than the majority of the gentry, to whose ranks she was admitted by virtue of her father's profession.

Jane Austen had a great many clergy relatives. Her maternal grandfather and her great uncle had been clergymen; so were her godfather, one of her uncles, two of her brothers and four of her cousins. Her sister became engaged to a clergyman and of the young men who are known or believed to have been Jane's suitors three were clergy. She was acquainted with a great many other clergymen, for they were thick on the ground in rural areas, where the rest of the population was small. A young woman travelling to different parts of southern England, as Jane Austen did, would meet clergymen as a matter of course at the houses of relatives and friends, for they were in great demand at card parties, dinner parties and dances: Jane's published correspondence alone mentions over ninety clergymen with whom she was acquainted. She became knowledgeable on all aspects of clergy life in country parishes, especially the intricacies of patronage: the clergy who appear in her novels are an important source of information for historians of the church and of late eighteenth-century and Regency England. Vicarages were the kind of house she knew best: as Nikolaus Pevsner pointed out, she decribed them in her novels in much greater detail than she accorded to gentry houses.[3] Above all, she became imbued with the modes of thought which characterised the mainstream of the Church of England to which she belonged.

Jane's father, the Revd George Austen, was born in 1731 and educated at Oxford in the 1740s and 1750s, when the Enlightenment was a major influence. Generations of historians have made the mistake of assuming that, although England gave birth to the Enlightenment in the works of Isaac Newton and John Locke, Englishmen promptly abandoned the movement to writers on the continent of Europe whose readers were in greater need of it. At the same time, undue reliance on the memoirs of Edward Gibbon has led many to the conclusion that the universities of Oxford and Cambridge, though ostensibly devoted to training clergymen for the Church of England, were in fact given over to idleness and dissipation. This is far from the truth. England shared to the full the increasing respect for human nature and the growing confidence in human abilities which led to more civilised attitudes. Enthusiasm for Newtonian science, especially astronomy, spread rapidly among the educated public, both male and female, and Locke's ideas on education were paramount throughout the eighteenth century. The vigorous defence of the rights of Parliament and the ever-increasing diffusion of newspapers and journals made England a model of freedom for many people on the Continent, including Voltaire. At the universities, idleness and dissipation were confined in the main to gentlemen commoners and their hangers on. Less privileged undergraduates, with more concern for their future careers, received conscientious guidance from tutors in the colleges. The physical sciences were not taught as a specific part of the undergraduate syllabus at either university, but this hardly mattered at a time when scientific discoveries were considered a part of general knowledge which could be incorporated into other branches of learning. Both Oxford and Cambridge remained staunch in defence of the established faith, yet their theologians, unlike their counterparts on the Continent, were not hostile to the new learning. On the contrary, they produced, in the work of such writers as Richard Watson, William Paley and Joseph Butler, an interpretation of Christian doctrine which reconciled belief in the scriptures with the evidence of science and philosophy.[4]

The many benefits bestowed by the Enlightenment included a growing respect for individuals as equal participants in a common humanity. Within families, the husband's power over the wife and the father's power over his children markedly declined, although the former was still embodied in the laws of property and the latter was difficult to escape until children could finance their own independence. It was increasingly regarded as contemptible for parents to force a young woman or pressurise a young man into an uncongenial partnership for their own gain. The dangers inherent in this new attitude were not ignored: much emphasis was placed on the need for personal desires to be guided by reason. In England, the Established Church was in a strong position to promote the ideal of a middle way. In the wedding service, marriage was likened to 'the mystical union that is betwixt Christ and his Church', which implied that the relationship should have both a loving and a practical content. Many couples found the balance difficult to achieve, and Jane Austen was to be as adept in revealing the tensions which ensued as she was convincing in her support of the church's ideal. The new ideas regarding the relationships between parents and children also raised problems. Patriarchal tyranny was condemned, but obedience on the part of the children was believed to be necessary if fatherly guidance and protection were to be maintained. The church still taught the law of Moses: 'Honour thy father and thy mother, that thy days may be long in the land which the Lord thy God giveth thee.' It was beginning to be recognised, however, that a law designed to safeguard the inheritance of property could not reasonably be applied in all circumstances. The church had not yet officially adapted its teaching to this view, but a clergyman of sense could arrive at a compromise, as the Revd Mr Morland does when confronted with Henry Tilney's rebellion against his father's unjustifiable demands.[5] Jane Austen's awareness of these nuances made it possible for her to introduce her readers to families which, for all their different customs and conventions, have remained recognisable to this day.

During the middle ages, the parish clergy had been expected to do little beyond administer the sacraments and preside over rites of passage. The religious troubles of the seventeenth century made the leaders of the Church of England aware of the need to expand these duties to include instructing the nation in Protestant doctrine, as envisaged at the Reformation.[6] With this in mind, the clergy in the course of the eighteenth century became a graduate profession. The sermon was given prominence in church services by being preached from a high pulpit, often in the middle of the congregation. Cooperation with the ruling classes in a mission that was believed to be of mutual benefit was symbolised by a special pew for the local squire and his family, either in the chancel or at the front of the nave.

George Austen brought up his large family in the humane, thoughtful, searching tradition he had himself encountered at Oxford – a tradition to which Jane was particularly responsive. The books she was given to read as a child, and others to which she had access in her father's library as a girl, had a profound influence on the cast of her mind. Under her father's guidance, Jane learnt to regard Christianity as a reasonable and practical doctrine which made sense in this world as well as offering hope for the next. She was encouraged to seek proofs of the existence and beneficence of God not only by reading religious works but by observing nature and studying human behaviour: her interest in landscape and in theories of the Picturesque stemmed from this teaching, as did her delight in observing ordinary men and women of the professional and gentry classes in their domestic surroundings. She was encouraged to strengthen her faith by prayer and worship, but to make her witness in the world through her behaviour to others rather than by preaching: in her writings, as in her life, she was to be typically reticent with regard to religious devotion and to concentrate instead on providing examples of good and evil in people's conduct towards each other and in their attitude to society at large. Morality is a major concern of all her novels.

Among so numerous a body as the clergy of the Church of England there were bound to be differences of intellect and attitude, just as, among the gentry, there would be some who were not prepared to listen to long discourses and achieve familiarity with the work of leading divines. George Austen was typical of a certain section of the clergy in the second half of the eighteenth century, in that he aspired to win respect for his profession and influence for his teaching not by joining with the local gentry in boisterous country pursuits but by adopting a cultivated style of living. His wife, Cassandra Leigh, came from an appropriate background, both scholarly and genteel. Between them they brought up Jane to move in the same circles. They naturally hoped she would marry, but this did not mean that her training was either exclusively domestic or entirely frivolous. As an Enlightenment scholar, George Austen believed that Jane should use her reasoning powers to enlarge her understanding and, as a Christian, he knew that it was her duty to improve her talent. Both he and his wife encouraged her writing, and George Austen was liberal enough to try and help her to become a published author.

The last years of Jane's life at Steventon coincided with Britain's war against Revolutionary France, which ended with the Peace of Amiens in 1802, the year after her father retired. This phase of the conflict, more than the fight against Napoleon which followed, was regarded in many quarters as a religious war, and George Austen, along with the clergy in general, was called upon to play a part in the nation's war effort. Thanks to his own learning and his wife's connections, he had also managed to educate his sons to enter gentlemanly professions: hence, when war broke out, Jane had two brothers serving as officers in the navy; and a third was soon to take a commission in the militia. Whilst the two sailor brothers acquainted her with the hazards and excitements of war, Henry Austen, as a militia officer, introduced her to its glamour. She also experienced the tragedy of war, for her sister's fiancé died in 1797 on one of Britain's ill-fated expeditions to the West Indies. She had not needed this experience to arouse her hatred of the enemy, for her first cousin, Eliza, whom she dearly loved, was visiting England when it was learnt that her husband, a captain in the French army, had been guillotined by the Jacobins.

In spite of her knowledge of the war, Jane never used it as a major theme of a novel. She does, however, provide numerous insights into it. Interestingly, although her brothers Frank and Charles continued to serve in the navy throughout the wars – Frank commanding a battleship in the great chase after Villeneuve across the Atlantic and winning commendation from Nelson – it is her brothers' experiences in the early, Revolutionary phase of the war, fought whilst Jane was at Steventon, that feature most clearly in her novels.

The clergy of the Church of England varied enormously in wealth.[7] In country parishes, their income came mainly from glebe (an area of land which had been donated to the church by faithful parishioners for the benefit of the incumbent) and tithe (the right of the clergy to receive a tenth of the annual gross product of all cultivated land in the parish). In some parishes the glebe consisted of a mere field whilst in others it could amount to sixty acres or more. The value of tithe varied not only with the fertility of the land in the parish but with the area it covered. The majority of England's 10,000 parishes were tiny. During a discussion in Parliament in 1802 it was ascertained that, for one reason and another, 1000 of the benefices in the country were worth less than £100 a year, whilst a further 3000 ranged between £100 and £150, at a time when the latter sum was thought insufficient to provide more than the barest necessities for a single man. Incomes could be increased by securing more than one parish, but this seldom resulted in affluence. The Revd Edmund Nelson, with three parishes in Norfolk, would probably not have been able to meet the expense of sending a son to sea: Horatio was fortunate in having an uncle who, as Captain of a naval vessel, could take him on board under his own protection.[8] The wealthiest clergy were those who either possessed a private income, as was the case with Jane Austen's friend Tom Chute of The Vyne, or were lucky enough to secure a cathedral appointment along with a clutch of parishes. One of Jane's uncles, the Revd Dr Edward Cooper, was in this latter category and could afford to give his daughter every advantage in life.

George Austen, whose income from one small parish rose from £110 a year at the outset to perhaps £600 at the end of his career, was not amongst the poorest of clergy as his family grew up; but money was usually in short supply. Jane could expect no dowry. At first, this does not seem to have mattered to her a great deal. Her family had many friends amongst the gentry in the neighbourhood of Steventon: she was invited to parties and balls, and looked forward to the years ahead with spirit and confidence. Discussions on marriage, which had often taken place at the parsonage, encouraged her to think that she would meet someone she could love – someone who would love her in return and who would have the means to support her. Unfortunately, the acumen which enabled her to reproduce in her novels the subtle class distinctions operating in gentry society gradually made her aware – perhaps too much aware – of her position on its fringes. This was especially the case when she stayed with her brother Edward in Kent, among families wealthier than those in the neighbourhood of Steventon. Her self-confidence deteriorated rapidly when her father retired and she no longer had the backing of his position as parish priest: in the next few years she is thought to have turned down two advantageous proposals of marriage, possibly, in part at least, because she did not want to figure as socially inferior to her husband.

It is tempting in a more secular age to assume that life in a religious household was dull and repressive and that any liveliness and initiative shown by Jane were signs of rebellion. There is no evidence that this was the case. On the contrary, there is every reason to believe that her life as a parson's daughter was disciplined but also fun, and that she appreciated it to the full. Family networks were of great importance in the eighteenth century: it was expected of Jane that she would visit relatives elsewhere whenever possible. Her father was also happy to have her visit Bath (a popular resort of clergy families) and London too, when occasion offered. George Austen was not alone amongst the clergy in encouraging amateur dramatics. He was probably not alone, either, in his enjoyment of novels (including the popular gothic mysteries of the time), although he was among a minority of men prepared to admit to reading them. The twenty-five years that Jane spent as the parson's daughter at Steventon should leave us with no surprise that her novels are both serious of purpose and entertaining to read. It was during this period, as James Edward Austen-Leigh saw, that 'the real foundations of her fame were laid'.[9]

QUID DULCIUS HOMINUM GENERI A
NATURA DATUM EST, QUAM SUI CUIQUE
LIBERI?

CICERO.

Epigram facing title page of *A Father's Instructions to his Children* (1776). 'What sweeter thing is given by nature to men than their own children?'

Chapter 1

A Goodly Heritage

In the summer of 1775, Mrs Cassandra Austen wrote from her husband's rectory at Steventon in Hampshire to her sister-in-law Susannah Walter at Tonbridge with the news that she was pregnant and expected to be confined 'some time in November'. She wrote cheerfully, but childbirth was a dangerous business in the eighteenth century and she had probably already arranged for her other sister-in-law, Philadelphia Hancock, to come from London to assist with the nursing. London, on account of the reputed skill of its doctors, was considered at the time to be quite the best place for a confinement; and although Mrs Austen, unlike Mrs Shandy, was too much of a countrywoman to wish to go to London for her lying-in, she liked to secure attention from someone well versed in the latest medical practices there.[1]

To the surprise of all concerned in the matter, November came and went without sign of the expected birth. It was not until mid December that the Revd George Austen was able to assure Mrs Walter that all was well and that he and his wife now had a baby girl whom they were going to call Jenny. 'You have doubtless been for some time in expectation of hearing from Hampshire, and perhaps wondered a little that we were in our old age grown such bad reckoners', he wrote. She might indeed have wondered, for her step-brother George and his wife, though not exactly old at forty-four and thirty-six, were not inexperienced either: this was their seventh child. Mrs Austen had had trouble with some of her pregnancies in the past, but this time all had gone well: the birth had been rapid and the mother had been pronounced out of danger on the very next day. Judging by his letter, George Austen was delighted to have a little girl this time: five of the other six children were boys, and his little Cassy, almost three, needed a playmate.[2]

Father and mother gave the new baby all possible care, for the times were hazardous for infants. Of the 20,514 deaths recorded by the *Annual Register* for the year of Jane Austen's birth, almost half were of children under the age of five. George Austen, in accordance with the best practice of the church, baptised the child on the day after her birth. The custom of swaddling babies in tight bands had disappeared from all but the most backward homes, and even stays were becoming uncommon except in the form of a long, quilted bodice; but it was still believed necessary to protect babies from every breeze that blew. The winter of Jane Austen's birth being exceptionally severe, with strong winds uprooting trees and deep snow obliterating lanes and hedgerows, she was kept snugly indoors until the spring.[3]

The parsonage in which she was born, and in which she was to live for the first twenty-five years of her life, was pulled down shortly after her death and nobody can be sure just what it was like. It had been in existence as a clergyman's dwelling since at least the end of the seventeenth century, when it was mentioned in a diocesan report. George Austen saw it for the first time in 1761, when he was appointed rector of the parish by a kinsman, Thomas Knight of Godmersham. It apparently struck him as being a poor place. Like the majority of parsonages, it was probably little better than a labourer's cottage, for the clergy had long been expected to make do with the peasant accommodation that had satisfied their celibate predecessors before the Reformation. Attitudes were changing, but improvement had not yet reached Steventon. In more than half the parishes in England the landowner had the sole right of appointing the parish priest, and as landowners grew more prosperous they sometimes invested in the future by refurbishing or rebuilding their parsonages. A commodious and handsome house, it was thought, would be the more likely to attract an incumbent of education and breeding, fit to dine at his benefactor's table and assist him in his various duties as employer, counsellor and often magistrate in the locality. Unfortunately, the gentleman who owned the vast estate of which Steventon was a part, and whose right it was to appoint the parish priest, did not reside in the area. Thomas Knight of Godmersham, who had inherited the land and the advowson in 1738 from a distant relative of his wife's, continued to live in Kent, spending much of his time rebuilding his own mansion in Palladian style. He appears to have had little interest in Steventon or in any of the other parishes over which he exercised patronage, except as a means of fulfilling his obligations to members of his wife's family. In 1757 he had appointed one of the latter, the Revd Henry Austen, as rector of Steventon. Henry Austen showed no more intention than his benefactor of living in the parish: like many another rector, he let out the glebe for rent, appointed a deputy to collect the tithes and left the duties of the parish to be carried out by a curate, to whom he gave a modest stipend out of his own pocket. The curate – a less favoured relative, the Revd Thomas Bathurst – was a bachelor, with neither the incentive nor the means to improve his dwelling.[4]

When in 1761 Henry Austen resigned the living at Steventon for pastures new, the position was handed on to Mrs Knight's second cousin, the Revd George Austen, a young man she could scarcely, if ever, have met. After swearing before a magistrate the required oath of loyalty to King George III, George Austen was instituted as rector of Steventon in the parish church of St Nicholas and proceeded to look around his domain. He was not unduly dismayed by the dilapidated state of the parsonage house, for he too had no immediate intention of residing in the parish. He was happily employed as assistant chaplain and tutor in classics at St John's College, Oxford. All dons liked to have a parish to their name as an added dignity, a supplement to their income, and an alternative occupation and place of residence should they wish to leave their celibate profession. Until such a time came, George Austen could simply take over the rents and tithes at Steventon from the previous rector and employ the Revd Thomas Bathurst to take services as usual.

George Austen's ambitions had long been focused on an academic career. He had advanced in life by means of his academic abilities, for although he was descended from wealthy clothiers who had later become landowners in Kent his own branch of the family had suffered hard times. His grandfather, John Austen, had spent money lavishly as a young man and then died before coming into his inheritance. His widow had brought up their young children as best she could. The eldest, another John, eventually inherited the family estate at Broadford; a second son, Francis, was apprenticed to a lawyer, did well, married profitably and became rich; but another, William (later George's father), was obliged to be content with becoming a surgeon – a profession not well thought of at the time. He too died young, leaving no provision in his will for his children by his first wife. His second wife promptly cast them off. The daughter, Philadelphia, was looked after by an aunt until she was old enough to be shipped out to India to find a husband; her brother George fared rather better in that he was taken up by his rich Uncle Francis, who paid for him to be educated at Tonbridge School. At the age of sixteen, George was nominated to one of the school's scholarships to St John's College, Oxford, where he took a B.A. degree in 1751. Elected to a Fellowship, he decided to stay on at college and study divinity until he was old enough at twenty-three to enter the church. After ordination and a brief spell as assistant master at his old school, he returned in 1758 to St John's. A taste for university politics brought him to the notice of fellow dons; a year as Junior Proctor marked him out for further advancement. If he had remained unmarried, he might have stayed at Oxford for the rest of his life.[5]

His good fortune in obtaining the rectorship of Steventon, at a time when a superfluity of clergy doomed many to remain as curates all their lives, opened up new possibilities for him. The parish he had been lucky enough to obtain was small and poorly endowed; but the income was what was known as 'improvable'. The glebe covered only three acres, but Thomas Knight had other land to let out: the incumbent would have no difficulty in setting up as a gentleman farmer. The tithes yielded only £100 a year, which was hardly enough to enable a cultured man to maintain a decent standard of living; but the area was fertile, the farmers were enclosing land and, with advances in agriculture rapidly gaining ground, the yields were likely in the future to be far from contemptible. There was the possibility too of combining the parish with that of Ashe or Deane. The patrons of both these nearby parishes had been known in the past to sell their right to choose the incumbent – a practice so common among patrons that interested persons (such as John Dashwood in *Sense and Sensibility*)[6] were able to make a rough estimate of the possible market price for any such transaction, based on the yield from tithes and glebe, the value of the parsonage and the life expectancy of the existing incumbent. George Austen reckoned that, if the presentation to Ashe or Deane should come on the market again, Uncle Francis could perhaps be persuaded to buy one or the other for the benefit of his nephew. In the event he bought both, in order to be able to present George to the one whose incumbent died first. There would be no difficulty in getting the bishop's approval for so mild a degree of pluralism. At least a third of the clergy of the Church of England held more than one parish, and who could blame them if it was the only way of making a decent living?[7]

Steventon was better off than a great many other parishes in that there was at least a parsonage house of sorts, which Thomas Knight as patron could be expected to improve if George Austen decided to take a wife and move in. Provided it were made spacious enough, the couple could adopt a practice that was becoming increasingly common among clergy in country parishes and set up a school for paying pupils. At university the clergy followed the same syllabus as all undergraduates other than a few studying law or medcine; hence, they were considered admirably suited to the task of educating gentlemen's sons.

When it came to seeking a bride, George Austen had other assets

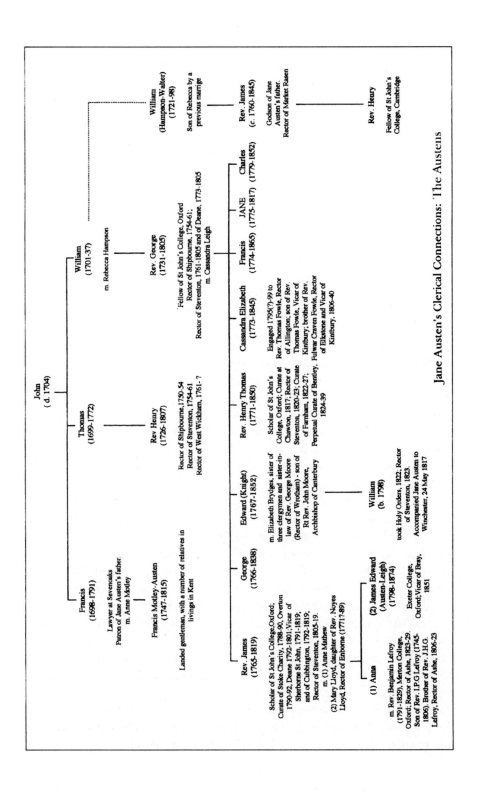

John
(d. 1704)

Francis
(1698-1791)

Lawyer at Sevenoaks
Patron of Jane Austen's father.
m. Anne Motley

Francis Motley-Austen
(1747-1815)

Landed gentleman, with a number of relatives in
living in Kent

William
(1701-37)

m Rebecca Hampson

Thomas
(1699-1772)

Rev. Henry
(1726-1807)

Rector of Shipbourne,1750-54
Rector of Steventon, 1754-61
Rector of West Wickham, 1761- ?

Rev. George
(1731-1805)

Fellow of St John's College, Oxford
Rector of Shipbourne, 1754-61;
Rector of Steventon, 1761-1805 and of Deane, 1773-1805.
m. Cassandra Leigh

William
(Hampson-Walter)
(1721-96)

Son of Rebecca by a
previous marrige

Rev. James
(c. 1760-1845)

Godson of Jane
Austen's father.
Rector of Market Rasen

George
(1766-1838)

Edward (Knight)
(1767-1852)

m. Elizabeth Brydges, sister of
three clergymen and sister-in-
law of Rev. George Moore
(Rector of Wrotham) - son of
Rt Rev. John Moore,
Archbishop of Canterbury

Rev. Henry Thomas
(1771-1830)

Scholar of St John's
College, Oxford; Curate at
Chawton, 1817; Rector of
Steventon, 1820-23; Curate
of Farnham, 1822-27;
Perpetual Curate of Bentley.
1824-39

Cassandra Elizabeth
(1773-1845)

Engaged 1795(?)-99 to
Rev. Thomas Fowle, Rector
of Allington; son of Rev.
Thomas Fowle, Vicar of
Kintbury; brother of Rev.
Fulwar Craven Fowle, Rector
of Elkstone and Vicar of
Kintbury, 1806-40

Francis
(1774-1865)

JANE
(1775-1817)

Charles
(1779-1852)

Rev. Henry
Fellow of St John's
College, Cambridge

Rev. James
(1765-1819)

Scholar of St John's College,Oxford;
Curate of Stoke Charity, 1788-90, Overton
1790-92, Deane 1792-1801;Vicar of
Sherborne St. John, 1791-1819;
and of Cubbington, 1792-1819;
Rector of Steventon, 1805-19.
m. (1) Anne Mathew
(2) Mary Lloyd, daughter of Rev. Noyes
Lloyd, Rector of Enborne (1712-89)

(1) Anna

m. Rev. Benjamin Lefroy
(1791-1829), Merton College,
Oxford; Rector of Ashe, 1823-29.
Son of Rev. I.P.G Lefroy (1745-
1806). Brother of Rev. J.H.G.
Lefroy, Rector of Ashe, 1806-23

(2) James Edward
(Austen-Leigh)
(1798-1874)

Exeter College,
Oxford; Vicar of Bray,
1851

William
(b. 1798)

took Holy Orders, 1822; Rector
of Steventon, 1823.
Accompanied Jane Austen to
Winchester, 24 May 1817

Jane Austen's Clerical Connections: The Austens

besides his parochial prospects. He was tall and handsome, with a fine head of light-brown curly hair and remarkably bright dark eyes: during his year of office he had been known at Oxford as 'the Handsome Proctor'. He was well-mannered and conversable, with a strong sense of humour and a lively interest in his fellow men. He was *persona grata* wherever he went.

By 1763 he had met and become engaged to Cassandra, younger daughter of the Revd Thomas Leigh, rector of Harpsden near Henley-on-Thames. She was an amusing and intelligent woman, accustomed to the conversation of learned men. Her uncle, Theophilus Leigh, was Master of Balliol and a legend throughout the university for his wit; her father had been elected a Fellow of All Souls at so early an age that he was ever afterwards called 'Chick' Leigh. Cassandra also prided herself on her descent from Sir Thomas Leigh, Lord Mayor of London in Queen Elizabeth's time and founder of a family which included the titled Leighs of Stoneleigh Abbey. Her own branch of the family, the Adlestrop Leighs, remained at a more modest gentry level, though one member, her grandfather, had married a sister-in-law of Cassandra, Duchess of Chandos, and bequeathed the name to the family as a reminder of the connection. The Revd Thomas Leigh and his wife, in short, counted both Oxford scholars and county families among their friends and associates. Such a background was important to George Austen in choosing a wife, for if he was to become a parish priest he intended to be one of a new type just coming into prominence: no longer a yeoman farmer but a scholar and a gentleman. Jane Austen in *Persuasion* was to assign the same ambition to Charles Hayter, one of her fictional clergymen she intended her readers to admire.[8]

Until comparatively recent times, most of the clergy occupying the small parishes of rural England had come from peasant families and had been notoriously unlearned. Those who had attended university had done so as 'poor scholars', obtaining free board and lodging in return for service at meals and in chapel. Though not uneducated, they could fairly be described as uncultured. They married servant girls and farmers' daughters, for no gentleman would risk marrying his daughter to a clergyman whilst there was still a threat of reversion to Roman Catholicism and its celibate priesthood. By the mid eighteenth century, however, young men from middle-class professional and property-owning families were entering the church in greater numbers. They were both more ambitious than their predecessors and more aware of the learning and culture prevalent in fashionable circles. After associating at university with men destined for the highest ranks of government

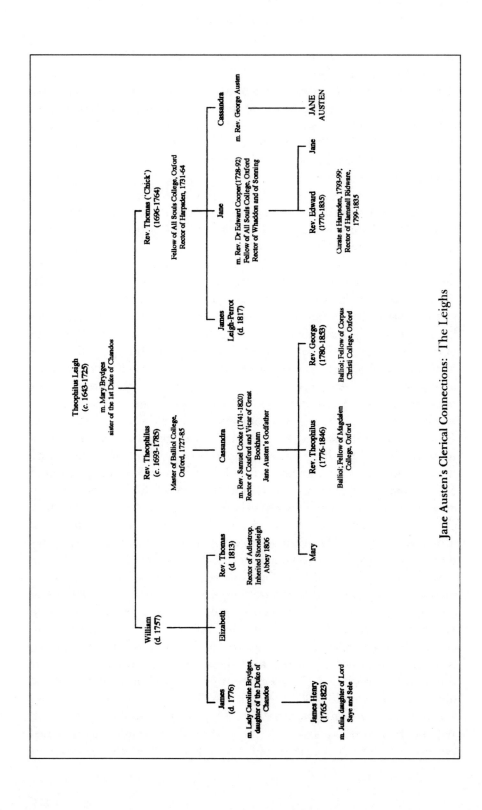

Theophilus Leigh
(c. 1643-1725)

m. Mary Brydges
sister of the 1st Duke of Chandos

Rev. Theophilus
(c. 1693-1785)

Master of Balliol College,
Oxford, 1727-85

Rev. Thomas ('Chick')
(1696-1764)

Fellow of All Souls College, Oxford
Rector of Harpsden, 1731-64

William
(d. 1757)

Cassandra

m. Rev. Samuel Cooke (1741-1820)
Rector of Cotsford and Vicar of Great
Bookham
Jane Austen's Godfather

Jane

m. Rev. Dr Edward Cooper(1728-92)
Fellow of All Souls College, Oxford
Rector of Whaddon and of Sonning

Cassandra

m. Rev. George Austen

James
Leigh-Perrot
(d. 1817)

Elizabeth

Rev. Thomas
(d. 1813)

Rector of Adlestrop.
Inherited Stoneleigh
Abbey 1806

JANE
AUSTEN

Jane

Rev. Edward
(1770-1835)

Curate at Harpsden, 1793-99;
Rector of Hamstall Ridware,
1799-1835

James
(d. 1776)

m. Lady Caroline Brydges,
daughter of the Duke of
Chandos

Rev. Theophilus
(1776-1846)

Balliol; Fellow of Magdalen
College, Oxford

Rev. George
(1780-1833)

Balliol; Fellow of Corpus
Christi College, Oxford

Mary

James Henry
(1765-1823)

m. Julia, daughter of Lord
Saye and Sele

Jane Austen's Clerical Connections: The Leighs

and society, they hoped to win respect for their profession and enter the most genteel circles in their locality. They needed wives who could not only provide them with intelligent companionship in their remote country vicarages but who could be introduced without embarrassment to the families of the neighbouring gentry. With the defeat of Jacobitism in the '45 rebellion, the Protestant ascendancy was safe at last, and clergymen could begin to present themselves to the gentry as suitable marriage prospects for their daughters. The Revd Thomas Leigh, in his late sixties and about to retire to Bath for his health, had two daughters still unmarried. They had excellent credentials but little money. He naturally welcomed the addresses of a respectable clergyman to the younger of the two sisters.[9]

George and Cassandra were married on 26 April 1764 at the smart new classical-style church of St Swithin in the parish of Walcot in Bath, the bride fashionably dressed in a suit of scarlet cloth, the jacket flared at the waist. The ceremony was performed by a friend of the bride's family, the Revd Thomas Powys, younger son of Philip Lybbe-Powys of Hardwick House, Oxfordshire. Powys had recently been given the living of Fawley in Buckinghamshire and was supplementing his income by taking pupils, as George Austen intended to do. One of his pupils later became Marquis of Camden, with valuable patronage to bestow on his former tutor: under his aegis, Tom rose rapidly in the church hierarchy. It is thought that Cassandra Leigh had once turned down an offer of marriage from him: if so, his subsequent wealth seems to have caused her no regrets.[10] Her marriage with George Austen was happy enough to withstand the normal strains and stresses of life without loss of affection or respect. The lady was of a determined and managing nature, cheerful when active but inclined to worry unduly about problems in which she could not intervene – characteristics to which the gentleman's more serene disposition was a perfect foil.

Still wearing her bridal outfit, Cassandra left with her husband immediately after the wedding ceremony for their new home, spending only one night at Andover on the way. George Austen had visited Steventon sometime during the previous year to arrange for the termination of Thomas Bathurst's curacy, and to find temporary accommodation for himself and his wife whilst their house was being not merely repaired but upgraded. By good fortune, the parsonage house in the neighbouring parish of Deane was available for a modest rent, not because there was no parson but because the incumbent, the Revd William Hillman, like many of the better-off clergymen of the time, preferred to let out his parochial dwelling and rent more prestigious accommodation for himself elsewhere (in his case Ashe Park, a Georgian bow-windowed house whose well-proportioned drawing-room Jane Austen as a young woman greatly admired). Deane parsonage was not ideal for a couple with aspirations to gentility, for the rooms were small, damp and badly arranged, but the Austens were prepared to make the best of it whilst awaiting something better.[11]

No sooner had they arrived than they found themselves obliged to welcome Cassandra's mother, now widowed, bringing with her a small boy she and her husband had been asked to look after. Mrs Leigh was to remain with her daughter and son-in-law until her death four years later. The seven-year-old boy who had arrived with her was the son of Warren Hastings, sent to England by his father to be educated under the supervision of his former neighbours, the Leighs. As though these charges were not enough, the Austens also found themselves responsible for seeking a home in the village for Cassandra's brother Thomas, who was mentally retarded and needed care. The elder Leigh brother, James, who had inherited considerable wealth from a great uncle on the sole condition of adding the latter's surname Perrot to his own, was happy enough to make an allowance towards the expense of looking after Thomas, but his sister and her clergyman-husband were to be left with the trouble. All these burdens had been shouldered cheerfully when, to Mrs Austen's great grief, little George Hastings died of 'a putrid sore throat' (probably diphtheria). She had grown fond of the boy, and he had promised well as a future pupil for her husband. His father, who had sailed from India without knowing that his son was ill, arrived too late to see him. He attributed no blame to the Austens. On the contrary, he became a firm friend of George Austen, with whom he shared a love of Latin poetry. In future years, Warren Hastings' skill at translation was to be held up as a model to pupils at Steventon parsonage.[12]

Three children were born to the Austens at Deane: James in 1765, George in 1766 and Edward in 1767. Not until the summer of 1768 was the parsonage at Steventon ready for occupation. The fact that the renovations took four years to complete suggests that George Austen paid for most of them himself – a procedure which would be unheard of for a clergyman nowadays but which had become increasingly common as the eighteenth century proceeded. The ground plan of the house seems to have remained the same as before, with the addition of an attic floor and perhaps even a bedroom floor to what may have been a single-storey foundation. The balanced Georgian front to the house was clearly new, and was probably a gesture on the part of the patron of the living to improve the appearance of the building. The bow window at the back, which was said to have flooded Mr Austen's study with sunshine, must also have been an addition – fashionable at the time but soon to be despised by connoisseurs such as General Tilney for its 'patched on' appearance.[13]

James Austen's daughter Anna, who moved into the parsonage with her parents when her grandfather retired, made a drawing of the front elevation which suggests that the house remained a fairly humble dwelling, with a single window on either side of a paltry latticed porch, three windows on the first floor and two dormers in the roof. Her step-brother James Edward, who also lived there as a boy, rejected this drawing when in 1870 he was seeking illustrations for a biographical sketch of his aunt Jane, and used instead a picture which made the house look larger and more impressive, with two windows on each side of the front door and more windows to the upper floors. Other grandchildren remembered an entrance parlour, another parlour to the left of it and a kitchen to the right, a private study for the rector and a few domestic offices at the back, seven bedrooms on the first floor and three rooms in the attic. A drawing by Anna of the back of the house shows two projecting wings in which some of these rooms may have been accommodated, but they would have needed to be small.

By the time he described Steventon rectory in his memoir, James Edward had become accustomed to the grandeur of Victorian parsonages and contemplated with wonder the more modest expectations of a previous age. Convention forbade him to mention the primitive sanitation of the times, or the single well in the courtyard from which all water for drinking, cooking, bathing and cleaning had to be drawn by hand. He described with distaste, however, the lack of interior finish to the rooms – the walls without cornices, and the beams which supported the upper floors protruding into the rooms below. He wrote, too, of the inadequacy of the kitchen quarters and the lack of a servants' hall – defects which his aunt Jane had accepted without complaint, much as Catherine Morland, in *Northanger Abbey*, was to accept the few 'shapeless pantries' and the 'comfortless scullery' in her father's parsonage at Fullerton. More important to George Austen as a prospective teacher was the fact that the house could be considered 'well-connected' (well arranged), for the rector's study, instead of opening out of the family dining room as in many parsonages, was approached privately along a passage running behind the parlour from a door at the side of the house.[14]

Jane Austen as she grew up became acquainted with several parsonages much more imposing than her father's. The one occupied by her godfather, the Revd Samuel Cooke, at Great Bookham in Surrey, was a positive mansion; the house provided for her cousin, the Revd Edward Cooper, at Hamstall-Ridware in Staffordshire was the last word in elegance; the rectory in which she visited one of her father's former pupils, the Revd Richard Buller, at Colyton in Devon, was a large Tudor residence bearing the arms of Henry VIII and Catherine of Aragon over the doorway. She knew, however, that these were exceptions to the general run of clergy residences. In *Mansfield Park*, set in the early nineteenth century, Henry Crawford still expects a parsonage to be either 'a scrambling collection of low single rooms, with as many roofs as windows' or a building 'cramped into the vulgar compactness of a square farmhouse'. Jane thought that a parson's house ought to be 'superior in appearance to those of the yeomen and the labourers', yet she never shared the enthusiasm for 'improvement' which led some clergy and their patrons to 'build for glory', as the Revd Sydney Smith put it. At Thornton Lacey she approves of Edmund Bertram's plan to remove a farmyard which obscured the view of the parsonage house from the road but, since the house was already a 'solid-walled, roomy, mansion-like building', she cannot allow Henry Crawford to impose his grandiose ideas for turning it round by forty-five degrees, planting a new garden, diverting a stream and giving travellers along the road the impression that they are approaching the residence of a great landowner. She abhorred pretension. Moreover, it had to be remembered before building too large a house that a clergyman was himself responsible for repairs and that, if he failed to carry them out, there could be acrimonious claims from his successor for 'dilapidations'. Mrs Norris and Dr Grant, her husband's successor as vicar of Mansfield, never got on with each other, their acquaintance having 'begun in dilapidations'.[15]

Whatever later generations may have thought of the parsonage house at Steventon, George Austen, whose tastes were as unpretentious as they were refined, enjoyed in it for more than thirty years the scholarly, cultivated existence he had chosen. It was a better house than any he could otherwise have afforded. It marked his status as a gentleman and helped to make his children more acceptable in society than they might otherwise have been. Jane was happy in it and loved it.

Along the side of the house, a tree-lined path or 'walk' led to the twelfth-century church of St Nicholas and also to the Tudor manor house, occupied by Hugh Digweed and his wife Ruth. The rest of the inhabitants of the village (some thirty households) were farm labourers, whose wives hired themselves out as domestic servants or stayed at home and took in washing, or spun flax or wool. Their cottages, each with its vegetable garden and fruit tree, straggled along a single lane, unsurfaced, unpaved and undrained. Beyond the village, a network of similar lanes, impassable in wet weather other than on horseback or in heavy farm vehicles, led to a circle of similar villages – Ashe, Deane, Oakley and Dummer. To the north and south, post roads fanning out from Basingstoke ran to Andover and Winchester, but these played a comparatively small part in everyday life. Journeys by stagecoach or hired chaise were arduous and time-consuming, and hence were only undertaken when special items (such as furniture, clothing or writing materials) needed to be purchased. The vast majority of England's population lived in villages no larger and often smaller than Steventon. Most people accepted the life uncomplainingly; many, like the Austens, loved it. English gentlemen, to the astonishment of the French nobility, were happiest living on their estates in the country, with the result that English towns, with the exception of a few aristocratic haunts such as Bath, were left to grow haphazardly and to degenerate quickly into squalor.

Mrs Austen professed to find the countryside around Steventon, with its sunken lanes, tall hedgerows and thin-trunked trees, shabby compared with the beauty of the Thames valley; but she had no wish at this stage in her life to move into a town. After one of her rare visits to London she commented disparagingly: ' 'tis a sad place, I would not live in it on any account: one has not time to do one's duty to God or man'.[16] On arrival at Steventon she busied herself cheerfully and competently with one of the accepted tasks of a parson's wife in the country, which was to run a poultry yard and a dairy. Earlier in the century it had been not uncommon for a parson's wife, like Fielding's Mrs Trulliber, to help with milking the cows and churning the butter. There is no evidence that Mrs Austen performed such menial tasks, but she certainly supervised the work and was soon to be heard discussing dairy matters with the frankness of any farmer's wife. In 1770 she wrote to her sister-in-law:

> My Alderney ... turns out tolerably well, and makes more butter than we use, and I have just bought another of the same sort, but as her calf is but just gone, cannot say what she will be good for yet ...[17]

In 1775, when she was pregnant with Jane, she was able to add to her personal news a knowledgeable account of her husband's farming:

The wheat promises to be very good this year, but we have had a most sad wet time for getting it in, however, we got the last load in yesterday, just four weeks after we first began reaping. I am afraid the weather is not likely to mend for it rains very much today, and we want dry weather for our peas and oats; I don't hear of any barley ripe yet, so I am afraid it will be very late before harvest is over.[18]

Until George Austen arrived in Hampshire he had thought of himself purely as a scholar. As a beneficed clergyman, however, he was aware that he had been entrusted with glebeland so that he could cultivate it to feed his family. Feeding the family could mean more than simply using the produce in his own kitchen; it could justify taking up farming on a larger scale and entering the market. George Austen, like many liberal-minded incumbents, preferred to do this rather than concentrate too much on tithes, which were unpopular with farmers in the parish. Instead of negotiating for tithes every time another piece of land was brought under cultivation and pressing farmers for larger payments every time their harvests increased, he embarked on making money by taking a lease on 200 acres of land at nearby Cheesedown, famous for its pigs. There are no stories of George Austen attending hogs to fair as Parson Trulliber was said to do, but he became keen enough on pig-breeding to pay attention to market prices and to listen with interest to accounts of elaborate pig-styes erected by his neighbour, Lord Bolton. An inventory made in 1801 of his farming stock and equipment – five cart horses, three sows, twenty-two pigs, three market waggons, four ploughs, eight harrows, and much else – is evidence of activity on a considerable scale.[19]

The farm and the poultry yard were not only important sources of income to a couple whose private means were limited; they were also an important source of food supply in a village which had no grocer, baker, butcher or shop of any kind. Equally significant was the contact they created with neighbours. George Austen soon found himself patronising ploughing matches and discussing yields with other landowners, whilst dairy farming was a pursuit which attracted women in all walks of life: from the lady of the manor, for whom it was a traditional source of pin-money, to the farmer's wife, for whom it was work. Without such contacts, George Austen could easily have felt isolated in his remote village, most of whose inhabitants were incapable of providing him with companionship. In *Persuasion*, Henrietta Musgrove speaks feelingly of the plight of the Revd Dr Shirley, living in the village of Uppercross with only her own family to talk to.[20]

At Steventon the only 'family' considered worthy of the name was headed by Hugh Digweed, who rented the manor house and farmed most of the land in the area by arrangement with Thomas Knight. George Austen shared with Hugh Digweed the lordship of the manor, which gave him the right to hunt and shoot over the Knights' land – a privilege which meant little to him personally, since he was not a sporting man, but was to be important to his sons. Beyond the village was the 'neighbourhood': a scattering of families sufficiently equal in social standing and living near enough to each other to meet for entertainment and companionship. The concept of the neighbourhood, which involved an elaborate ritual of social breakfasts, dinner parties, picnics and balls, was to play an important part in Jane Austen's adult life and novels. George Austen and his wife could not afford to join in the more expensive activities on any scale whilst their children were young, but Mrs Austen nevertheless instilled, into her daughters especially, their duty to play their part in the social life of the neighbourhood. The term 'neighbour' had biblical connotations which obliged Christians to show a concern for persons with whom they were thrown into contact whether they liked them or not, an obligation of which Elinor Dashwood in *Sense and Sensibility* frequently reminds her sister Marianne. George Austen kept no carriage, but his wife, dressed in her old wedding outfit, was prepared to walk several miles in fine weather to pay polite calls upon her neighbours. The very term 'paying calls' indicated to foreigners that the English regarded short visits to acquaintances as a debt to be discharged to society.[21]

In 1771 Mrs Austen gave a warm welcome to 'two very young single gentlemen': the brothers William and James Holder, who had made money in the West Indies and returned to England to replace the Revd William Hillman as tenants of Ashe Park. James Holder was to hand on his newspaper regularly to his neighbours at Steventon parsonage – a particularly welcome service when the affairs of Antigua became a cause for concern during the war of 1776–82 between Britain and America. The educated public of the late eighteenth century was interested in all colonial and maritime matters, and George Austen had a special interest in Antigua, for a former pupil from his Oxford days, James Langford Nibbs, owned a plantation there. When Nibbs married and set up as a country gentleman in England, he appointed George Austen as trustee of his distant estate and stood as godfather to George's first-born son, James. A map of Antigua may well have hung on the parsonage walls, for Jane Austen was later to make use in her novels of some of the names found on such a map published at the time.[22]

The Austens had already become acquainted with John Harwood of Deane House whilst living in the same parish. Squire Harwood, reputed to have been the original of Squire Western in Fielding's *Tom Jones*, was typical of many of England's gentry in being uneducated and in lacking any cultural interest. Many a young clergyman, arriving in a country parish and finding some such raucous farmer-squire as his sole companion, succumbed to similar habits and disgraced his profession by overindulgence at the table and the bottle. Squire Harwood, finding that George Austen was not of this type, showed a respect amounting to awe for his learning, but would clearly have been happier with what Wilberforce was later to call a 'buck' parson – a hard drinker and a bruising rider to hounds. Mrs Austen, however, commended herself to him as a woman of robust temperament, not likely to be put off by his down to earth language; and on this basis they got on well enough.[23] Whilst living at Deane, the Austens had also struck up a friendly relationship with the young Mr Wither Bramston, patron of Deane church and a member of the ramified clan of Withers, Bramstons and Biggs ubiquitous in the area.

Further afield, grander persons such as William Chute of The Vyne, William Portal of Laverstoke, Lord Bolton of Hackwood and Lord Portsmouth of Hurstbourne Park were known to George Austen not only through a mutual concern for agriculture but on account of his involvement in politics. The curious franchises of the day, which differentiated between county and borough constituencies and gave votes to specified sections of the population in each, allowed the rector of Steventon to vote along with the 'forty-shilling freeholders' of his county (owners of land to the annual value of forty shillings or more) in elections for two Knights of the Shire to represent Hampshire in the House of Commons. In fact, county elections were seldom contested, matters being arranged instead by negotiation among the clergy and gentlemen at race meetings, assizes and other local gatherings. In Hampshire, where the temper of the freeholders was notoriously conservative, a potential Whig candidate as formidable as Lord John Russell once withdrew after confronting a group of clergy and gentry at a nomination meeting.[24] Much expense was thereby avoided. County elections, if contested, were extremely expensive on account of all the entertaining and canvassing that had to be done; and the cost fell entirely on the candidates or their patrons.

Lord Portsmouth sent his son, a little fellow not yet six, to Steventon parsonage to be coached and looked after by the rector and his wife as their first pupil. Mrs Austen pronounced the young Lord Lymington backward for his age but decided that her own boys, Jemmy and Neddy, aged eight and five at the time, would be happy enough to have him as a playmate. They had scarcely got used to him when his mother whisked him off to London to receive treatment for a bad stammer.[25] George Austen was thereafter free to take in rather older boarding pupils, starting in 1773 with the fourteen-year-old Master William Vanderstegen, son of one of Mrs Austen's girlhood friends. For the next twenty years he was to take in five or six at a time and make their fees a significant part of his income.

The Austens had been at Steventon parsonage three years when their fourth son, Henry, was born in 1771. Their first daughter, Cassandra, followed in 1773 and a fifth son, Frank, in 1774. By the time Jane was born, on 16 December 1775, Mrs Austen had developed her own well-tried methods of bringing up children. Like the parsonage house itself, they were to be described with a certain amount of disapproval by her grandson James Edward, Jane's first biographer.

Chapter 2

Upbringing

George Austen's choice of a wife with claims to academic ability and social standing had its effect on the rearing of his children. Mrs Austen took a considerable part in the running of her husband's school. In addition to catering for the material needs of the pupils, it was she who organised their study time and supervised their behaviour. It was she who enticed reluctant pupils back to school, intervened in quarrels between the boys and generally kept things running as smoothly as possible. At the same time, as a relative of the titled Leighs, she liked to keep abreast of practices in aristocratic households. In upper-class families it had long been common for mothers to put their children out to nurse from the day of their birth for a varying period which might last as long as five years. Usually such infants were 'brought up by hand' from the beginning, although it sometimes happened that a surrogate mother who had recently given birth to a child would breast-feed both babies. Whatever the initial process of feeding, the foster child stayed with its surrogate mother until its natural parents saw fit to take it back – often not until it was ready to be handed over to a governess or sent to school.[1]

In the course of the eighteenth century, fostering came increasingly under attack, not on psychological grounds but for the sake of health and morals. Medical experts, with good reason, declared breast-feeding to be infinitely more hygienic than feeding by hand on the milk of cows or goats; yet so intimate was the process of breast-feeding that it was hard to imagine any woman of proper feeling allowing the task to be fulfilled by a wet-nurse. The argument implied that mother's milk provided more than physical sustenance and, in the intellectual climate of the times, it was assumed that the additional properties were of a moral nature. Wet-nurses came from the lower-classes: their morals could not be relied upon. They might harbour 'depraved inclinations' which could be inculcated into the infant with the milk from their breasts. Earlier in the century, John Locke had argued that the initial upbringing of children was a part of their education and that the objective throughout should be morality. This implied that fostering children upon lower-class women was undesirable even if it did not involve wet-nursing. In 1762 Rousseau's treatise *Emile* drew together these ideas and proclaimed a mother's care for her children from the day of their birth to be the only sure way of producing moral citizens.[2]

Jonas Hanway predicted that upper-class women would be either too debilitated by leisure or too addicted to pleasure to take on the care of their own children. The new ideas were nevertheless widely canvassed in nursing journals and became well known among the reading public. As the wife of a clergyman whose religion placed great emphasis on morality, Mrs Austen is bound to have been impressed by the moral urgency of the anti-fostering campaign. At the same time, she was a busy woman and one who would not have wanted to adopt sentimental middle-class attitudes. Under these circumstances, she struck a compromise: she suckled her babies herself for the first three months (this being the length of time experts such as Cadogan, in his popular *Essay upon Nursing and the Management of Children*, regarded as suitable for breast-feeding) and then put them out to be nursed by a 'good woman', in one of the peasant cottages nearby, until they could walk and talk and be regarded as rational beings.[3]

The emotional effect such a process may have had on the children can only be imagined. It has been suggested that Jane's lack of warmth towards her mother, which is evident in her letters, was caused by it, yet her sister and her brothers seem to have suffered no such consequence. Jane Austen's nephew, writing in the mid Victorian period, was clearly embarrassed by his grandmother's readiness to farm out her children, which by his day had become a totally unacceptable practice. 'The infant was daily visited by one or both of its parents, and frequently brought to them at the parsonage,' he wrote, 'but the cottage was its home.' One of the Austen boys, he said, continued even as an adult to speak of his foster mother as 'Movie', the name by which he had called her in his infancy. Mrs Austen herself had no qualms about the practice. The period of time her children spent with their foster mother, learning to walk and talk, was to her an accepted stage in their progress: on 6 June 1773 she reported proudly to her sister-in-law that her daughter Cassy, born on 9 January, had already been settled at 'a good woman's at Deane' for eight weeks – almost as though she had gone to school.[4]

According to Rousseau, foster parents were always downgraded by the natural parents so that the latter could reassert their own pre-eminence. Deliberately or not, some such process occurred in the Austen family. Evidence suggests that the 'good woman' employed by Mrs Austen was Elizabeth Littleworth, the wife of a farmworker at Cheesedown, part way between Deane and Steventon. Elizabeth and her husband John were honest country folk who brought up children in a sensible fashion. They remained closely connected with the Austens for many years to come: in 1789 Jane acted as godmother to their eldest grandchild and in 1796 stood as witness at the wedding of John Littleworth's brother, 'testy old Uncle Will'. Yet they were always treated as poor neighbours, belonging to an inferior station in life. When their youngest daughter Bet, who had been of an age to play with Edward Austen during his childhood at the cottage, called on him later in life at his stately home in Kent, he saw to it that she was treated kindly; but it was the servants whom he ordered to make much of her. Frank Austen was teased by his brothers and sisters throughout life because as a child he had continued to speak in the Hampshire dialect he had learnt at Cheesedown.[5]

Jane Austen, it seems, was kept at home with her mother a little longer than the usual three months, for she was not brought out of the parsonage until 5 April 1776, when she was arrayed in a square-necked, sleeveless gown of fine cotton and taken along the tree-lined walk to the church of St Nicholas for her christening. How long she then spent with the Littleworths depends on how long it took her to learn to walk and talk. Her brother Henry had been back home after fourteen months, 'and a fine stout little fellow he is, and can run anywhere', wrote his mother. Cassy had stayed until she was just over two years old, when she was reported to be 'talking all day long' and 'almost ready to run away'. Frank, who was running about at thirteen months, was probably brought home quite early.[6]

Assuming Jane, like Cassy, to have come home from the Littleworths at the age of two, she had five years of childhood at home before being sent away again, this time to school. There is every reason to believe that the atmosphere at the parsonage was relaxed and happy. Puritan attitudes were being revived in Evangelical homes, resulting in strict and even harsh control of children for their souls' good, but George Austen, as a true son of the Enlightenment, continued to believe in natural intercourse between parents and their offspring. He and his wife addressed their children by pet names, allowed them to eat at the same table as themselves and took them with them on visits to relations and friends. George Austen's considerable learning was combined with an affectionate nature and a deep love of family life. He hated being alone in the house when his wife went away to visit relatives; and it grieved him a little to realise that his children missed their parents much less than he would have missed them if he had been obliged to leave them. Most Oxford scholars of his day admired John Locke. In George Austen's case, the ideas put forward by that most liberal of educational thinkers could only have strengthened a natural inclination to give his children plenty of freedom and to make them his friends at an early age.[7]

Mrs Austen, though sharp-tongued and quick-tempered, was at her best when her children were young. She was proud of her growing brood, which she tended to refer to in the same vein as the young livestock in her farmyard. Urging her sister-in-law Mrs Walter to visit Steventon in the summer of 1773 she wrote eagerly: 'I want to show you my Henry and my Cassy, who are both reckoned fine children ... I have got a nice dairy fitted up and am now worth a bull and six cows, and you would laugh to see them for they are not much bigger than Jack-asses ... In short you must come, and, like Hezekiah, I will show you all my riches.' As an inducement to Mrs Walter to bring her young daughter Philadelphia with her, she assured her that there were 'ducks and chicken for Philly's amusement'. Mrs Austen assumed that all children, and especially little girls, liked playing with the small creatures on a farm – in which case Jane may have disappointed her, for there are no stories connecting her with pets.[8]

Like many mothers at the time, Mrs Austen recorded her children's progress in terms of dress. When Cassandra was taken out of her long gown and put instead into 'petticoats' (a frock and slip which finished at the ankles), her mother regarded it as a sign that she had left babyhood and would soon be learning to walk. From the petticoat stage, there was little change in girls' clothing, except that the waistline of the frock went higher and the neckline lower. Her brothers would also have progressed from gowns into petticoats, but for them there was a significant further step at the age of four, when they were breeched. 'Henry has been breeched some months and thinks himself near as good a man as his brother Neddy', wrote Mrs Austen in August 1775. The breeches that were in fashion for all boys until the 1780s were held up by a band around the waist and continued to below the knees, where they ended in further bands with buckles at the front or side. They were accompanied by a waistcoat reaching to the hips, and over it a coat which fastened with a single button at the top and flared out at the waist into a skirt reaching to the knees: a few years later, the skirt would be cut away at the front so that it remained only as a tail at the back. Henry might well have thought himself a man, for such an outfit was a small replica of the clothes worn not only by his elder brothers but by adult males of all ages. Not until the 1790s did trousers begin to replace breeches for men's daytime wear.[9]

In *Northanger Abbey*, Jane Austen describes another parson's daughter, the young Catherine Morland, as having been 'noisy and wild', preferring boys' games to playing with dolls, hating to stay indoors, reluctant to wash her hands and face, and liking nothing so much as to roll down the green slope at the back of the house. There is no evidence that Jane herself grew up to be quite so hoydenish, but it is reasonable to suppose that she romped about a good deal in her childhood. Accounts of the garden at Steventon vary between James Edward's recollections of a homely mixture of flowers and vegetables, bounded by a thatched mud wall, and Anna Austen's lyrical descriptions of a grassy walk leading to a sundial, and a tall silver fir up which the sweet-smelling honeysuckle climbed; but it seems that there really was a green slope at the southern end of the parsonage garden which Jane may well have rolled down in competition with her brother Frank. Eighteen months older than Jane and not yet immured in the schoolroom, Frank became her earliest playmate. He was by her own account a fearless little boy whose golden curls and engaging smile carried him through many a mischievous exploit. Mrs Austen relied a good deal on Cassandra to look after them both. Mr Austen had known, when Jane was born, that Cassandra would be delighted to play with a real baby instead of her dolls, and for many years the kind and sensible child was a little mother to her younger sister. Not until Jane was three and a half did Mrs Austen have another baby, Charles, whom the two girls could adopt as their joint plaything.[10]

To Jane and Cassandra, the arrival of Charles in June 1779 probably more than made up for the departure of their eldest brother James, with his superior airs, to Oxford, where he matriculated at the beginning of the following month. To a gentleman of modest means the education of five promising sons would have created formidable obstacles, but George Austen had the advantage of being able to prepare his own boys for university along with his paying pupils. His wife's descent from Sir Thomas White, the sixteenth-century founder of St John's College, Oxford, could then be invoked to provide them with scholarships reserved for Founder's Kin. By these means James entered St John's at the early age of fourteen, and his father was able to turn his attention to younger sons. The next in line, Edward, seemed unlikely to take to scholarly pursuits, but he was well-mannered and reasonably intelligent and there could be no harm in giving him the classical education considered suitable for a gentleman. Henry, aged eight, was not very studious either, but his father believed him to be the cleverest of the family. George Austen was too astute to map out careers for his boys before they knew their own minds. James fancied himself as a poet and might wish to try for a literary career; Henry was sufficiently lively to try for almost anything. In the background there was the knowledge that they could fall back on their most likely prospect – a career in the church.[11]

As time went on, Jane became aware of another boy, almost grown up, who did not live with the family but who was nonetheless her brother. George Austen, his father's namesake, was twelve or thirteen when Jane, as a toddler, may have been considered old enough to be taken to see him; but he could neither have heard her nor spoken to her properly, for he was both deaf and dumb. There were other serious problems, too. He had started to have fits shortly after being put out to nurse. Many children suffered fits during the teething process and there was hope that George would get over them, especially when he went for a year without trouble. Sadly, the hope was not fulfilled. By the time he was four, his mother had resigned herself to the fact that he was epileptic.

Medical science at the time held out so little hope of effective treatment for epilepsy that even doctors were likely to resort to such old wives' remedies as infusions of mistletoe. Persistent epileptics were classed as mentally defective. Under these circumstances, the Austens' chief concern was not so much to secure medical attention for poor George as to make arrangements for him to be taken into care. The idea that they might look after him themselves at home never occurred to them, for it was not the practice of the times in any but the poorest families. A gentleman-scholar's house seemed unlikely to be a suitable environment for him: he would be happier in one of the cottages nearby, from which he could move about the village among people who would accept his strange behaviour.[12]

The boy's godfather (George Austen's brother-in-law, Tysoe Saul Hancock) believed that the cost of putting him into care would become overwhelmingly burdensome as years went by, and was consequently filled with dismay as reports of rapid increases in the Austen family reached him from time to time at his post in India.[13] The parents themselves never mentioned the cost. The only comment the Revd George Austen is known to have made on the whole sad situation came in a letter to his sister-in-law, Susannah Walter, and reflects by its strange mixture of ideas the distress he never put into words:

I am much obliged to you for your kind wish of George's improvement. God knows only how far it will come to pass, but from the best judgement I can form at present, we must not be too sanguine on this head; be it as it may, we have this comfort, he cannot be a bad or a wicked child.[14]

Epilepsy, because of its sudden and violent manifestations, had long been attributed either to the presence of evil spirits or to divine punishment for sin. Such ideas, though undermined by the Enlightenment, could never be wholly destroyed whilst doctors were unsure of the causes of the malady. Yet they could surely not be applied to little George Austen, baptised on the day of his birth and hardly responsible since then for any of his actions. His father, for all his learning, found comfort in the thought.

If the fate of this strange brother puzzled Jane and sometimes worried her, there is no sign that she dwelt on it. There were other boys at the parsonage who helped to make life varied and interesting – boys who slept in the attic, ate in the kitchen and disappeared into the parson's study with Jane's older brothers each day for lessons. The boarding pupils were a mixed bunch, for George Austen needed the money and promising candidates were not easy to come by. They included, during Jane's childhood, the strong-minded Fulwar Craven Fowle, whom her brother James greatly admired. She never much liked Fulwar, for he was overbearing and got cross when beaten at games. Mrs Austen regarded him as the cleverest of the pupils and made a favourite of him, to the annoyance of another member of the class, Frank Stuart, who sulked openly over the matter. Not so Gilbert East, eldest son of Sir William East of Hall Place, neighbour to Mrs Austen's brother James in Berkshire. Gilbert was too busy enjoying himself to bear grudges. He loved dancing and would skive off Latin lessons without a qualm if there was an opportunity of attending a ball. By and by, Fulwar went to Oxford and was replaced in the schoolroom by his sixteen-year-old brother Tom, a gentle young man whom Jane and Cassandra both liked – the latter especially. In the same year the group was joined by George Nibbs, the son of George Austen's friend from Antigua. This young man was later to cause his father such anxieties that he was to send him off to Antigua in order to separate him from undesirable acquaintances, thereby providing Jane Austen with a precedent for Sir Thomas Bertram's treatment of his son in *Mansfield Park*.[15]

A houseful of boys provided Jane, as she grew up, with a fund of boisterous humour and cheerful lunacy which emerged in her early writing. It also gave her mother plenty to do. Fortunately, a clergyman's wife was not yet expected to preside over a Sunday School and numerous parish organisations as she did in Victorian times. On the other hand, in *Northanger Abbey* Jane Austen takes it for granted that, in a clergyman's family such as her own, it would be the mother who taught the children to read. We are told how Mrs Morland, in her country vicarage, slaved away at the task with all her ten children as one after the other reached the age of four or five. Mrs Austen probably did the same for her James, Edward, Henry, Cassandra, Frank, Jane and Charles. Hornbooks (tiny primers backed with horn) were available from which to teach young pupils to recognise and recite two-letter combinations, followed by words of one syllable, two syllables, and so on. In Thomas Dyche's much reprinted *Guide to the English Tongue*, apparently known to Jane since Mrs Allen quotes it in *Northanger Abbey*, the words thus painstakingly built up were combined into moral axioms which it was thought would be useful to the young pupils throughout life.

As a further step to fluent reading, Mrs Morland introduced her children to a simple history book, thereby once more killing two birds with one stone. Mrs Austen probably did the same, for Jane Austen showed later that she was well acquainted with the type of book commonly used. John Newbery, an enterprising publisher of children's books, produced a number of relevant titles. Authors commissioned to write such books attempted to make the contents not only accessible to stumbling readers but manageable by their untrained teachers. With these laudable objectives, they moved rapidly through English history monarch by monarch, describing how they came to the throne, listing a few events of their reign, recording the circumstances of their demise, and ending with a summary judgement. Illustrations consisted of portraits, or 'heads', of the various monarchs, as in Newbery's *Complete History of England with Heads of Thirty Kings and Queens*. At the age of fifteen, Jane entertained the members of her family by producing a parody of the genre. In her *History of England*, monarchs ascend the throne by fair means or foul, preside over a very small number of events, and die naturally or unnaturally in the space of a few lines. Cassandra painted a comic 'head' to accompany each monarch, leaving out Edward V on the grounds that, according to Jane, 'this unfortunate prince lived so little a while that no body had time to draw his picture'.[16]

In many clergy families, including that of George Austen's friend the Revd Noyes Lloyd, children were expected to confine any further reading to the pages of the Bible. In many others, the standard work purchased was Watts's *Divine Songs*, which called down the wrath of God upon children's heads for the slightest misdemeanour:

FABLES.

FABLE L.

The HARE and many FRIENDS.

FRiendſhip, like love, is but a name,
    Unleſs to one you ſtint the flame.
The child, whom many fathers ſhare,
Hath ſeldom known a father's care;
'Tis thus in friendſhips; who depend
On many, rarely find a friend.

Opening lines of the poem Catherine Morland learnt 'as quickly as any girl in England'. From John Gay, *Fables* (1727).

Have you not heard what dreadful plagues
Are threatened by the Lord,
To him who breaks his father's law
Or mocks his mother's word?

What heavy guilt upon him lies!
How cursèd is his name!
The ravens shall pick out his eyes,
And eagles eat the same.[17]

This Puritan tradition, which was undergoing a revival at the hands of Evangelical teachers, produced several new editions of James Janeway's *A Token for Children*, whose accounts of deathbed utterances by pious children were designed to frighten young readers into good behaviour with warnings that they might die and go to hell before they had had time to repent.[18] Mr and Mrs Austen inflicted none of these popular horrors on their children, adopting instead the more liberal policy of providing a certain amount of secular literature. Of the two types available they avoided the chapbooks, whose stories of giants and dragons, superhuman heroes and miraculous events were criticised by Enlightenment theorists on account of their irrational and amoral attitudes, and purchased instead a newer type of literature regarded as entertaining whilst being also 'improving' in the moral sense.

This included, inevitably, *The History of Little Goody Two-Shoes,* first published by John Newbery in 1765 and kept in print by his successors to the end of the following century. Addressed to 'all Young Gentlemen, and Ladies, who are good, or intend to be good', the story of Mistress Margery's rise from poverty and neglect to wealth and influence is so heavily overlaid with moral lessons that modern critics have found it hard to understand how any children could have taken her to their hearts. Yet generations of adults remembered with nostalgia the many hours spent with *Goody Two-Shoes* in their infant days. Jane Austen's copy of the tiny book was bound between the charming gilt and flowered 'Dutch' paper boards which were John Newbery's special gift to the publishing trade. Not only was the frontispiece lovingly if crudely coloured in a childish hand; the front page was firmly inscribed 'Jane Austen' by her at a later date. The text undoubtedly had its engaging features. The poor little girl who becomes mistress of a Dame School invites her young readers to join in the word games she has devised for her pupils and to admire the pictures of the various birds and animals she has rescued from cruelty – a raven, a pigeon, a skylark ('see, here he is …'), a dog, a lamb ('and a pretty fellow he is; do look at him ...'). Mistress Margery's eventual marriage with a rich gentleman who very soon dies and leaves her all his money was equally bound to please. John Newbery described himself to his young readers as 'their old friend in St John's Church-Yard' and addressed his tale not only to those who desired to be good but also to those

> Who from a State of Rags and Care,
> And having Shoes but half a Pair;
> Their fortune and their Fame would fix,
> And gallop in a Coach and Six.

The idea that good behaviour brings earthly rewards was, after all, as old as the biblical Book of Proverbs, holding a place in George Austen's religious teaching alongside the irreconcilable example of the fate of Jesus Christ.[19]

Whilst fairies were frowned upon, talking animals were considered efficacious. John Locke had advised parents to give their children Aesop's Fables to read as soon as they had learnt the alphabet, on the grounds that the moral teaching they contained would last through life. Locke's idea of morality was a reasoned understanding, neither sentimental nor cynical, of how to live amicably within a community, and Aesop's Fables were admirable illustrations. By the late eighteenth century, however, their author had been overtaken in popularity by John Gay, whose fables in verse were easier to learn by heart. The ability to 'repeat' *The Hare and Many Friends*, which Catherine Morland acquired 'as quickly as any girl in England', became something of a benchmark by which parents could boast of their children's academic attainments. In many families, Gay's verses were handed down by word of mouth: Jane Austen may have learnt them in this way rather than from having possessed a copy of the work. In either case, the example of the hare, based on shrewd observation of human behaviour, taught her at an early age to look doubtingly on people who made friends too easily. Emma Woodhouse was to find ready familiarity a fault in Mr Weston, and Jane Austen herself disliked the trait when she detected it in Miss Armstrong at Lyme.[20]

Other than Watts's *Divine Songs* and John Gay's *Fables* there was little poetry available specifically for children. 'The Beggar's Petition', which Catherine Morland failed to master in spite of three months' drilling by her mother, was one of the poems Jane had read in a book given her by her brother Edward: Dr Thomas Percival's collection of *Tales, Fables and Reflections: Designed to Promote the Love of Virtue, a Taste for Knowledge and an Early Acquaintance with the Works of Nature*. It was a

strange gift for a teenage boy to choose for his sister, but Jane Austen
cherished it and was clearly delighted when she ran across Percival's
son more than twenty years later. 'We have got a new Physician,' she
wrote to Cassandra from Southampton in 1808, 'a Dr Percival, the son
of a famous Dr Percival of Manchester, who wrote moral tales for
Edward to give to me.' The main title of the book, *A Father's Instruction
to his Children*, indicated that it was meant to be used for teaching
purposes. Each passage, seldom more than a hundred words in length,
was intended to form the basis of a separate lesson, to be followed by
discussion on another day. Of the three objectives listed in the title,
morality took clear precedence over knowledge and the works of nature.
Childish offences such as 'taking of birds' nests' and 'crying upon trifling
occasions' were castigated alongside adult enormities such as drunkenness and brutality, with consequences ranging from remorse to severe
punishment. Again, the appeal throughout was to observation and
reflection; even the beggar, whose petition defeated Catherine Morland's learning capacity, founded his plea for help on a reminder that
misfortune can strike where least expected, and that the rich man may
one day be in the same plight as the poor. Thus was Jane Austen's
moral rationalism nurtured at an early age.[21]

The name of Thomas Percival, an active member of the Manchester
Literary and Philosophical Society and a friend of Enlightenment
writers such as Diderot and Voltaire, was well known in scholarly circles
throughout England.[22] Edward had probably bought Dr Percival's *Tales*
on the advice of his father, given in answer to the predictable question,
'What can I get Jane for her birthday?' Any further part played by
George Austen in his young daughter's early training can only be
guessed at. Writing (which was taught separately from reading) and
accounts (arithmetic) were considered technical subjects, best taught by
a man. Often an itinerant master was employed for the purpose. The
Revd Richard Morland, however, taught both subjects to his daughter
Catherine, and it may be that George Austen took time off from his
teenage classes to teach them, first to Henry and Cassandra and then
to Frank and Jane. Henry Austen certainly believed that it was from
her father that Jane acquired 'at a very early age' her enthusiasm for
the English language and her sensitivity to literary style.[23]

When lessons were over there was a good deal of fun and laughter
at the parsonage, for the Austens were fond of story-telling and of
charades and party games. Mrs Austen, who at the age of six had been
described by her uncle Theophilus Leigh, the Master of Balliol, as
'already the poet of the family', was especially good at producing comic

verse.[24] Card-playing was a popular stand-by: even in Evangelical circles, card games were not regarded as leading inevitably to the gaming dens. There were times of special excitement too, as when James Austen returned from Oxford towards the end of 1782 with the idea of brightening up the Christmas holiday for everybody by producing a play. The scheme was no doubt welcomed by Mrs Austen as a means of giving her young people something to do: the Christmas festival itself offered few distractions in those days, and outdoor activities were curtailed by the extreme muddiness of all the surrounding lanes at such a season. The chosen play, *Matilda* by Dr Thomas Francklin, needed no more than six players and could therefore have been performed at one end of the parsonage dining-room with the remaining members of the household arranged as audience against the wall at the other. It was a ranting melodrama in blank verse, set at the time of the Norman Conquest. George Austen, who was amused by all forms of popular literature, obviously raised no objections. James wrote a poetic prologue, recited by Edward, and a somewhat comic epilogue which was entrusted to Tom Fowle. Both boys may also have been assigned parts in the play along with Henry and a couple of Mr Austen's pupils, or perhaps the Digweed boys over from the Manor House. The part of the heroine was probably played by a boy, since there is no record of a visit to the parsonage by any female cousins at the time. Cassandra was approaching ten years of age and may have been considered old enough to play the part of Bertha, the heroine's friend, thereby increasing the excitement for Jane, who would have had the fun of helping her sister to dress up.[25]

This was the last occasion on which the whole of the Austen family was to be together, for Edward was to go away the following year for good. He had for some time been in the habit of going to stay with relatives for the whole of the summer. The practice stemmed from a day in 1779 when a fashionably dressed lady, with finely-wrought features and a kind but searching gaze, called at the parsonage with her husband in the course of their wedding tour. She took a fancy to the eleven-year-old Edward and persuaded her husband to let her take him with them on the rest of their journey. The Austens made no demur, for the visiting couple were the son and daughter-in-law of Thomas Knight of Godmersham, George Austen's revered benefactor and patron of the living. The Knights had other parishes in their gift: their goodwill might be useful to James and Henry in the future. Edward was brought back to the parsonage in time to resume his studies in the autumn and little more was thought of the episode until the following year, when a letter arrived from the young couple asking if Edward could again spend his summer holidays with them. Edward's brother Henry, already sharp-eared and quick-witted at the age of eight, heard and remembered the conversation which ensued between his parents. Mr Austen had intended to make sure that Edward stuck to his Latin grammar over the summer, but Mrs Austen, who was normally as keen as her husband on keeping boys at their studies, on this occasion had her eye on the main chance and persuaded her husband that he had 'better oblige his cousins and let the Child go'. Edward was accordingly waved off along the lane, riding on a pony beside the coachman who had been sent to fetch him. From then on, it was gradually taken for granted that he would spend all his holidays with the Knights and that as soon as his schooling was over he would go and live with them.[26]

Children were given away for a variety of reasons in the eighteenth century: the fact that Elizabeth Knight, though she had been married only a few years and was barely thirty years old, had concluded that her marriage was destined to be childless would have seemed to relatives and acquaintances of the Austens reason enough. The Knights owned large estates; they needed an heir, and the Austens had sons enough to supply the need. When formal adoption took place in 1783, Edward was sixteen and of an age to leave home anyway.

Other, more emotional attitudes to motherhood and the family were beginning to take root as Rousseau's doctrines led on to a more Romantic age. Did they result in some criticism of what the Austens had done? 'There is something so shocking in a child's being taken away from his parents and natural home!' exclaims the sentimental Isabella Knightley in *Emma*. 'To give up one's child! I really never could think well of anybody who proposed such a thing.' Did Jane and more particularly Cassandra, who had been Edward's closest companion, miss him when he left home? Fanny Price, adopted by Sir Thomas Bertram of Mansfield Park, is heartbroken at having to leave her brother William. Yet it ultimately becomes clear that Fanny's adoption has been for everybody's good and that she has secured as close a relationship with her brother as she could ever have had if she had remained at home. In this, as in many other matters, Jane Austen was poised between two generations.[27]

Chapter 3

School

The departure of Edward to live with the Knights eased the pressure on space at the parsonage, which had become very crowded in recent years. Yet Charles was growing up to take his place: at the age of four the conventions of the time no longer allowed him to enter his parents' bedroom, let alone sleep there. In termtime, the house had to accommodate seven members of the family, four or five boarding pupils and three servants. Theoretically, the boarding pupils could have been sent away; in practice, George Austen needed the money they brought in. His income had increased a little in 1773, when the rector of Deane died and the living, which his uncle had purchased for him, at last came his way; but equally his financial commitments had increased as his family grew larger. James had graduated at Oxford in 1783, but but it would be some years yet before he needed to make up his mind about seeking ordination. Meanwhile, he wished to take up the option available to him as Founder's Kin and stay on at his college. It was a sensible enough course, for it would allow him to prepare for a possible career in the church by commending himself to fellow graduates whose fathers had parishes at their disposal, and perhaps even to secure one of the parishes in the gift of the college; but it meant that his father would have to continue for another seven or eight years to find the subsidies he had sent him twice a year since his matriculation. Mr Austen had already twice borrowed sizeable sums of money from his wife's brother, James Leigh-Perrot; the first debt had had to be cancelled because he could see no prospect of paying and the second sum had not yet been fully redeemed. The boarding pupils obviously had to stay.[1]

Shortage of space at the parsonage was doubtless one of the reasons why, in the spring of 1783, it was decided to send Cassandra and Jane away to school; but it is unlikely that George Austen would have agreed to any such plan had it not offered educational advantages too. The girls, unlike their brothers, could not be taken into their father's classes, and he had no time to teach them separately. To do so, he would have needed to reorientate his teaching entirely, for the emphasis with the boys was heavily upon the classical training needed for university, and educational pundits and religious writers were at one in regarding classical languages as unnecessary for the female sex and pagan literature as unsuitable.

Even so, George Austen was surely reluctant to lose his girls, as he called them. The initiative for the move probably came in the end from the Coopers, at whose house in Bath Cassandra had been to stay in the summer of 1782. Jane, dragging little Charles by the hand, had run excitedly along the lane to meet the coach in which her father brought Cassandra home – little realising what effect the visit was to have on future plans.[2]

Jane Cooper was Mrs Austen's sister. She was beautiful, wealthy, socially accomplished and much admired by Mrs Austen, whose only claims to comparable achievement were that she had married younger and produced more children. Jane Leigh had reached the age of thirty-two before marrying the Revd Dr Edward Cooper, a Fellow of All Souls College, Oxford, whose parental home, Phyllis Court, was near to her father's rectory in Oxfordshire. The Coopers had spent the first few years of their married life moving between London, where their son Edward was born, and a large country house in Berkshire where their daughter Jane was born. Mrs Austen was right in suspecting that, after two difficult confinements in less than a year, her sister had 'done breeding': Mrs Cooper and her husband thereafter moved to Bath, where the Reverend Doctor's private means, supplemented by income from a couple of small neighbouring parishes and a prebendal stall at Wells, enabled them to live in style, first at No. 12 in the newly-built Royal Crescent and then at No. 14 Bennett Street, fashionably situated oppposite the Upper Rooms. Here they were glad to have their niece Cassandra Austen visit them and make friends with their daughter Jane.[3]

The latter was going on twelve when her father decided that she should go to Oxford to be educated under the care of his sister Ann Cawley, whose husband, a former Principal of Brasenose College, had recently died, leaving her to fend for herself by exploiting the growing popularity of young ladies' schooling. A suggestion that Cassandra should accompany her well-off cousin would obviously have appealed to Mrs Austen and may not have been wholly unwelcome to her husband, who cherished fond memories of his *alma mater*. There were boarding schools near to Steventon to which the girls could have gone, but the Austen parents perhaps preferred the service offered by Mrs Cawley, who looked after her charges in her own home and found visiting tutors for them from among Oxford's impecunious scholars. Cassandra, at the age of ten, may have been thought more or less old enough to go to boarding school, but Jane, at seven, was by the standards of the time too young. Yet, if a bedroom was to be vacated at the parsonage, both girls would have to go. Oxford would at least have the advantage that James would be at hand to see that the girls were settled in.[4]

Whether Jane was excited or apprehensive about her first experience of leaving home can only be conjectured. A reference in *Emma* to school as a place where 'girls could be sent to be out of the way' suggests that she had overheard the conversation about bedroom space. Unfortunately, the atmosphere which the two little girls encountered on reaching their new abode was not reassuring. Mrs Austen had known Ann Cawley in younger days, but may not have been aware that her old playmate had become a stiff-mannered woman incapable of inspiring her pupils with trust and affection. James did his best to welcome his sisters, but his efforts were not well judged; eager to impress them with the glories of the great seat of learning at which they had arrived, he took them on a sight-seeing tour which deadened their young hearts and wearied their small legs. Jane afterwards teased him about it in one of her early satirical writings:

> I never, but once, was in Oxford in my life and I am sure I never wish to go there again – they dragged me through so many dismal chapels, dusty libraries, and greasy halls, that it gave me the vapours for two days afterwards.[5]

In April 1783 Mr Austen paid Mrs Cawley £30 in advance for a year's care of his two daughters. They cannot have received much instruction in Oxford when for some unknown reason she decided to move to Southampton, taking the girls with her. They had been there only a few weeks when the town was swept by one of its periodic epidemics of typhus fever, brought by troops arriving at the port from Gibraltar in overcrowded, insanitary ships. Mrs Cawley kept quiet about the danger, but in September Jane Cooper wrote home with the alarming news that her two cousins had been taken ill. Mrs Cooper and Mrs Austen set off at once for Southampton, where they paid Mrs Cawley such fees as were outstanding and took their daughters home. Jane Austen is believed to have been dangerously ill. Happily she recovered, but Mrs Cooper had by then caught the fever and died on her return to Bath. Her husband, heartbroken, resigned his Wiltshire livings, sub-let his house in Bennett Street and returned to the Berkshire area he had known in his youth. He gave Cassandra a diamond ring, by which to remember her aunt, and Jane a headband which she was still pleased to wear many years later at a local ball. The whole unfortunate episode had lasted a mere five months.[6]

The three girls were less seriously affected by the experience than their parents might have feared. In retrospect it could even have taken on an air of excitement comparable to the dramatic rescue by Mr Darcy of his young sister from the care of the unsatisfactory Mrs Younge.[7] At least they were not wholly put off from the idea of going away to school. This was fortunate, for Dr Cooper was likely to have felt more keenly than ever the need to provide some suitable education for his daughter, now motherless; and if he again sent his Jane to school she was bound to want her cousin Cassandra to go with her. Until his affairs were settled, however, the Austen girls must get on as best they could at home, receiving such instruction as their parents had time to give them. As it turned out, nearly two years elapsed before there were any more plans for school.

While many parents, including some clergymen and their wives, thought only of equipping their daughters with a show of accomplishments which would enable them to compete in the marriage market, Mr and Mrs Austen looked beyond this objective. There was of course no question of educating them for careers, which for women hardly existed. The most enlightened of aims could merely be that of educating them to become good wives. In future years their most likely suitors would be clergymen, for the latter frequently looked to daughters of other clergy as their partners, in the expectation that they would have experienced a more academic background than many daughters of the gentry and that they would be prepared to marry with fewer social ambitions. So common was the practice that clergymen's daughters tended to look upon any young ordinands who entered the neighbourhood as their natural prey. Mary Crawford is sure that Edmund Bertram will be captured by one of the sisters of a fellow ordinand with whom he goes to stay:

> Their father is a clergyman, and their brother is a clergyman, and they are all clergymen together. He is their lawful property – he fairly belongs to them ...

she tells Fanny Price.[8] Clergymen who already had the prospect of a parish were often particularly eager to marry. Their wives were guaranteed entry into neighbourhood society by virtue of their husband's position, but they also found themselves immediately responsible for a household which had to be run as economically as possible. Lady Catherine de Bourgh's excellent if officious advice to Mr Collins made clear the qualities required:

> Choose a gentlewoman, for my sake and for your own; let her be an active, useful sort of person, not brought up high, but able to make a small income go a long way ... Find such a woman as soon as you can, bring her to Hunsford, and I will visit her.[9]

To fit them to be clergymen's wives, Cassandra and Jane were to be taught a number of household skills, mainly of a supervisory kind. They would not be required to do any cooking (it is in one of Mrs Bennet's cattier moments that she suggests that Charlotte Lucas may have had to hurry home to see about the mince pies); but they must be taught to manage affairs in the kitchen and control the servants. At the same time their manners and interests must be cultivated in such a way that they would be able to associate with the wives and daughters of the surrounding gentry, and their intellects nurtured so as to enable them to provide a clergyman husband with companionship in the inevitable loneliness of a country parish. With these considerations in mind, the two girls were to be encouraged to entertain themselves in their leisure hours with such cultural pursuits as took their fancy and, above all, to broaden their minds by conversation and reading.[10]

One of the problems from a teaching point of view was their difference in age. Any instruction that they were given jointly would be likely for some time to benefit Cassandra more than Jane. They may both have attended the art lessons given by the young John Claude Nattes when the latter, not yet famous as a watercolourist, was hired by George Austen to include Steventon parsonage in his travels as an itinerant teacher in the Basingstoke area; but, although Henry Austen thought that Jane had shown great potential as an artist, it was Cassandra who excelled. It was also Cassandra who won her mother's approval in all matters of household management. Jane, set aside as not yet old enough to cope properly, learnt ruefully to accept the assumption that she was incompetent in practical affairs. Hence, although the three household servants shared the family kitchen during the day, they formed no more than a background to Jane's life. In her novels she was to mention at least a hundred servants, but none of her heroines is to be seen actively involved in their management. It was also Cassandra, and not Jane, who grew up to share their mother's interest in farming. 'You know my ignorance in such matters', Jane once wrote, when trying to explain to Cassandra some changes which had been made among their father's employees. In *Sense and Sensibility*, Elinor Dashwood, when married to a clergyman, is reported to be seeking more pasturage for her cows; but happily for Jane no further details were required, for the novel ends there.[11]

At this stage, a good deal of Mrs Austen's time was no doubt taken up with teaching the four-year-old Charles to read. Jane might have found herself neglected as an 'in-between' had not the need to give special tuition to her brother Frank provided her with his companionship. It was clear that Frank, though by no means unintelligent, was neither as studious as James nor as quick-witted as Henry. Of the careers open to young men of the gentry and professional classes – the church, law, medicine and the armed forces – the latter seemed likely to be the most suitable for him. The navy was in some ways an obvious choice: Hampshire was traditionally a sea-faring county, well ahead of the rest of England in the proportion of naval officers its population supplied. It was a popular profession, too, for clergymen's sons, who formed the third largest social grouping among naval officers (after the sons of the gentry and of former sailors).[12] Frank would make a good officer, for he was not only practical, energetic and courageous but also socially presentable: taken by his parents on a visit to his Austen relatives in East Kent whilst Cassandra and Jane were at Oxford, he had won the approval even of his censorious cousin Phila.[13]

Unfortunately the Austen and Leigh families had no previous connections with the sea: there was no naval captain they could rely upon to take Frank on board his ship as an apprentice officer. They would need instead to enter him at the Royal Naval Academy at Portsmouth, which took boys from the age of twelve and prepared them to sail as 'volunteers by order' two or three years later. To obtain admission, he would have to undergo an examination by the Headmaster of the Academy in the presence of the Governor. Report had it that the examination, which took the form of a half-hour interview, was no great barrier. Nevertheless, it was typical of George Austen that he should have started to prepare his son for some of the subjects taught at the Academy. These were listed as 'Writing, Arithmetic, Drawing, Navigation, Gunnery, Fortification, other useful parts of the mathematics, French, Dancing, Fencing, and the exercise of the firelock'.[14] Hence, when Jane was presented with a French primer in December 1783, she found herself sharing it with Frank.[15]

It was characteristic of the period that even lessons in French grammar were regarded as an opportunity to inculcate morality. The

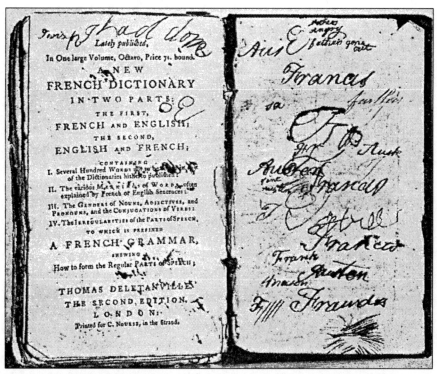

Endpaper of the French primer, *Fables choisies*, Jane shared with her brother Frank. (*Private Collection*)

ninety-nine pieces of prose which formed the exercises in Jane's French primer were all fables. Neither she nor Frank grumbled on this account, but the book was nevertheless not a success. Years later, Frank admitted that he was never any good at languages, and there is no sign that Jane, either, made much progress with French whilst the two of them were studying together.[16] In moments of tedium, perhaps when doing homework under a rule of silence, she scribbled messages to her brother on the last page of the book: 'I wish I had done', or 'Mothers angry fathers gone out' [*sic*]. This last suggests that, although Mr Austen prescribed the course of study, Mrs Austen supervised the work in hand.[17]

In the matter of discipline, neither parent is reputed to have adopted the extremes sometimes found at the time. Mrs Mary Sherwood, born in the same year as Jane Austen and later to become famous as the author of *The Fairchild Family*, tells us that her brother, tutored by their father the Revd Dr George Butt, was allowed to do exactly as he pleased and in consequence fell behind in his studies. Mary herself, meanwhile, underwent strict discipline at the hands of her mother, who made her sit at lessons wearing boards at her back, strapped to an iron collar round her neck, to improve her deportment. George Austen seems to have followed the advice of Locke in avoiding corporal punishment but to have ignored his injunction that all lessons should be pleasurable. Oliver Goldsmith, who was well thought of in the Austen household, doubted whether such an objective was attainable and whether it would serve any useful purpose if it were. Mr Austen kept his pupils at their *Eton Latin Grammar* whether they liked it or not, yet many of them regarded him with sufficient affection to visit him after they had left school. Mrs Austen, for her part, could not put up with children who idled their time away; but her brisk manner and sharp tongue were sufficient to discipline her charges without recourse to the harsh restraints which Mary Sherwood says were 'the fashion' in her day.[18]

The atmosphere at Steventon parsonage during the first few months after Jane's return from school certainly favoured serious study. The family was in deep mourning for Mrs Austen's sister, and even when Christmas came there could be no repetition of the theatricals inaugurated the previous year. Not until the spring of 1784 did the clouds begin to lift. Mrs Austen appeared at last to have recovered from the shock of her sister's death and plans were made for a lively party when James came home from Oxford for the summer. No more tragedies were to be enacted on the Steventon stage, James decided: henceforth, the Austen players would follow the fashion of amateur thespians everywhere and produce only comedy, farce or pantomime. In July 1784 Sheridan's recent London success, *The Rivals*, was performed in the Revd George Austen's dining room. Since the play required about a dozen characters, it seems likely that the eligible members of the Austen family were joined by one or two of the Digweed brothers from the Manor House and also by Jane Cooper and her brother Edward, who was on holiday from Eton. It may well have been on this occasion that the subject of school was again discussed.[19]

Jane Cooper may indeed already have been entered, for the establishment chosen was one which would have had an immediate appeal to her father. The latter was now settled at Sonning and would inevitably have been drawn into the circle of intellectual notabilities cultivated by the ambitious Dr Richard Valpy, recently appointed as Headmaster of nearby Reading School. Valpy's boys often had sisters of school age, which meant that it was in his interests to boost the reputation not only of his own establishment but also that of the neighbouring girls' school housed in the gateway of Reading's ruined abbey. He did so by sending masters from his own school to help with the teaching of the more academic subjects at the Abbey School and by entertaining favoured pupils at his home as occasion offered. Mr and Mrs Austen were apparently ready enough to agree that Cassandra should join her cousin at the Abbey School in the autumn of 1785, but they considered Jane too young to benefit from so smart an establishment. However, Jane made such an outcry at the thought of being separated from her sister that it was agreed both girls should go, Mrs Austen opining somewhat peevishly that 'if Cassandra's head had been going to be cut off, Jane would have her's cut off too'. She could hardly be expected to understand that, without Cassandra, Jane would not only be deprived of her model but left at the mercy of her mother's impatience.[20]

Jane Austen is generally believed to have had the Abbey School in mind when she emphasised that Mrs Goddard was the mistress merely of a school:

> not of a seminar, or an establishment, or anything which professed, in long sentences of refined nonsense, to combine liberal requirements with elegant morality, upon new principals and new systems, and where young ladies for enormous pay might be screwed out of health and into vanity, but a real, honest, old-fashioned boarding school, where a reasonable quantity of accomplishments were sold at a reasonable price, and where girls might be sent to ... scramble themselves into a little education without any danger of coming back prodigies.[21]

It was certainly not one of the schools that Hannah More denounced for teaching nothing but ornamental fripperies and sending girls home to despise their mothers; nor was it one of those establishments which ruined its pupils' health in the effort to turn them out as prodigies. Like all schools professing to cater for the leisured classes, it aimed to prepare its pupils for marriage whilst avoiding subjects which might be classed as housewifery: Mr Knightley, in his straightforward way, describes Harriet Smith as having had 'an indifferent education' and learnt 'nothing useful' at Mrs Goddard's school.[22] Richard Valpy would not have been pleased at the aspersion thus cast upon the record of the Reading Ladies Boarding School, as the Abbey was more formally called; but his own contrary claims as to its exceptional merits were probably somewhat inflated.

The subjects offered – sewing, drawing, dancing and music on the one hand and writing, arithmetic, French, history and a little geography on the other – were those normally provided by girls' boarding schools at the end of the eighteenth century, and were doubtless conducted in the usual fashion. As far as the practical subjects were concerned, the inordinate amount of time once spent on needlework had abated over the past few decades, but the kind of sewing taught had not changed very much. It was still common for girls to take home a number of landscapes embroidered in silk 'in proof of . . . having spent seven years at a great school in town to some effect', as Mrs Jennings's daughter did a few years later. The drawing, dancing and music lessons which now competed with needlework were a mixed blessing, for they were promoted without regard for talent or inclination, and parents were urged to pay extra fees for tuition from a whole series of hired masters, each of whom concentrated on a particular branch of his subject. Jane Austen believed everybody should be taught to dance, but she took great delight in *Pride and Prejudice* in having Elizabeth inform Lady Catherine de Bourgh that none of the Bennet sisters had been made to draw or play the piano unless they had particularly wished to do so.[23]

Meanwhile, academic subjects were tailored to suit what was believed to be the usual run of feminine needs. Mathematics was confined to simple arithmetic, since neither algebra nor geometry was needed to compile household accounts.[24] Writing lessons consisted of penmanship, orthography and the art of letter writing. Females were believed to have a natural gift for keeping up friendships by correspondence, but girls needed to be taught to write a clear hand, to spell, and to open and close their letters with suitable phrases if, like Lady Bertram, they were to develop a 'competent, commonplace, amplifying style' which enabled them to make much out of what was thought to be the small amount of matter at their disposal.[25] French was taught more seriously than English, since it was widely regarded as a mark of gentility: according to Maria Edgeworth, any good inn on the London road could produce a landlady's daughter who had learnt to sustain a dialogue in French 'in the question and answer manner' as proof of a superior education.[26] History, too, was accorded serious attention, for the surprising reason that it would provide girls with a fund of moral examples and genteel topics of conversation – a view Catherine Morland was to contradict by describing history as a catalogue of unsavoury characters and unseemly events: 'the quarrels of popes and kings, with wars or pestilences, in every page; the men all so good-for-nothing and hardly any women at all'.[27]

Whatever the merits of the Abbey School may have been, Jane Austen was not in a position to take full advantage of them. It was only the older girls who were given the privilege of tutorials with the visiting masters and who enjoyed French conversation with Miss Pitts, the school's most competent linguist. Cassandra, at thirteen, probably qualified for this specialist treatment: it was she, and not Jane, who many years later subscribed to the fund-raising effort aimed at establishing Miss Pitts, with her émigré husband, in a school of her own in London. Jane, at ten, is more likely to have been among the 'set of little people and inferior pupils' taught in the classroom by the junior mistresses. These were probably not in any way superior to the sentimental Miss Nash and her colleagues at Highbury. Efforts had been made since the beginning of the eighteenth century to provide some sort of training for teachers in charity schools, but mistresses in boarding schools – often impecunious gentlewomen – were given none at all.[28]

The Abbey School was run by a Mrs La Tournelle, who, like Mrs Goddard, saw to the physical needs of the pupils and left most of the teaching to others. She slept the girls two in a bed for warmth, as was common at the time, but she also provided them with good food, ensured that they got plenty of fresh air, and gave them a more adequate supply of clean linen than was vouchsafed in most boarding schools.[29] Indeed, she was so concerned about cleanliness that at morning prayers she could be heard whispering 'Make haste! make haste!' to the mistress in charge when she saw that the laundress had arrived. She was a stout, middle-aged, good-natured woman who took care of the little girls and left the older ones as much as possible to their own devices. Newcomers were fascinated by the agility with which she trotted around on her cork leg: no one knew how she had come to lose the real one. There was a mystery about her name, too, for she was born Esther Hackitt and had never married. Romantic teenage notions were probably responsible for her changing Esther to Sarah ('for which young lady of common sensibility will reach the age of sixteen without altering her name as far as she can?' asks Jane Austen in *Northanger Abbey*),[30] but the surname La Tournelle is less easily explained. Until 1780 it was known only to belong to the widow of a local Huguenot pastor, with whom Miss Hackitt was totally unconnected. Mary Butt (later Mrs Mary Sherwood), who entered the school a few years after the Austen sisters, thought that Miss Hackitt must have been employed originally as a French teacher and been given the name La Tournelle to impress parents; but, as she apparently knew no word of French, this seems unlikely. Her half-sister owned the school: it is probable that, having been employed to help with the domestic arrangements, she adopted the French name on her own initiative, in anticipation of the day when she would inherit the establishment. In addition to retaining a streak of romance in her nature, which led her to drape the walls of her drawing-room with chenille hangings representing tombs and weeping willows, she was a shrewd businesswoman. As such, she would have known that French ideas had been successfully infiltrating the English educational scene since the middle of the eighteenth century and that a French name would give a cachet to her establishment.[31]

Like Mrs Goddard, she believed that she worked hard enough in general to be entitled to take time off now and again; but whereas the former merely accepted an occasional invitation out to tea or supper Mrs La Tournelle disappeared from view every afternoon. Discipline was none too rigid, at least as far as the older girls were concerned. They were expected to take part in morning prayers in the classroom, but no one minded if they were late. They were required to attend lessons for the rest of the morning but were then free to spend the afternoon as they wished, roaming about the old house, strolling in the garden or gazing out of the window at boys crossing the Forbury from Dr Valpy's school at the other side. They were not supposed to leave the grounds, but nobody took much trouble to keep an eye on them. Fortunately, good sense prevailed: there were none of the elopements which a contemporary writer described as a 'dismal and desperate' feature of boarding school life and which Jane was to make use of in her novels.[32]

Neither Jane nor Cassandra spent weeks of their summer holiday visiting classmates, as Harriet Smith is reported to have done in *Emma*.[33] Nor did they make any lasting friendships among their contemporaries.

This need not suggest that they were unhappy at the school. There is no reason to suppose that they felt out of place, for, although the Abbey attracted a few wealthy girls, the majority came from small gentry and professional backgrounds not unlike their own. A few, like the Martin sisters at Mrs Goddard's school, were daughters of farmers. The only reference Jane ever made to the school in her subsequent correspondence with Cassandra gives the impression that the pair whispered and giggled happily with the other girls:

> The letter which I have this moment received from you has diverted me beyond moderation. I could die of laughter at it, as they used to say at school.[34]

There was plenty that a couple of cheerful girls might have enjoyed at the Abbey. The gateway building was unlike any ordinary house. Two vast stairways with the remains of gilt on the balustrades led to the rooms above. These were connected by narrow passages, full of nooks and crannies, to the adjoining schoolhouse – a rambling two-storey building shaded by huge trees under which the younger children played on summer evenings. An embankment on two sides of the garden gave a view of the ruins of the twelfth-century abbey, where ghosts were said to have been seen, whilst more prosaically the gateway itself gave on to the Forbury, once the forecourt of the great abbey church and now an open space where fairs were held. The girls were allowed to receive visitors. On one occasion their mother's cousin, the Revd Thomas Leigh, called in on his way home from London to Adlestrop and gave Cassandra and Jane some pocket money; on another, their brother Edward, who was about to leave England on the Grand Tour, came with his cousin Edward Cooper and took all three girls out to dinner at an inn. Then there was the excitement of breaking up for holidays in the summer and again at Christmas. Sometimes one of the masters would give a ball; at other times the dance-room would be fitted up as a theatre with footlights and curtain, and the girls would produce a play to which boys from Dr Valpy's school were invited. Mrs La Tournelle in the course of her mysterious earlier life had had her head turned by the theatre: there was nothing she liked better than to regale the girls with stories of actors and green rooms.

If Cassandra and Jane were disappointed when they were withdrawn from school after little more than a twelvemonth, they recorded no sign of it. The reason for their withdrawal is unknown but was probably unremarkable. There was after all the expense to be considered. Mrs La Tournelle's charges, like Mrs Goddard's, could have been described as moderate, but at £35 a year for each pupil they swallowed up the amount George Austen earned from any two of his teenage pupils. He could afford the expenditure whilst his affairs prospered, but the severe winter of 1785–86, which brought snowdrifts ten feet high in Hampshire during the girls' Christmas holiday, made hay, straw and turnips very scarce and thereby caused cattle to die or to become too emaciated to sell profitably. In May and June of 1786, frost and blight decimated fruit crops, and in the following months good weather produced a plentiful harvest which lowered the price of wheat. These problems came at the very time when George Austen had taken on the cost of sending Frank to naval college (£25 a year in boarding fees, with incidental expenses which might total another £25 to £30, plus the cost of providing a new uniform every twelve months on the King's birthday).[35]

Girls were frequently sent to boarding school for a short time only, to acquire a few social graces. At the end of two years, Mary Butt felt that the school had given her greater poise and self-confidence than she could have acquired in a country vicarage: 'I was not the same awkward girl I had been', she wrote.[36] Perhaps the Austen parents thought that Cassandra, at nearly fourteen years of age, was equally ready to face life's challenges without further polish and that Jane, not yet eleven, was too young to be subjected to a 'finishing' process. Moreover, their brother James, who liked to pontificate on the subject of girls' education, was vehemently critical of the kind of syllabus offered at most schools. This may have been the reason why no further thought was given to sending Jane either to the Abbey or anywhere else. By Christmas 1786 both girls were back home for good.

Chapter 4

Reason and Godliness

If morning prayers had been a somewhat casual affair at the Abbey School, Jane was unlikely to have found them so when she got home, for her father, in spite of his farm and his school, was above all a clergyman. 'The first & most important of all considerations to a human Being is Religion', George Austen told his son Frank, when the latter was preparing to go to sea.[1] Unlike Fielding's Parson Trulliber, who was 'a parson on Sundays, but on all other six might properly be called a farmer', Jane's father relied upon a steward, John Bond, to carry out the day to day supervision of his acres, much as Mr Knightley in *Emma* relies on William Larkins. The school, certainly, required him to spend a large part of each day teaching, but this was regarded by contemporaries as a legitimate use of a clergyman's time, since it helped him to increase his influence with the neighbouring gentry and to inculcate Christian principles into a rising generation of the ruling class.

George Austen was appointed rector of Steventon in the diocese of Winchester in the same year that the famous – or, as some would have said, infamous – Benjamin Hoadly, bishop of the diocese, died. The latter's relaxed attitude to doctrine and church discipline was already being superseded, and in ensuing years archdeacons were to circulate some firm charges to the clergy reminding them of their spiritual obligations and of the importance of their position in the life of the community.[2] Such parochial records as have survived show that George Austen was exemplary in the performance of the duties required of a parish priest at that time. In the course of thirty-seven years as rector of Steventon he rarely called upon a substitute. All but a handful of births, marriages and deaths were registered by him. He visited parishioners in their homes to baptise their new-born infants before a second Sunday had passed, as the Prayer Book then required. He held services of Morning and Evening Prayer in church every Sunday, and administered the sacrament of Holy Communion often enough for his parishioners to fulfil their obligation to partake of it at least three times a year, one of which had to be Easter. Visitation returns testify that he kept the chancel of his church in good repair, as was his duty, and saw to it that the wardens fulfilled their obligation to maintain the nave, if necessary by levying a rate. The Church of England had not yet adopted the more exalted role designed for the clergy by Evangelicals and Tractarians alike, but George Austen took no narrow view of his duties. The knowledge which his daughter later showed of the needs of the poor and lonely in the parish suggests that he knew his parishioners personally and well.[3]

Jane Austen was descended from clergymen, closely related to ten other clergymen and acquainted with a great many more. She was aware that their specific training for clerical duties was minimal. There were no theological colleges for them to attend. The majority took an ordinary rather than an honours degree, after which a hurried perusal of a few theological texts was well known to be all that was required to prepare a candidate for the few questions he would be asked by the bishop prior to ordination.[4] The idiosyncrasies and absurdities displayed by the clergy provided her with much amusement and some scope for moralising in her novels. Yet she was never in doubt that the church was served on the whole by a decent body of clergy who performed their duties to the satisfaction of their flocks and for the good of the nation. Of the twelve clergy characters appearing in her novels (Edward Ferrars and the enigmatic Dr Davies in *Sense and Sensibility*, Mr Collins in *Pride and Prejudice*, Henry Tilney and Mr Morland in *Northanger Abbey*, Edmund Bertram, Mr Norris and Dr Grant in *Mansfield Park*, Mr Elton in *Emma* and Charles Hayter, Dr Shirley and the shadowy Mr Wentworth in *Persuasion*) only three – Dr Grant, Mr Collins and Mr Elton – receive any criticism at her hands, and all three are pilloried for personal faults rather than for any deficiency in performing their duties. Dr Grant is too fond of eating, but his gourmet habits do not prevent him from being a satisfactory parish priest. He resides in his vicarage, practises hospitality and preaches excellent sermons. Mr Collins and Mr Elton are mercenary-minded, and lack the discrimination in behaviour which was regarded as the hallmark of a gentleman; but Mr Collins has announced at the beginning of his ministry that he will be 'ever ready to perform those rites and ceremonies which are instituted by the Church of England', and he is a man of his word; whilst Mr Elton, for all his silliness in the presence of women, is pronounced by no less an authority than Mr Knightley to be 'a very respectable vicar of Highbury'. He is consulted by the magistrates and churchwardens; persons in need can appeal to him at any time; the teachers at Mrs Goddard's school are impressed by his sermons; and his conduct in church is admired by the whole parish.[5]

With the possible exception of Edward Ferrars, who says that he always wanted to be a clergyman, Jane Austen's fictional clergy show no particular sense of vocation. This is because no such experience was required of candidates seeking ordination, nor were they encouraged when priested to regard themselves as having been endowed with personal qualities of an exceptional nature. They were simply qualified to administer the sacraments of the church, which were in themselves a sufficient means of salvation. Emma Woodhouse may not have wished to invite Mr Elton to dinner, but she raises no objection to his performing the service in which she marries Mr Knightley.[6]

The ministry of the church was a profession like any other, attracting large numbers of candidates at a time when few professions were sufficiently well organised to compete in popularity. Over 50 per cent of all graduates of Oxford and Cambridge took Holy Orders. Many middle-class families had one or two sons in the ministry; George Crabbe, the poet, told Walter Scott that he had put two of his sons into the church because he could not think of anything else to do with them.[7] Inevitably there were some clergymen who performed their duties in a mechanical fashion and took advantage of the fact that the obligations were not numerous. A few notorious cynics and loose-livers were gleefully tracked down and exposed for the entertainment of readers in a journal entitled *Public Characters*, produced annually towards the end of the century.[8] In spite of such embarrassing revelations, James Froude regretted the change which took place in public life when the Oxford Movement produced a more ostentatiously zealous clergy. Looking back nostalgically upon the modest claims that had been made for the clergy earlier in the century, he wrote:

> They [the clergy] were Protestants to the backbone. They knew nothing and cared nothing about the Apostolic Succession. They had no sacerdotal pretensions; they made no claims to be essentially distinguished from the laity. They affected neither austerity nor singularity. They rode, shot, hunted, ate and drank like other people ... In dress and habit they were simply a superior class of small country gentlemen: very far from immaculate, but, taken altogether, wholesome and solid members of practical English life ... The parson of the old school, however outwardly worldly in character, did sincerely and faithfully believe in the truth of the Christian religion; and the congregation which he addressed was troubled with as few doubts as himself.[9]

The religious training Jane received at her father's hands was neither lenient on the one hand nor repressive on the other. Religious duties were presented as inescapable but acceptable. In accordance with the Book of Common Prayer, the emphasis at her baptism had been on the need to cleanse her from the stain of original sin, but George Austen, unlike the more Evangelical clergy of the time, was not obsessed by the inherent depravity of mankind. He did not share the view, prevalent since Puritan times, that God's grace was soon used up and the baptismal state of innocence quickly eroded. He saw no need to break his children's wills in order to make them obedient to God. He did not take them to visit the dying or view the dead in order that they should be aware of their own mortality. His chief insistence was that they should say 'their prayers' (as the phrase went) night and morning, thanking God for the blessings they had received and humbly seeking his continued protection.[10] As a baby, Jane would have had such prayers said for her over her cradle. When she grew a little older, she would have joined the rest of the family each morning in the parlour or in her father's study whilst he read the service from the Prayer Book; in the evening she would have said her prayers as she was put to bed by her mother or by the most trusted of the family's servants. The boarding pupils were equally expected to be faithful in prayer.[11] Even in this important matter, however, George Austen never expected too much. He reminded his son Frank that he must regard prayer night and morning as 'a Duty which nothing can excuse the omission of'; yet, being a reasonable man, he added that in times of great pressure 'a short Ejaculation to the Almighty, when it comes from the heart will be as acceptable to him as the most elegant and studied form of Words'.[12]

When she was considered old enough – perhaps five or six – Jane would have been allowed on Sunday mornings to accompany Cassandra and her brothers to church, where they would have squashed into the pew reserved for the rector's family, glad in winter to be able to huddle together for warmth in the unheated building. Unless the Digweed boys peeped at the rest of the congregation through the wooden tracery of the squire's high box pew, which occupied a privileged place at the front of the nave, there could have been little to entertain a child. The church, mainly dating from the thirteenth century, was very plain. There is unlikely to have been any music, for the hymns of Watts and Wesley which Evangelical clergy were introducing into their services had not yet reached the main body of the church, especially in rural areas. Even the singing of Sternhold's metrical version of the Psalms had largely been discarded in favour of antiphonal recitation, with the clerk dolefully calling out each line for the benefit of illiterate members of the congregation. The service – Morning Prayer, Litany and Ante-Communion – lasted anything up to three hours if accompanied by a sermon; mercifully, Jane as a youngster may have been allowed to leave at the end of the three Collects. Along with the rest of the congregation, she would have begun the service by repeating after her father the general confession of sins and hearing him pronounce God's forgiveness. This was followed by a psalm of praise and thanksgiving and by readings (or 'Lessons') from the Old and New Testaments, after which everybody stood up to say the Apostles' Creed. Three prayers, a blessing, and a little girl was free to emerge into the churchyard, where grass and wild flowers grew among the lopsided gravestones.

Jane's religious training probably began in earnest on her return from Southampton and continued when she returned from the Abbey School. Her three godparents, who had promised at her public baptism that they would encourage her to hear sermons and make sure that she learnt the Creed, the Lord's Prayer, the Ten Commandments, and 'all other things which a Christian ought to know for his soul's health', are unlikely to have been any more active in their duties than the majority of godparents have ever been. They were all three at a distance. Samuel Cooke (Mrs Austen's cousin by marriage) was vicar of Great Bookham in Surrey; the elderly Jane Austen (the wife of Mr Austen's benefactor, Uncle Francis) lived at Sevenoaks; Jane Musgrave was the wife of Mrs Austen's cousin James, who was rector of Chinnor.[13] They may even have made their baptismal promises by proxy, and doubtless felt happy enough to leave their goddaughter's training in her father's hands.

As a vehicle for teaching the basic truths of the Christian religion in accordance with the doctrines of the Church of England, George Austen used the Catechism – the list of questions and answers set out in the Book of Common Prayer.

Question. What is your name?

Answer. N. or M.

Question. Who gave you this name?

Answer. My Godfathers and Godmothers in my Baptism, wherein I was made a member of Christ, a child of God, and an inheritor of the kingdom of heaven.

Question. What did your Godfathers and Godmothers then for you?

Answer. They did promise and vow three things in my name. First, that
I should renounce the devil and all his works, the pomps and vanities
of this wicked world, and all the sinful lusts of the flesh ...

So it went on, at a length of some 1800 words, until the Cathechist
had assured himself that his pupil could enumerate the sacraments,
describe their purpose and recite the Lord's Prayer, the Ten Commandments and the Apostles' Creed. In using this apparently
old-fashioned instrument, George Austen was in fact abreast of the
times, for catechising had been adandoned by many of the clergy during
the first half of the eighteenth century and restored to popularity only
in recent years, as a result of the successful use made of it by Evangelical
teachers.[14]

To George Austen, the object behind the mere learning of the answers
by heart was that the pupil should thoroughly understand his or her
duty to God, to neighbours and to self. From the Catechism Jane learnt
that the first four Commandments required her to love, honour, trust
and worship God and to serve him truly all the days of her life, whilst
the remaining six involved loving her neighbour as herself and treating
others as she would like them to treat her. There were no words
outlining her duty to herself: it was George Austen's own understanding,
as a Christian and as a scholar of the Enlightenment, that if she lived
in harmony with God and her fellow men she would arrive at self-
fulfilment without having to give further thought to the matter. It was
an understanding that was to form the moral framework of all Jane's
novels: her characters who experience true happiness are those who
think about others. She did not always, however, take kindly to her
fellow men. In her novels, she is sometimes at pains to point out that
we cannot be expected to love them in the way we love our closest
friends and that we ought not to give the appearance of doing so. As
Emma Woodhouse decides after observing Mr Weston:

A little less of open-heartedness would have made him a higher character.
General benevolence, not general friendship, made a man what he ought
to be.[15]

For our relationship with neighbours, we need the imaginative concern
that Mr Knightley shows for Mr Woodhouse and Miss Bates – a concern
that the Prayer Book calls charity. The Catechism urges diligent prayer
as the only means of acquiring the special grace needed to maintain a
charitable approach. Jane Austen's reticence about religion precluded

her from mentioning this in her novels, but in her daily life she never failed to carry out the Catechist's advice.

For further instruction, George Austen relied upon one of several compilations by Vicesimus Knox, the headmaster of his old school at Tunbridge. Knox advocated what he believed to be a 'liberal education'. For all godly purposes, he said, it was enough that, having learnt the Catechism, children should study the Bible and read sermons. Care must be taken, however, to shield them from the emotional outpourings of Evangelical divines.[16] To aid parents and teachers in making a proper selection, Knox's *Elegant Extracts in Prose* included a section designated as 'Moral and Religious'. This began with articles reproduced from the *Spectator*, the *Rambler*, and the *Idler* on such topics as 'Providence', 'The Immortality of the Soul' and 'Motives to Piety and Virtue'. These were followed by commentaries on various parts of the Book of Common Prayer and selections from the works of contemporary writers such as Hugh Blair and Mrs Hester Chapone.[17] The book appeared in 1783 when Jane was seven. Her father thought so highly of it that five years later he gave the fourteen-year-old Frank a copy of it to take with him on board ship bound for the East Indies, assuring him that its passages from approved authors would furnish him with 'every requisite for belief and practice'.[18] A further copy remained at home. In its closely printed pages, Jane could have seen discussed at length a precept she was to apply to Henry Crawford and several other characters in her novels – that 'idleness is the most fruitful source of crimes and evils' and that a private income brings no exemption from useful employment:

> Every man has something to do which he neglects; every man has faults to conquer which he delays to combat ... The social virtues may find a man business more than the most active station in life. To advise the ignorant, relieve the needy, comfort the afflicted, are duties that fall in our way almost every day of our lives.[19]

Elizabeth Bennet discovers during her visit to Pemberley that Mr Darcy has a great many social virtues; on the whole, however, Jane Austen was so impressed by the temptations to idleness besetting the wealthy that she came near to describing even 'a competence' as an evil in itself. Elinor Dashwood, meditiating on 'the irreparable injury which too early an independence' has inflicted on the 'naturally open and honest disposition' of Willoughby, concludes that it is 'the world', rather than his own selfishness, which has made him extravagant and vain.[20]

From Hugh Blair, Jane learnt what was meant by 'taste' in relation to preaching, and how to distinguish proper feeling from embarrassing emotion. She grew up to be an assiduous reader of sermons and a sharp critic of those she heard delivered from the pulpit. By the time she wrote *Mansfield Park* she may even have encountered the five volumes of Blair's sermons, but it seems unlikely that Mary Crawford had done more than read the few passages in *Elegant Extracts* when she wished that country clergymen would have 'the good sense to prefer Blair's sermons to their own'.[21]

On her return from school, Jane would have been considered old enough to attend church not only on Sunday mornings but in the late afternoon too, to hear her father read Evening Prayer. If the weather was very bad, however, the family and servants would gather instead in the parlour whilst Mrs Austen, or one of the older boys should any be at home, read the service from the Prayer Book. As the well-chosen words of the Anglican liturgy became familiar, they made their impression on Jane's receptive mind. In her young days there were very few criticisms of the Prayer Book abroad. Later, when objections to its 'redundancies and repetitions' began to be heard, Jane regarded them as superficial – the kind of criticism a man like Henry Crawford would be likely to advance. The prayers which she herself wrote for use at family services were firmly based not only on the teaching of the Prayer Book but on its rhythms and diction, including its use of 'Thee' and 'Thou' when addressing God. The only improvement in the church's services that she was willing to consider as being at all necessary was that parsons should try to be more audible.[22]

As far as sermons were concerned, most of those she heard at Steventon are likely to have been chosen from published collections and expounded to the congregation with whatever explanation seemed appropriate and necessary. Jane had no objection to the use of published texts, which were regarded at the time as a means of introducing congregations to the work of great divines such as Tillotson and Sherlock. The same sermons were often used again and again in country churches: Parson Woodforde, for instance, preached modified versions of Tillotson's famous discourse on 'The Precepts of Christianity not Grievous' many times over; and even, sometimes, read the whole text verbatim.[23] Books of sermons were too expensive to buy in any great number (Samuel Johnson charged £2 a time merely to hire his); and in any case, if we are to believe George Eliot, congregations liked to hear sermons they already knew.[24] Country clergymen were not expected to produce original compositions except on very rare occasions. Mr Collins of *Pride and Prejudice*, who preached two of his own sermons in the first six months of his ministry, was in this matter, as in most others, ludicrously overzealous in the performance of his duties.[25]

Of George Austen's sermons, only one survived his death. The dates in the margin indicated that he preached it eight times at Steventon and seven at Deane. The text was from Psalm 5, urging God to protect his followers from the wiles of unbelievers: 'For there is no faithfulness in their mouth; their inward part is very wickedness; their throat is an open sepulchre; they flatter with their tongue.'[26] The temptations most often denounced in sermons at this time were those later known as consumerism – an addiction to purchasing the latest manufactured products simply because they were available. Although the word for the craze had not yet been invented, its existence as a social evil was an obsession with preachers, and it may well have been as a result of hearing about it from the pulpit that Jane came to attribute it to General Tilney in *Northanger Abbey*:

> The elegance of the breakfast set forced itself on Catherine's notice when they were seated at table; and, luckily, it had been the General's choice. He was enchanted by her approbation of his taste, confessed it to be neat and simple, thought it right to encourage the manufacture of his country; and for his part, to his uncritical palate, the tea was as well flavoured from the clay of Staffordshire, as from that of Dresden or Sêve. But this was quite an old set, purchased two years ago. The manufacture was much improved since that time; he had seen some beautiful specimens when last in town, and had he not been perfectly without vanity of that kind, might have been tempted to order a new set.[27]

George Austen's sermon was probably preached by him on occasions (of which there were two or three every year) when the psalm in question was appointed for recitation by the congregation at Morning Prayer. Like much of his teaching, it may have ended, as did the psalm itself, on a note of promise to the faithful: 'For thou, Lord, wilt bless the righteous; with favour wilt thou compass him as with a shield.'

During Jane's girlhood, her father would have ridden off on horseback at some point every Sunday to take at least one service in his other church at Deane. This was then a simple building with nave and chancel, a south porch and a tiny bell tower at the west end. Here the most imposing pews were occupied by current members of the Harwood, Bramston and Wither families, whose dead ancestors were commemorated in tablets on the walls. At neither Steventon nor Deane were there regular services on any day during the week. Apart from Easter Sunday and Christmas Day, there were few parishes where feast days and holy days were kept. Lent simply required a few changes in the prayers on Sundays; and Ash Wednesday and Good Friday usually passed without services in church. The population of George Austen's two parishes combined was so small – a mere 284 as late as 1801 – that rites of passage occupied him on average a mere six times a year.[28] Funerals could take place on a Sunday. They were often marked by most of the women in the village wearing black bombazine, whilst the men carried the coffin from the deceased's house to the church. It was on a Sunday spent in her brother's house in Kent that Jane 'saw Mr Claringbould's funeral go by'.[29]

Weddings were usually simple affairs, with only the immediate family attending as guests. These, too, could take place on a Sunday, and if by any chance there was more than one couple they could be married in the same ceremony. The church at Steventon having no vestry, and the key to the main door being kept, as everyone knew, in the hollow of a yew tree in the churchyard, George Austen probably took the marriage registers home with him after services. At some time when she was about sixteen, Jane amused herself by writing mock entries in the specimen pages. She filled in the application form for banns with the names of 'Henry Frederick Howard Fitzwilliam of London' and 'Jane Austen of Steventon', and recorded a marriage as having taken place between 'Arthur William Mortimer of Liverpool' and the same Jane Austen of Steventon. Inspiration then ran out, leaving 'Jack Smith' to marry 'Jane Smith, late Austen', in the presence of further Smiths.[30]

To an enlightened clergyman such as George Austen, the emphasis in religious teaching, both at home and from the pulpit, was no longer on the mystical aspects of Christianity but on its reasonableness, which was believed to be such as to make it acceptable to anyone prepared to use ordinary reasoning powers. Newton's explanation of the workings of gravity seemed to have proved that God had created a universe which obeyed fixed laws, the nature of which could be elucidated by a process of observation and deduction. The human beings who formed a part of this universe must also have been given divine laws which, if obeyed, would result in their lives running as smoothly as the daily course of the world around them. These too were discoverable by the use of common sense. They could be inculcated into children by means of fables and stories rather than by drilling them in admonitions laid down by the church. At a more adult level they could be illustrated by studying the behaviour of human beings in society as effectively as by reading religious works – in which context, history was an important subject at Steventon parsonage.

The Form of an Entry of Publication of Banns.

The Banns of Marriage between *A. B.* of *[London]*
and *C. D.* of *[Steventon]*   were duly publifhed in this

Church for the {firft / fecond / third} Time, on Sunday the

Day of   in the Year One Thoufand Seven
Hundred and

                              J. J. Rector ⎤
                                       Vicar ⎬
                                       Curate ⎦

The Form of an Entry of a Marriage.

A. B. of *[Steventon]*   and *C. D.* of *[   ]*

were married in this Church by {Banns / Licenfe*} this
Day of   in the Year One Thoufand Seven
Hundred and   by me
                              J. J. Rector ⎤
                                       Vicar ⎬
                                       Curate ⎦
This Marriage was folemnized between us *A. B. C. B.* late *C. D.*
in the Prefence of *E. F. G. H.*

* Infert thefe Words, viz. *with Confent of* {*Parents* / *Guardians*} where both, or either
of the Parties to be married *by Licenfe*, are under Age.

Specimen page of the Steventon Marriage Register, filled in fictitiously by Jane
Austen. (*Hampshire Record Office*)

Above all, God's Word, it was thought, could be received by observing the wonders of nature. James Thomson's sensationally popular cycle of poems entitled *The Seasons* (from which Catherine Morland learnt to quote extracts in order to qualify as a heroine) inaugurated the idea that the spectacle of uncontrolled power presented by fierce weather and harsh landscapes evoked awesome reverence for the great Creator, whilst the teeming wildlife and luscious fruits of gentler environments witnessed to God's beneficence. Thomson was very probably a deist, but *The Seasons*, extensively quoted in a second volume of *Elegant Extracts*, was read in Christian households as a genuinely devotional work. Not least of its merits were the sections which implied that God's goodness to his people required them to show a comparable concern for each other.[31]

Evangelical writers complained that Christian parents were often as intent on preparing their children for this life as for the next.[32] If this was a fault, George Austen was certainly guilty of it. He brought up all his children to be intensely practical and to improve on such talents as God had given them. He believed wholeheartedly in the spirit of the passage from the Book of Proverbs, which he read from the lectern once a year to his evening congregation:

> My son, forget not my law; but let thine heart
>   keep my commandments:
> For length of days, and long life, and peace
>   shall they add to thee.
> Let not mercy and truth forsake thee: bind them about
>   thy neck, write them upon the table of thine heart:
> So shalt thou find favour and good understanding
>   in the sight of God and man.[33]

He reminded his Midshipman son that, since his success in the navy was dependent wholly on God's dispensation, it was out of 'interest' as well as 'duty' that he should address himself night and morning to God in prayer. Prudence, defined in the Old Testament as synonymous with Wisdom, both spiritual and worldly, would show him how to rise in the world. Good humour, unselfishness, affability and devotion to duty would win him the esteem and support of officers and men alike. Frank was also recommended, for the sake of his 'Health, Morals and Fortune', to maintain Sobriety and, for the sake of his comfort in the hot climate to which he was going, to pay attention to personal cleanliness. In particular he was reminded to take care of his teeth. Frank thought so highly of his father's letter that it remained with him on board ship, through fire and water, to the end of his career.[34]

Its combination of godliness and good sense was to guide Jane Austen also as she prepared for her adult life, when it would be displayed both in her conduct and in her novels. The optimism which pervaded it, and which was typical of the Enlightenment attitudes which prevailed during George Austen's university days, must sometimes have appeared to fly in the face of the evidence, but it was based on a faith in the ultimate sureness of God's promises which she tried hard to accept. She also learnt to share her father's acceptance of the current structure of earthly society. 'The little world, of which you are going to become an inhabitant, will consist of three Orders of Men', George Austen told Frank.[35] His commander and other superior officers on the ship would forward his career if he showed them obedience and respect; his messmates and other persons of equal standing would be won over by a genial and helpful manner on his part; the ordinary seamen would respond to benevolence:

> With your Inferiors perhaps you will have but little intercourse, but when it does occur, there is a sort of kindness they have a claim on you for, & which, you may believe me, will not be thrown away on them.

Some years were to elapse before Mrs Alexander penned her famous words

> The rich man in his castle,
> The poor man at his gate,
> God made them high or lowly,
> He ordered their estate ...

but the sentiment was already well known. It derived from the instruction in the Catechism to do one's duty in that state of life into which it should please God to call one. It was never intended to deter people from striving honourably to rise in the social scale: Jane Austen ridicules Sir Walter Elliot for criticising the navy 'as being the means of bringing persons of obscure birth into distinction'.[36] It meant rather that, since equality of circumstances may be unattainable and possibly undesirable, people should conduct themselves usefully in the situation in which they found themselves and not question God's Providence by envying the more fortunate or despising the less. So, at least, Jane was instructed by her favourite religious manual.[37] The fact that a complicated code of behaviour and a multitude of mistaken attitudes had grown up around society's divisions was to provide her with endless material for her novels.

Sketch of the back of Steventon parsonage by Jane's niece Anna Austen (later
Lefroy). Dated 1814. (*Private Collection*)

Chapter 5

Reading and Learning

In most secular subjects, Jane was left to instruct herself by reading as much as she wished in her father's library. George Austen bought books whenever he could afford them (and, sometimes, whether he could afford them or not), until by the time he retired he had some five hundred volumes, housed in a handsome Hepplewhite bookcase. The catalogue Jane made of them has unfortunately disappeared, and only one item bearing George Austen's bookplate and signature – a copy of Charlotte Brooke's *Reliques of Irish Poetry* (Dublin, 1789) – has been traced.[1] In his later years he became, like many clergymen, fond of the works of William Cowper, but until then he had probably not bought much poetry. Poems other than Latin verse were not on the whole considered manly reading and are unlikely, therefore, to have figured in the school curriculum at Steventon.[2] Jane's early writings show that as a girl she was acquainted with Pope, Gray and Thomson, as well as with Shakespeare; but her knowledge of prose writers was clearly much more extensive. Whether, as a girl, she had actually read the works of the fifty or more authors whose ideas can be detected in her juvenile writings is another matter.[3] Her brother Henry wrote of her admiration for Samuel Johnson, but the only one of his works she is known to have possessed in her early years (apart from portions reproduced in *Elegant Extracts*) is the novel *Rasselas*, which is hardly typical.[4] In her own novels she adopts many of the ideas of Locke, including his belief that the major part of an adult's character, for good or evil, is the result of education: the Bertram girls have 'no positive ill nature' but are led astray by Mrs Norris's malign influence on their upbringing; and even Mr Collins's 'weak head', Jane thinks, became worse under the guidance of 'an ignorant father'.[5] Yet she may not have read Locke's famous *Thoughts Concerning Education* so much as heard his ideas discussed, for they were common currency.

> Pray, sir, in all the reading which you have ever read, did you ever read such a book as Locke's *Essay upon the Human Understanding?*

asks Tristram Shandy of an imagined critic.

> Don't answer me rashly, because many, I know, quote the book who have not read it.[6]

Conversation was highly prized as an instrument of education in the eighteenth century: Johnson, for one, actively sought opportunities for extending his knowledge by discussion. In adult life, Jane was often disappointed by the standard of conversation she met with in the houses of the gentry. Combined, as it was, with a new fashion which allowed guests to divert themselves with reading, letter-writing, sewing or playing an instrument, conversation was often desultory. Among families that she knew and had grown fond of, Jane could accept a dull evening with tolerance, reporting kindly to Cassandra on an evening at Ashe Park:

> Mrs Bramston talked a good deal of nonsense, which Mr Bramston and Mr Clerk seemed almost equally to enjoy. There was whist & a casino table, & six outsiders. – Rice and Lucy made love, Mat: Robinson fell asleep, James & Mrs Augusta alternately read Dr Jenner's pamphlet on the cow pox, & I bestowed my company by turns on all. On enquiring of Mrs Clerk, I find that Mrs Heathcote made a great blunder in her news of the Crooks & Morleys; it is young Mr Crooke who is to marry the second Miss Morley – & it is the Miss Morleys instead of the second Miss Crooke, who were the beauties at the Music meeting ...[7]

She was less indulgent towards persons with social pretensions whom she met during her visits to her brother at Godmersham: an afternoon visit to Lady Fagg and her family at Mystole was reported to Cassandra as 'stupidish; ... there was a lack of Talk altogether'; whilst in another letter she could find nothing to say about a morning call from Lady Elizabeth Hatton and her daughter except that 'they came & they sat & they went'.[8] She is equally discriminating in her novels. Emma Woodhouse finds a dinner-party at the Coleses' reassuringly ordinary, with 'the usual rate of conversation; a few clever things said, a few downright silly, but by much the larger proportion neither one nor the other – nothing worse than everyday remarks, dull repetitions, old news, and heavy jokes'. On the other hand, Mrs Ferrars, we are told bitingly, was 'not a woman of many words; for unlike people in general, she proportioned them to her ideas'.[9]

The overall impression given by Jane Austen's letters and novels is that conversation in gentry circles was limited by narrow horizons: the men interested in sport and agriculture, the women in household matters and local gossip. Politics, which she attributes to men as an interest in *Sense and Sensibility*, was widely regarded as an unsuitable topic to introduce in mixed company. Clergymen could not all share the conversational brilliance of Henry Tilney, but there was a reasonable chance that they had read books and could express themselves intelligently. Jane was usually more appreciative of the clergymen than of the other people she met amongst her brother's Kentish neighbours: Mr Moore, rector of Wrotham, who had certain arrogant traits but could 'tell a story well'; Mr Sherer, vicar of Godmersham, whose opinion of her novels she sought; or Mr Chisholme, rector of Eastwell, with whom she indulged in persiflage when sitting next to him at dinner.[10] She would have been the first to admit how much she had benefited, as a girl, from the conversation of her parents and siblings in the parlour at Steventon Rectory.

Her brother Henry and her nephew James Edward, who were the first to write of her home background, mentioned particularly her early interest in the Picturesque and her detailed knowledge of Samuel Richardson's voluminous novel *The History of Sir Charles Grandison*.[11] William Gilpin, the originator of the idea of the Picturesque, was vicar of Boldre, a country parish to the south of the New Forest in the Austens' own county of Hampshire. From 1768 onwards, he published a series of 'observations' on his travels through various parts of Great Britain, commending himself to many of his fellow clergymen by assessing the aesthetic merit of landscape in accordance with its variety and balance – a sure sign of the handiwork of the divine creator. He insisted that to qualify as Picturesque (that is, suitable to form a picture) a landscape must display contrasting areas of light and shade, with a tangled foreground forming a frame for a smooth background. Unlike Edmund Burke, who relied for appreciation of landscape on the variety of emotions it aroused in the beholder, Gilpin set out rules which could be learnt for the purpose. This lent itself to a certain amount of jargon, which Henry Tilney in *Northanger Abbey* was to rattle off to the amazement of Catherine Morland.[12] In contrast, Marianne Dashwood in *Sense and Sensibility* was to deplore it when measured against her own emotional responses.[13]

Whereas Burke identified only two types of landscape, the beautiful (which was light and smooth, thereby creating sensations of peace and serenity) and the sublime (rough and dark, inspiring wonder and awe), Gilpin added a third, the 'horrid', consisting of towering rocks and cavernous depths, inspiring terror and disgust. Of the landscape near Castleton, in Derbyshire, Gilpin wrote:

> A combination of more horrid ideas is rarely found than this place affords ... The inhabitants of these scenes are as savage as the scenes themselves ... Few places have more the air of the poetical regions of Tartarus.[14]

Descriptions of similarly harsh landscapes, supposedly to be found in the Pyrenees, were soon to be exploited by Mrs Ann Radcliffe as settings for her 'horrid' novels.

Although 'enamoured of the picturesque', as her brother put it, at an early age, Jane was also aware of its comic potential. She was to make fun of Gilpin's rules about variety and mock his 'horrid' scenery in an early sketch, 'Evelyn'.[15] In her first attempt at a novel, later revised and published as *Sense and Sensibility*, she was to credit Edward Ferrars with a gently amusing response to Marianne's rapturous outbursts over wild landscapes:

> I like a fine prospect, but not on picturesque principles. I do not like crooked, twisted, blasted trees. I admire them much more if they are tall, straight and flourishing. I do not like ruined, tattered cottages. I am not fond of nettles, or thistles, or heath blossoms. I have more pleasure in a snug farm-house than a watch-tower – and a troop of tidy, happy villagers please me better than the finest banditti in the world.[16]

She nevertheless associated a love of the Picturesque with a cultivated gentlemanly taste, and hence in *Pride and Prejudice* she locates Darcy's ancestral home in the Peak District of Derbyshire, one of Gilpin's Picturesque areas of the country *par excellence*.

If Gilpin's *Observations* are now seldom read, Samuel Richardson's *Sir Charles Grandison* is widely regarded as unreadable. Its heightened vocabulary, outdated moralising and inordinate length, which runs to over a million and a half words, are enough to deter all but the most persevering. Yet to Jane Austen it was a cherished favourite of her childhood, whose every detail was remembered long afterwards. Her nephew believed that she knew the characters in the story as well as if they were her living friends. Therein lay its chief attraction: it was the first of all domestic comedies, providing a model for the type of fiction to which she was to make so distinguished a contribution. Again, however, she could see the comic potential of a novel that Richardson had intended to be taken seriously. The eponymous hero, designed to set the highest standards of gentlemanly behaviour, is so perfect in every respect as to be not only unrealistic but ludicrous. In her early tale of *Jack and Alice*, written when she was about fourteen, Jane produced a parody of him in the person of the youthful Charles Adams, who announces solemnly:

> I look upon myself to be Sir a perfect Beauty – where would you see a finer figure or a more charming face. Then, sir I imagine my Manners & Address to be of the most polished kind; there is a certain elegance, a peculiar sweetness in them that I never saw equalled & cannot describe. Partiality aside, I am certainly more accomplished in every Language, every Science, every Art and every thing than any other person in Europe. My temper is even, my virtues innumerable, my self unparalleled ... I expect nothing more in my wife than my wife will find in me – Perfection.[17]

Yet she appreciated Sir Charles Grandison's virtues, underpinned as they were by a firm though reticent faith in Christianity. As a model for the heroes of her own novels, she preferred him to Fielding's attractive rogue Tom Jones (with whom she was also acquainted at an early age). Sir Charles's virtues were to be transferred to Mr Darcy, as described by his housekeeper at Pemberley – the best of sons, brothers, friends, landlords, employers. His personal assets were also to be transferred to Darcy, who like Grandison is young, handsome, rich and aristocratic, with huge estates, an elegant mansion and tastefully landscaped grounds. Jane was not prepared to have her hero pray at the deathbed of a repentant Mr Wickham, as Grandison does at that of Sir Hargrave Pollexfen, but Darcy attends church dutifully at Rosings (in spite of his disgust at the parson's obsequiousness) and he ends his long letter to Elizabeth Bennet by invoking God's blessing upon her.[18]

For a girl to be left to educate herself by reading may sound to the modern ear very much like neglect, yet Jane Austen came to believe that it was the best kind of education anyone could have had. She was aware of the problems arising from a situation which lacked the discipline of the classroom: Elizabeth Bennet, brought up with her sisters on the same principle, admits to the disapproving Lady Catherine de Bourgh that 'those who chose to be idle certainly might'.[19] For others, however, reading could be 'an education in itself', especially if there were someone at hand with whom to discuss the books. James Austen was accredited by his son, James Edward Austen-Leigh, with having performed such a role as Jane was growing up, but this may have been wishful thinking. If James had indeed fulfilled it, Jane repaid him handsomely by writing with great appreciation of a similar service performed by Edmund Bertram for Fanny Price at Mansfield Park:

> he [Edmund] recommended the books which charmed her leisure hours, he encouraged her taste, and corrected her judgement; he made reading useful by talking to her of what she read, and heightened its attraction by judicious praise.[20]

It seems that there were two subjects, however, which even Fanny Price could not be left to study on her own: she had to be allowed to have her cousins' governess to teach her French and hear her 'read the daily portion of History'.[21] Jane had begun to receive instruction in French along with her brother Frank before he left for the Royal Naval Academy; evidence suggests that she also received history lessons with him, under the guidance of her father, and that these may have been continued after Frank had left. The lessons included both European and British history, though possibly of selected periods only. Whatever textbook George Austen used for European history, it appears to have had both a patriotic and a Protestant bias, for when Frank in 1813 was commanding a battleship, on its way to Sweden to convey Bernadotte's troops to fight against Napoleon in Germany, Jane wrote to him:

> It must be a real enjoyment to you, since you are obliged to leave England, to be where you are, seeing something of a new Country, & one that has been so distinguished as Sweden. Gustavus-Vasa, & Charles 12th, & Christina, & Linneus – do their Ghosts rise up before You? I have a great respect for former Sweden. So zealous as it was for Prot-estanism [*sic*]! And I have always fancied it more like England than many Countries.[22]

The mention of Linnaeus is a particular tribute to her father's teach-ing, for Enlightenment thinkers at Oxford in his day had regarded the Swedish naturalist as a key figure in their attempts to reconcile science with religion. Linnaeus himself had believed that his intricate classifi-cation of species, far from helping to undermine religion as many continental thinkers declared, proved that the natural world was created by a judicious, all-seeing, efficient and beneficent God. The 'natural religion' which such a view encouraged lies behind Fanny Price's eu-logies upon the harmony of nature and the intended harmony among human beings, evoked by the beauty of the moonlit landscape at Mansfield Park:

> 'Here's harmony!', said she, 'Here's repose! Here's what may tranquillize

every care, and lift the heart to rapture! When I look out on such a night as this, I feel as if there could be neither wickedness not sorrow in the world; and there certainly would be less of both if the sublimity of Nature were more attended to, and people were carried more out of themselves by contemplating such a scene.' [23]

The star-gazing which Fanny and Edmund were engaged in at the time was also a tribute to Enlightenment teaching. Contemplation of the heavens through the newly-invented telescopes convinced many viewers that God was less remote than he had once seemed to be; hence the study of astronomy was recommended by archdeacons to the clergy as a suitable occupation for their leisure hours. George Austen, unlike many wealthier gentlemen of the time, was not in a position to have an observatory built at the top of his house, but he had 'a small astronomical instrument' which he presumably used in his teaching and which Jane believed to be 'a Compass & Sun-dial'. He also had a microscope and a terrestrial globe which revealed further wonders of God's creation and were classed at the time as philosophical rather than scientific instruments. [24]

For English history the textbook which had been used at Steventon parsonage ever since James was a boy was Oliver Goldsmith's four-volume *History of England from the Earliest Times to the Death of George II*. Certain sections of this were now heavily annotated by Jane, and dates were written in the margins, indicating the portion to be studied for each lesson. [25] There is no reason to suppose that she seriously resented the work, for she retained a love of history to the end of her days; but Goldsmith's methods left much to be desired and were to become one of her targets in the little history book she wrote at the age of fifteen for the amusement of her family. [26]

Goldsmith professed his intention of avoiding the approach which made history into an unpalatable list of dates and facts, and of enlivening his account with personal and cultural detail. Jane accordingly declared that her history book would have very few dates, and a reference to Lady Jane Grey's intellectual pursuits is ludicrously dragged into the account of her journey to the scaffold. [27]

In spite of having four volumes at his disposal, Goldsmith was obliged to select his material. His criterion was to concentrate on those aspects of history which could be interpreted to show continuity between past and present, and to leave out developments which had proved retrogressive or short-lived. The method had two consequences, to both of which Jane was fully alive. The first, which was to give events of the past a significance they could not have had for contemporaries, she was willing to laugh at:

> He [the Duke of Somerset] was beheaded, of which he might with reason have been proud, had he known that such was the death of Mary Queen of Scotland [Jane's professed favourite]; but as it was impossible that he should be conscious of what had never happened, it does not appear that he felt particularly delighted with the manner of it.[28]

The second consequence she took more to heart. Goldsmith claimed to be without bias, yet his dismissive attitude to lost causes gave the impression that the triumph of the Whigs under George II had been God's ultimate purpose for Englishmen. On both counts, Jane thought he was wrong. Bias could only be avoided by someone prepared to take a superficial, debating attitude; in her little history, which she stated was by 'a partial, prejudiced, and ignorant historian', she harangues the reader on every page and openly supports the Yorkists against the Lancastrians, Mary Queen of Scots against Elizabeth I, and the Stuarts against all comers. Goldsmith's undeclared anti-Stuart bias had already provoked her into pencilling angry contradictions in the margins of his textbook, ending with her own weighty judgement on the dynasty:

> A family who were always ill-used, BETRAYED OR NEGLECTED, whose virtues are seldom allowed, while their errors are never forgotten.

This flamboyant display of devotion to the Stuarts was in part a legacy from her mother, who liked to remember that her ancestor Thomas Leigh had received a baronetcy for welcoming Charles I at Stoneleigh Abbey in 1643, when the gates of Coventry were closed against him. The 'loyal Leighs' had made gestures of devotion to successive Pretenders for over a century: Theophilus Leigh, father and son, drinking toasts over the water; and Sir Thomas Leigh, Baron of Stoneleigh, holding a room at the Abbey in readiness to receive Bonnie Prince Charlie in the '45.[29] No harm had resulted even then; and by the time Jane heard of the Stuart cause it had ceased to be a threat to the Hanoverian dynasty. During her girlhood it provided her with an element of romance, and she was prepared to stick to it in adult years as a piece of history she had made her own.

An attachment to the Tories and the Stuarts was in any case a tradition common to the clergy and gentry of the countryside. The Whigs supported religious toleration, which was seen as tantamount to favouring Catholics and Dissenters in opposition to the Church of England. At the same time, their control over the first two Hanoverian kings

Opening page of Jane Austen's *History of England* (*c.* 1790). (*British Library*)

threatened to increase the power of the aristocracy and great landowners over lesser men. By contrast, James I and Charles I were seen
as defenders of church and crown. The most commonly held occasional
services were those prescribed by the Prayer Book to be held annually
on 5 November and 30 January, when Jane could have had the thrill
of turning cold at mention of 'the most traitorous and bloody intended
Massacre by γυνποωδερ' and of the wickedness of 'cruel and bloody
men' in taking the life of a most noble king'. These pro-Stuart sentiments were combined with a fierce loyalty to George III, who had
broken with the Whigs at his accession in 1760 and associated himself
with his Stuart predecessors as a defender of throne and altar. There
was profound disquiet in the countryside when in 1788 the King suffered
his first (mercifully short) attack of madness and there was talk of a
Regency under the Prince of Wales, who had flirted with the Whigs in
opposition to his father. The Prince soon became well known in the
neighbourhood of Steventon, for in that same year he took a seven-year
lease on Kempshott Park as a hunting lodge and visited it annually
with a group of raffish friends. At least one young man known to Jane
Austen was drawn into the set, to the dismay of his parents.[30]

Though she may have heard of 'Regency bonnets' worn by the Prince's
female supporters in 1788, her political education began in earnest in
1790, when Hampshire was the scene of one of the fiercest electoral
contests of the reign, with Sir William Heathcote of Hursley Park and
William John Chute of The Vyne fighting to keep out the two Whig
candidates, whose programme of Catholic Relief and Parliamentary
Reform seemed to threaten both the Anglican supremacy and the
independence of small landholders. George Austen, canvassed for his
vote in the Tory interest, attended the 'elegant dinner' held at Basingstoke Town Hall and came home with the cry of 'Heathcote and Chute
for ever', long remembered by Jane as a catchword in the Austen
family.[31]

Her championship of Mary Queen of Scots is evidence of her wide
reading beyond the pages of the prescribed textbook. With the passing
of any real threat from Catholicism, the rights and wrongs of England's
treatment of this troublesome lady had become a matter of hot dispute
among historians and a fruitful source of historical romance. Jane had
read the Revd John Whitaker's voluminous *Vindication* of Mary and had
been moved to admiration and compassion at the thought of her
courage under persecution:

abandoned by her son, confined by her Cousin, Abused, reproached and villified by all, what must not her most noble mind have suffered when informed that Elizabeth had given orders for her Death! Yet she bore it with a most unshaken fortitude; firm in her Mind, Constant in her Religion ... And yet could you Reader have believed it possible that some hardened & zealous Protestants have even abused her for that Steadfastness in the Catholic Religion which reflected on her so much credit? But this is a striking proof of *their* narrow Souls & prejudiced Judgements who accuse her.[32]

Something of the same tone was to be repeated many years later in defence of another woman whom Jane believed to have been generally forsaken: Caroline of Brunswick, the Prince Regent's estranged wife. On 16 February 1813, when the Princess's affairs were front page news, Jane wrote to her friend Martha Lloyd:

Poor Woman, I shall support her as long as I can, because she is a Woman, & because I hate her Husband.

Obliged to admit that the Princess's behaviour left much to be desired, she added:

I am resolved at least always to think that she would have been respectable, if the Prince had behaved only tolerably by her at first.[33]

Parents who could not afford to employ a governess for their girls could purchase books which were supposed to act as a substitute by describing lessons said to have taken place between a governess and her pupils. Their objective, derived like most educational practices of the day from John Locke, was ostensibly to combine instruction in morality with the provision of useful knowledge. In fact the former had usually degenerated by this time into instruction in snobbish and patronising attitudes and the latter into strings of useless definitions. Jane was provided with one of the more popular specimens of the genre: Ann Murry's *Mentoria*, chosen perhaps because it was dedicated to the Princess Royal and had run through several editions within a few years of its first appearance in 1778.[34] Its wholly unnatural conversations between the priggish Mentoria and her two precocious pupils, Lady Mary and Lady Louisa, who constantly express satisfaction at their own achievements and surprise at the ignorance of their less fortunate friend Miss Simple, were to provide Jane with a model for the exchanges between Aunt Norris and the Bertram girls at the expense of their adopted cousin Fanny at Mansfield Park:

'Only think, my cousin cannot put the map of Europe together – or my cousin cannot tell the principal rivers in Russia – or she never heard of Asia Minor – or she does not know the difference between water-colours and crayons! How strange! Did you ever hear anything so stupid?'

'My dear,' their considerate aunt would reply, 'it is very bad, but you must not expect everybody to be as forward and quick at learning as yourself.'

'But, aunt, she is really so very ignorant! ... I cannot remember the time when I did not know a great deal that she has not the least notion of yet. How long ago it is, aunt, since we used to repeat the chronological order of the kings of England, with the dates of their accession, and most of the principal events of their reigns!'

'Yes,' added the other, 'and of the Roman emperors as low as Severus, besides a great deal of the heathen mythology, and all the metals, semi-metals, planets, and distinguished philosophers.'

'Very true, indeed, my dears, but you are blessed with wonderful memories, and your poor cousin has probably none at all. There is a vast deal of difference in memories, as well as everything else, and therefore you must make allowance for your cousin, and pity her defi-ciency. And remember that, if you are ever so forward and clever yourselves, you should always be modest; for much as you know already, there is a great deal more for you to learn.'[35]

The best that can be said for *Mentoria* is that it provided Jane unintentionally with amusement. By contrast, an aspect of her education which she found extremely tiresome was her exposure to manuals and magazines prescribing proper conduct for young ladies. Mothers were assumed to have a duty to bring up their daughters to behave with decorum, and Mrs Austen took her role seriously enough to subscribe to the *Mirror*, a journal whose inappropriate advice concerning accept-ance of one's humble status in life Mrs Morland prepares to seek out when her daughter Catherine returns from Northanger Abbey with a broken heart.[36] The parsonage bookshelves also held a copy of *Sermons to Young Women* by James Fordyce, whose pompous language and sheer horror at the thought of reading a novel from a circulating library were to help provide a model for Mr Collins in *Pride and Prejudice*.[37] Jane was not averse to receiving lessons in morality: what she could not stand were semi-political injunctions, issuing mostly from male writers, requir-ing young women, more than young men, to beware lest they shake the foundations of civilised society by failing to behave in a docile and respectful manner towards the powers that be. She was particularly irritated at being told that young ladies should avoid 'the insipid Vanities and idle Dissipations of the Metropolis of England' when she had very little chance of being exposed to them. After visiting London briefly when she was twelve, she never set foot there again until she was twenty, when she wrote gleefully to Cassandra, 'Here I am once more in this Scene of vice, and I begin already to find my Morals corrupted'.[38]

When she was eighteen or nineteen, Jane wrote a wickedly clever satire on the work of such 'conduct writers'. The infamous Lady Susan pursues her immoral ends by carrying out the advice of writers on female education and behaviour to the letter. She justifies her outrageous seduction of other women's husbands and lovers with hypocritically moral statements. Worst of all, her exuberant flouting of conventions makes her attractive not only to the men she captivates but to the reader. The story promised to be a gem of its kind, but Jane put it aside before it was finished, perhaps because she lost confidence in it. By the time she came to draft out *Pride and Prejudice* shortly afterwards, she had decided that there was some good in the conduct books after all. Among the Bennet sisters it was to be the foolish Lydia she allowed to scorn Fordyce's *Sermons*, just as in Sheridan's play *The Rivals*, which Jane had seen performed in her father's parlour, it is the stupid Lydia Languish who uses the pages of the book for curl papers.[39]

In the debate on the relationship between manners and morals which gathered momentum with Wilberforce's campaign of 1787 against unseemly behaviour, Jane came to think that manners were of some importance. Whilst genuine sensitivity to the feelings of others was necessary to produce the truly courteous behaviour seen in a man like Mr Knightley, lesser mortals could do worse than learn a few rules. In *Pride and Prejudice* she praises the training in civility which enables Sir William Lucas to listen politely to insulting remarks from Mrs Bennet; and in *Emma* she gives due credit to the similar training the heroine has received from Miss Taylor, without which she would undoubtedly have behaved throughout her adolescence like the spoiled child she really was.[40] In all matters of behaviour, Jane soon learnt to look to Cassandra as her guide and model. Cassandra was everything that she admired: serene, friendly, kind, practical, intelligent, good. Yet Jane was never afraid to approach her with her own fears and failings. Cassandra was always ready to listen, to understand, and to enter into her younger sister's hopes and disaapointments. 'Their affection for each other was extreme', their niece Anna recalled, 'it passed the common love of sisters.'[41] It would be untrue to say that Cassandra was a mother figure to Jane, for she was less distant. Yet she was more than a sister, companion, lover or friend. She was more nearly Jane's better self.

She was all the dearer in that at no time during her adolescence did Jane have a friend of her own age. Frank, the companion of her childhood, could come home from the Naval Academy only once a year, for three weeks either at Christmas or at Whitsuntide. Charles was four years her junior and had for so long been her plaything that, although she loved him dearly, he could not yet be more to her than her 'own particular little brother'. Struggling, on her return from school, to make her mark among her older siblings, it is not surprising that she sometimes seemed precocious and quaint – hardly like a young girl at all, thought her cousin Phila, who met her for the first time when she was twelve.[42] With grown-ups she could be painfully shy, as she afterwards remembered, but if any showed a particular interest in her she responded more readily than she did to acquaintances nearer her own age. Taken to visit the new incumbent of Ashe, the Revd I. P. George Lefroy, she showed no interest whatever in his young daughter Lucy but gave her whole heart to his wife, the fascinating 'Madam' Lefroy. Visiting her father's new tenants at Deane parsonage, she made lifelong friends not with Mary, the younger of the two Lloyd sisters at home, but with Martha, ten years older than herself.

Although Jane's education, in the deepest sense of the word, continued throughout her life, her Confirmation at the hands of the bishop signified the completion of her upbringing. She may well have had to wait until she was almost nineteen for this event to take place. Dioceses were vast, and bishops could get around only rarely to perform their sacramental duties. On 24 April 1794 she received a gift often bestowed on Confirmation candidates: a copy of William Vickers' *Companion to the Altar*, a guide to the private preparation to be undertaken in order to be worthy of receiving Holy Communion. Its keynote was its enormous emphasis on self-examination, 'that henceforward no secret sin may lie undiscovered and corrupt the soul'. This, like so much of Jane's reading, was to be applied to many of the characters in her novels, not least to the charming Elizabeth Bennet and Emma Woodhouse. According to members of Jane's family, she cherished the *Companion* and made constant use of the prayers and meditations included in it. She was to take her participation in the sacrament of Holy Communion seriously, as a cleansing from sin and a repeated welcome into the company of the faithful.[43]

Chapter 6

Dramatic Times

On their return from school at Reading, Jane and Cassandra were greeted with the exciting news that their cousin Eliza was coming to stay for Christmas. Jane had heard a great deal about Eliza, and it had all sounded so romantic that the prospect of her actual arrival at the parsonage gate was something to be contemplated with awe. Eliza's mother, Philadelphia Hancock, who was coming with her, also sounded like a character from a story book. She was George Austen's sister – the same Aunt Hancock who had perhaps assisted at Jane's birth. George Austen had had a protective attitude towards her ever since the two of them had been orphaned and cast upon the world in their infancy. Unfortunately, as a young man he had had no home to offer her, and had been unable therefore to save her from being shipped out to India, where a dowerless girl might hope to find a husband from among the European expatriates.

She had duly married Tysoe Saul Hancock, a surgeon with the East India Company twenty years her senior. They had spent some time in Calcutta, where they secured the lasting friendship of Warren Hastings: when their daughter Eliza was born they called her after Hastings' own daughter who had died young. Hastings stood godfather to her and poured such care and affection upon her that malicious gossip soon had it that she was his child. If Mr Hancock himself had suspicions, he was careful to show no sign of it. In 1765 he returned to England with his wife and four-year-old child, with every intention of devoting his remaining years to their welfare. He counted without his Phila's delightful but extravagant ways. The fortune he had made abroad soon disappeared and he was obliged to return to India, in increasing ill-health, to make what money he could for his family's support. He died in 1775 without ever having seen his wife and daughter again.

In accordance with her father's wishes, Eliza was educated to marry a gentleman. To ensure that she acquired an air of gentility, private masters were employed to teach her writing and arithmetic. She was given a pony to ride, and taught to play on her own harpsichord. When poor Mr Hancock began to have doubts about the wisdom of teaching her to dance and to speak French, when she might after all be condemned to marry a tradesman, Warren Hastings restored his resolve by pointing out that neither dancing nor French disqualified a woman from fulfilling her duties, whatever sphere of life she found herself in. Meanwhile, he set up a trust fund of £10,000 to enable Philadelphia Hancock to bring up her daughter to be a lady and to provide a dowry which would safeguard her from having to marry for money. The trustees were George Austen and Warren Hastings' brother-in-law, John Woodman. From then on, George Austen regarded himself as standing *in loco parentis* to Eliza.[1]

After her husband's death, Philadelphia soon discovered that the small amount of money he had garnered was insufficient to keep her in London in the style she seemed determined to enjoy. Since they had always intended Eliza's education to be finished in France, she now set out for the Continent with her fourteen-year-old daughter and her Indian maid to set up house in a country where stylish living was reputed to be cheaper than in England. By 1780 she had settled in Paris and had by some unknown means secured an entrée into the most privileged circles. Eliza's letters to her cousin Philadelphia Walter in Kent described a dazzling round of balls and soirées to which she had taken like a duck to water. The letters were sent on to Steventon, where the family gathered in the parlour to pour over accounts of Louis XVI's court:

> We were a few days ago at Versailles & had the honor of seeing their Majesties & all the royal family dine & sup. The Queen is a very fine woman, she has a most beautiful complexion, & is indeed exceedingly handsome; she was most elegantly dressed, she had on a corset & petticoat of pale green lutestring covered with a transparent silver gauze, the petticoat & sleeves puckered & confined in different places with large bunches of roses, & an amazing large bouquet of white lilac. The same flower, together with gauze, feathers, ribbon & diamonds intermixed with her hair. Her neck was entirely uncovered & ornamented by a most beautiful chain of diamonds, of which she had likewise very fine bracelets; she was without gloves, I suppose to shew her hands & arms which are without exception the whitest & most beautiful I ever beheld. The King was plainly dressed, he had however likewise some fine diamonds. The rest of the royal family was very elegant, & indeed I may say the court of France is, I believe, upon the whole one of the most magnificent in all Europe.[2]

1. The Revd George Austen, Jane's father, as a young man. (*Jane Austen Memorial Trust*)

2. The Revd George Austen in 1801, the year of his retirement. (*Jane Austen Memorial Trust*)

3. St John's College, Oxford, where George Austen and, later, his sons James and Henry were Fellows. (*Cambridge University Library*)

4. Jane Austen: steel engraving (1869) from Cassandra Austen's sketch.

5. The only known image of Mrs George Austen, Jane's mother. A silhouette, *c.* 1800. (*Jane Austen Memorial Trust*)

6. Eliza Hancock, Jane's cousin, a few years before her marriage to the Comte de Feuillide. (*Jane Austen Memorial Trust*)

7. Cassandra Austen, after her sister Jane's death. Undated silhouette. (*Private Collection*)

8. The Revd James Austen, Jane's eldest brother. A miniature, *c.* 1790. (*Jane Austen Memorial Trust*)

9. Jane's fourth brother, Henry, in preaching bands. A miniature, *c.* 1820. (*Jane Austen Memorial Trust*)

10. Jane's brother, Francis William (Frank). A miniature, 1796. (*Jane Austen Memorial Trust*)

11. Charles Austen, Jane's younger brother. A portrait, *c.* 1809. (*Jane Austen Memorial Trust*)

12. Sketch of the front of Steventon parsonage by Jane's niece Anna Austen (later Lefroy). Dated 1814. (*Private Collection*)

13. The Abbey School, Reading.

14. Portsmouth Harbour from Gosport . From R. Mudie, *Hampshire* (1838).

15. Portsmouth from Block House Point. From R. Mudie, *Hampshire* (1838).

16. A silhouette, showing Edward Austen, aged about twelve, being presented by his father to Mrs Knight for adoption a few years later. Mrs Austen looks up from her game of chess, whilst Thomas Knight stands behind her chair. (*Jane Austen Memorial Trust*)

17. Hackwood House, home of Lord Bolton, where Jane Austen attended balls and her father took an interest in pigstyes. From R. Mudie, *Hampshire* (1838).

18. The Vyne, home of William John Chute and his wife Elizabeth. G.F. Prosser, *Select Illustrations of Hampshire* (1833).

19. Manydown, the home of Jane Austen's friends, the Biggs. G.F. Prosser, *Select Illustrations of Hampshire* (1833).

20. On the right: The Paragon, Bath. Jane Austen stayed with her sister and mother at No. 1, the home of Uncle and Aunt Leigh-Perrot, in 1797. By J. C. Nattes. (*Bath City Library*)

21. The Pump Room, Bath, by J. C. Nattes. Here invalids such as Jane's uncle (and Mr Allen in *Northanger Abbey*) drank the waters whilst their friends walked about the room. A statue of Beau Nash presides from the alcove. (*Bath City Library*)

Such passages were varied with descriptions of the latest fashions in dress, hair styles and etiquette, and accounts of the pastoral life to which Eliza, like Marie-Antoinette, professed herself glad to retire in the summer months. The five-year-old Jane might scarcely have believed Eliza to be a real person had not one of the letters been accompanied by a miniature portrait dutifully addressed to Uncle George Austen. It revealed an elf-like creature with large dark eyes gazing appealingly from a small pointed face. 'It is reckoned here like what I am at present', wrote Eliza. 'The dress [of soft, white material trimmed with blue] is quite the present fashion & what I usually wear.'[3]

In the summer of 1781, George Austen was discovered frowning over the news that his niece was about to marry an officer in the French army. To an English country parson all foreigners were suspect; and the French were, after all, England's enemy in the war against America. They were also Catholic, which George Austen could not like. He learnt from John Woodman that Captain Jean-François Capot de Feuillide had no present fortune, and he could summon up no faith in what were said to be the gentleman's 'great expectations'. He probably suspected (rightly) that Eliza had boasted of her connection with the famous Warren Hastings of India and that the Captain thought he was marrying an heiress. Mercifully he may never have known that the Captain, as well as being penurious, had no valid claim to the title of Count which he assumed.[4]

For the first few years of her married life, Eliza was wonderfully happy. She told her English relatives quite plainly that on her side her marriage was not a love match, but she swore that her husband for his part adored her and that he was 'everyways amiable, both in mind and person'.[5] He was certainly not without initiative. Discovering that his wife's fortune was as slender as his own expectations, he followed the example of many a genuine aristocrat of the time and set about improving his prospects by his own enterprise. He secured from the King the grant of an area of marshland near to his hometown of Nérac and spent eighteen months (at the expense of his mother-in-law) draining it for future agriculture. Eliza installed herself in the nearby Château de Jourdan and looked forward with her usual optimism to immense profit and prestige.[6]

An English country clergyman, such as George Austen, had no time for French aristocrats, whose profligacy was believed to derive in some obscure way from their religion. By contrast, the romantic visions conjured up by the Countess's letters home appealed greatly to James Austen, idling his time away at Oxford and writing sonnets to Lady

Catherine Powlett, daughter of George Austen's landowning neighbour, the 6th Duke of Bolton. In addition to imagining himself in love with an aristocratic lady, James aspired to a fashionable life of continental travel. Perhaps from some little jealousy of his brother Edward, who was about to leave England on the Grand Tour, he planned to visit his cousins in their château in France early in the following year.[7]

Eliza for her part had long hoped to visit her English relatives. She had rejoiced when the signing of a peace treaty between England and France in 1782 made such a journey feasible, although she knew that the treaty in question, which recognised the independence of Britain's former American colonies, was unpopular with her English countrymen.[8] In January 1786 she discovered that she was pregnant. As her husband had expressed a wish that their child should be born in England, she began to make plans for the two of them to set out – only to find that month after month went by and the Count could still not bring himself to leave his land reclamations. When spring came, Eliza and her mother sailed for England without him. They had originally intended to stay only a few days in London before travelling on to Steventon, Uncle George having told Eliza that he could only accommodate visitors during the summer holidays; but in the event they had no sooner arrived in London than Eliza was brought to bed prematurely and on 25 June delivered of a son. By the time she recovered, the summer vacation was over.[9]

James Austen, meanwhile, had abandoned his idea of visiting France, on the assumption that neither Eliza nor her husband would be at the château to receive him. When Eliza arrived in England without the Count he renewed his enquiries. On learning that M. de Feuillide, in spite of his wife's absence, was perfectly willing to entertain her cousin, he started early in November on what was to be the one foreign journey of his life. He was still away from home when his parents opened their doors to the family for Christmas and the New Year.[10]

Mrs Hancock, with Eliza and her baby son Hastings, arrived at the parsonage on 21 December 1786 – presumably by post chaise, although the following year they were reported to be travelling everywhere in a carriage-and-four emblazoned with the Count's crest.[11] Mr and Mrs Austen loved receiving visits from relatives, and nothing could have delighted them more than the addition of a six-month-old child to the family party. A gathering of as many young people as possible was planned for the festive season. Henry, aged fifteen, and Charles, aged six, were at home; Cassandra, nearly fourteen, and Jane, nearly eleven, were back from school; and Frank, aged twelve and a half, was on annual leave from Portsmouth. Their cousins, Edward Cooper and his sister Jane, aged sixteen and fifteen, were to arrive for New Year's Day. Mrs Austen would dearly have liked her remaining niece, Philadelphia Walter, to come too, for Phila, at twenty, was the nearest in age to Eliza and had corresponded with her in terms of great affection for years, but she had little hope of persuading Philly's mother, who had become something of a recluse, to make the necessary effort of accompanying her young daughter into Hampshire. Eliza, fortunately, was not at all abashed by the youthfulness of the gathering, but became at once the life and soul of the party. Mrs Austen borrowed a piano for the occasion; Eliza played on it every day and also accompanied the 'snug little dance' that was held in the parlour on the second evening of the New Year.[12]

A few days later, Frank returned to the Royal Naval Academy and the Coopers returned home. This left Jane with plenty of time to take stock of her aunt and cousin, for the Hancocks stayed at the rectory for some six weeks. Mrs Hancock was a sentimental, impulsive woman, enterprising and efficient in large matters, unrealistic and scatter-brained in small. It is more than likely that Jane's impressions of her, stored away in her memory, played a part in the creation of Mrs Dashwood in *Sense and Sensibility*.[13] Eliza, for all her brilliance, was a warm-hearted young woman, grateful for appreciation and ever ready to respond to friendliness. Her delight in displaying her French sophistication could not hide her pleasure in rediscovering her English relatives. Seeing Jane's large hazel eyes fixed admiringly upon her, she responded gratefully, and the two loved each other from that time.

When Mrs Hancock's trunks were unpacked, there had emerged from them a twelve-volume set of Arnaud Berquin's *L'ami des enfants*, purchased, probably in London, as a present for Jane's eleventh birthday.[14] Opening the first of the dumpy little books which came to hand, the generous lady scrawled in it 'pour dear Jane Austen' – realising later, if at all, that she had written not in the opening volume but in the fifth. Berquin's tales had very recently taken both Paris and London by storm; for a young girl growing up in a country village they were a truly stylish present. The stories were didactic and childish, but they were charmingly written and their direct but elegant French prose made them an excellent choice for someone struggling to learn the language. Eliza may well have read them aloud and translated them for her young cousins. Her faultless pronunciation and the dazzling way in which she introduced French phrases into her English conversation could hardly have failed to attract Jane, who ultimately came to be able to read the

BELL'S EDITION.

THE

W O N D E R!

A

WOMAN keeps a SECRET.

A COMEDY, by Mrs. CENTLIVRE:

AS PERFORMED AT THE

𝔗𝔥𝔢𝔞𝔱𝔯𝔢=𝔕𝔬𝔶𝔞𝔩 𝔦𝔫 𝔇𝔯𝔲𝔯𝔶=𝔏𝔞𝔫𝔢.

Regulated from the Prompt-Book,

By PERMISSION of the MANAGERS,

By Mr. HOPKINS, Prompter.

L O N D O N:
Printed for JOHN BELL, near *Exeter-Exchange*, in the *Strand,*
and C. ETHERINGTON, at *York.*

MDCCLXXVI.

Title page of the play produced at Steventon parsonage, December 1787.

language with ease but could never pride herself on her ability to speak it.[15]

It was probably the desire to emulate Eliza which also made Jane eager to learn to play the piano. No other member of the family played – unless Mrs Austen had received some long-forgotten tuition in her girlhood. The latter now at least remembered an old song book, which she brought out possibly for Eliza's use at family sing-songs. Jane gradually appropriated it and added other tunes, carefully copied out from borrowed volumes.[16] She may have had a few music lessons at school which familiarised her with the notes. Unfortunately, a few years were to elapse before she acquired a piano and could start lessons from a visiting tutor. Mrs Austen, who was pleased enough to listen to Eliza's playing, regarded other things as more important for everyday.

Needlework, for instance. To be fair to Mrs Austen, proficiency in needlework, referred to simply as 'work', was generally considered to be a minimum requirement for the female sex. Even Fanny Price, neglected as her education had been, could 'read, work, and write' at the age of ten, although 'she had been taught nothing more'.[17] Great ladies, no less than labourers' wives, were expected to be able to sew: as is the way of the world, many of the former were more skilled in the art than some of the latter who needed it more. They frequently made shirts for their menfolk and bed linen for their households: Mrs Austen, who prided herself on her aristocratic lineage, saw nothing detrimental to her pretensions in being seen mending the family's clothes. She was long remembered by her grandchildren for the way she would sit, of an evening, in the common parlour (which was virtually an entrance hall opening on to the latticed porch at the front of the house), busily mending the household linen even when visitors arrived. It was not until Jane's later years that delicate items of embroidery were considered the only suitable occupation for elegant females.

Under her mother's eagle eye Jane began, as most girls did, by producing a sampler – an alphabet or a scriptural text set in cross-stitch on a rectangular piece of cloth. Samplers were a relic of the days when women spent a vast amount of time producing tapestries for walls and chair coverings and needed to produce a sample first. Choosing dark green and purple silks, Jane dutifully surrounded a ten-inch piece of linen with an intricate border, and proceeded to fill in the square with a medley of verses from the Psalms – nearly a hundred words in all – finishing off with her name and the date 1787 along with a few stylised trees and a bird. As time went on she became, through her own patience and dexterity, extremely accomplished at all forms of needlework both practical and ornamental – particularly satin stitch on muslin cloth and appliqué work on fine net. It was the only domestic skill in which she felt completely confident.[18]

Eliza, meanwhile, had taken up residence in a fashionable part of London, where she immediately became as prominent in society circles as she had been in Paris. The family at Steventon nevertheless remained very much in her thoughts. During her stay at the parsonage she had heard about their early efforts at amateur theatricals and nothing would now do but that she must return to Steventon the following Christmas, when James would be at home and at liberty to produce another play in which she could take the leading part. If James visited her when he returned from France, as would have been only polite, Eliza is sure to have enthralled him with her ambitious plans. Their combined efforts were to provide Jane Austen many years later with material for the famous play-acting sequence in *Mansfield Park*.

Amateur theatricals were at that time enjoying great popularity, especially among the aristocracy. This was not because there was any shortage of professional theatres or any reluctance to attend them but because play acting, with all the bustle of preparation, was found to be an excellent source of occupation for idle young men and women cooped up in a house party for days on end. Many participants had learnt the rudiments of stage craft at boarding school, where acting was considered useful as a training in elocution and grace of movement. Even Sir Thomas Bertram had encouraged it, to the extent that Tom Bertram could hardly remember the number of times he and Edmund had 'mourned over the body of Julius Caesar, and *to b'ed* and not *to b'ed*' for their father's satisfaction.[19]

The craze for performing soon spread down to the lesser gentry and professional classes, few of whose members had rooms at their disposal large enough to accommodate a stage. James Austen, whose romantic soul was attracted to aristocratic pursuits of all kinds, had no doubt heard that in such circumstances barns and coach houses were often adapted as temporary or even semi-permanent theatres. It was not long before Eliza learnt that her uncle's old tithe barn was being fitted up 'quite like a theatre' – presumably with a stage, a green baize curtain and a large quantity of oil lamps or candelabra, since it was the fashion to light both actors and audience with equal brilliance throughout the performance.[20] Scenery would also be needed. This usually consisted of flats brought in from the side of the stage or dropped from above. They were sometimes painted by a friend or a member of the family; otherwise a scene painter was hired from a nearby town. Cassandra was the recognised artist of the Austen family, but a girl of thirteen could hardly have been expected to cover a large expanse of canvas. A scene painter from Basingstoke or Overton must therefore have been employed to produce the sets, which were later listed among the items to be auctioned when George Austen retired.[21]

As a clergyman George Austen was not at all unusual in tolerating such activity; Mary Sherwood's father actually wrote prologues for the plays produced during her time at the Abbey School.[22] Yet attitudes towards amateur acting were often ambivalent. On the one hand, it could be regarded as traditional among the English, especially at the festive season. On the other, there were perceived to be disadvantages. 'Proper' behaviour for ladies and gentlemen required emotional restraint, whereas the stage conventions of the time not only encouraged actresses to swoon to excess and male actors to 'rant dreadfully', as Mr Yates was heard to do at Mansfield Park, but even required audiences to sigh, weep and groan without inhibition. For female participants there might be even greater dangers. Professional actresses were only just beginning to acquire a degree of respectability. There was still a widespread belief that they were likely to have been contaminated by the immorality of the parts they were sometimes required to play. If they managed to escape, it was only because they had been, as Edmund Bertram put it, 'bred to the trade' and could produce 'hardened acting' in which their own emotions were not involved. Amateurs had 'all the disadvantages of education and decorum to struggle through'; their self-consciousness drew even more attention to the improper emotions they were enacting than would otherwise have been the case.[23] Rousseau had condemned stage performances as unnatural and therefore immoral long before Evangelicals joined the hue and cry on religious grounds. Not only did most drama give undue emphasis to passions such as love and hatred; the closely confined atmosphere of the theatre and the unusual proximity of males and females were inducements to both actors and audience to participate vicariously in the situations and emotions displayed, Rousseau argued.[24] Amateur enthusiasts often tried to allay objections by confining performances to relatives and close friends. Jane Austen was perceptive enough at the age of twelve to see that the dangers might thereby be enhanced.

There was always likely to be difficulty in finding a play that would not only fit the number of available performers but gratify their various aspirations.[25] The stage conventions of the time placed a premium on leading roles, ignoring team work and attaching little importance to supporting parts. At Mansfield Park, we are told, the performers wanted a piece containing very few characters on the whole, but every character first-rate, and three principal women ... No piece could be proposed that did not supply somebody with a difficulty, and on one side or the other it was a continual repetition of, 'Oh! no, *that* will never do. Let us have no ranting tragedies. Too many characters – Not a tolerable woman's part in the play – Anything but *that*, my dear Tom. It would be impossible to fill it up – One could not expect anybody to take such a part – Nothing but buffoonery from beginning to end ... I have always thought it the most insipid play in the English language – I do not wish to make objections, I shall be happy to be of any use, but I think we could not choose worse.'

In September 1787 Eliza de Feuillide saw Mrs Cowley's *Which is the Man?* and Garrick's *Bon Ton* performed professionally at Tunbridge Wells, and from then on she looked forward to playing the leading lady in both comedies at Steventon. Finding that there were two parts that the Austens and Coopers between them would be unable to fill, she set about trying to recruit her cousin Philadelphia. Phila had already indicated that she would like to watch the performance but had neither the courage to take part nor the wish to acquire it. Eliza brushed aside all scruples with a determination equalled by that of Tom Bertram at Mansfield Park, and even stooped a little towards the blackmailing arts employed more crudely by Mrs Norris. She would be 'cruelly mortified', she said, if Phila refused to take part:

> I know you have engagements, but if you love me put them off to another year: consider it is the only Christmas we may pass together for many, many years, whereas you have it always in your power to be with your other friends, who I am sure are too reasonable to object to your taking this only opportunity of being with an affectionate relation from whom the sea will shortly divide you.

Phila's reply expressed panic at the thought of appearing in public, but this merely drew from Eliza an assurance that the performance would be 'by no means a publick one, since only a select party of friends would be present'. There could be no question of Phila staying at the parsonage unless she came prepared to act, she said, for their Aunt Austen had declared 'she has not room for *idle young* people'.[26] Unlike Fanny Price, who was pressurised into agreeing that she would at least understudy a small part in rehearsal at Mansfield Park, Philadelphia at her much greater distance stuck to her guns. It was perhaps because of this that the choice of play to be performed on 26 and 28 December 1787 was changed to an older comedy by Mrs Centlivre, *The Wonder:*

A Woman Keeps a Secret! It is to be hoped that the change was made before the carpenter and the scene painter began work, or George Austen would have incurred the kind of wasted expense chalked up to Sir Thomas Bertram for two unwanted doors in flat.[27]

Mrs Centlivre's play was sexually less explicit than the ones Eliza had set her heart on, but the Countess was an accomplished flirt and it was only to be expected that she would make the most of such opportunities as her role afforded to captivate her cousins James and Henry. James had now decided on a clerical career as far as to seek ordination, but the event required little preparation: after coming back from France in the late autumn of 1787 he had found time to discuss the approaching theatricals with Eliza before setting off for Pembrokeshire where he was ordained deacon at St David's Cathedral on 19 December. On his return to Steventon, he wrote a prologue and epilogue for *The Wonder* in which he celebrated the capacity of women to conquer men by their wit and charm. He was clearly fascinated by Eliza but, although his clerical vocation sat as lightly upon him as it did upon most young ordinands at that time, it is unreasonable to suggest that he was so lost to propriety as to harbour pretensions in regard to a married woman whose husband had recently shown him generous hospitality. Henry, who played Don Felix opposite Eliza's Violante, was of a nature to throw himself into the hero's rapturous love scene without embarrassment. As a lanky youth of sixteen he was bound to feel flattered by the attentions of a stylish and cosmopolitan lady of twenty-six but, far from dismissing thoughts of the lady's married state from his mind, he was planning to accompany her when she returned to France and to succeed his brother James as her husband's guest. There was nevertheless much to intrigue the silent Jane as she watched the rehearsals, and much that she would remember and reinterpret when she came to write her novels.

The installation of a theatre at the parsonage provided both an opportunity and an incentive for producing more plays when Eliza had gone. George Austen may have decided to follow fashion and experiment with drama as an educational exercise, for two performances of a simple nature were staged during termtime in 1788 and, with no older cousins present, some of the parts would have had to be taken by younger members of the family and by pupils. The first, which was not unlike a pantomime, featured Tom Thumb and may well have starred the nine-year-old Charles with his two sisters in supporting roles. The second, described as 'a private theatrical Exhibition', probably consisted of miscellaneous items devised by members of the cast. It may have been for this occasion that Jane wrote a very short play entitled *The Mystery*, which she dedicated to her father. Inspired by Sheridan's *The Critic*, it consisted of three whispering scenes, mocking the contemporary device whereby characters on the stage exchanged confidences with each other *sotto voce*, to the bewilderment of the audience.[28]

This burst of junior theatricals was brought to an end by a number of family events which occurred in July. Henry, who had been hoping for some time that a place for Founder's Kin would become vacant at St John's College, Oxford, learnt that his chance had come when he least wanted it: he was obliged to matriculate on 1 July 1788 and forego his plans to accompany Eliza when she returned to France.[29] James at about the same time secured a licence as curate of the tiny parish of Stoke Charity. He was lucky to obtain even this modest appointment so early in his career, for a fifth of all ordinands were obliged to give up the struggle after a few years of fruitless effort and take up other occupations, sometimes of a menial nature.[30] He was not required to devote much time to caring for the souls of the few parishioners at Stoke: an occasional sermon and a little help with the annual communions for the sick may have been all that was demanded of him. He welcomed the emolument, such as it was, as an aid to returning to the gentlemanly life at Oxford, where he joined his brother for the remainder of the year.

With only Charles and the two girls left at home, Mr and Mrs Austen seized the opportunity to take Cassandra and Jane on a visit of duty to their Great Uncle Francis in his beautiful late Stuart town house in Sevenoaks. Thinking to please them, the old man invited his niece, Susannah Walter, and her daughter Phila, who lived nearby, to dine with them one evening. Cassandra, like her brothers before her, came through the family inspection with flying colours. Jane, either because she was shy or because she was already prejudiced against both Great Uncle Francis and his relations, behaved in an odd, dislikeable fashion which Phila described first of all as 'prim' and later as 'whimsical and affected'.[31] She cannot have been unaware that Francis Austen was one of her father's benefactors. She may also have heard, however, that he was responsible for shipping Eliza's mother out to India to marry an unknown bridegroom – an act which filled her with revulsion. She may already have decided that his wealth, which he had derived in large measure from marrying two successive heiresses, was 'ill-gotten' (a term she later applied to it in a letter to Cassandra).[32] As for Aunt Susannah and the miserable Phila, she can have thought of them only as relatives who constantly declined invitations to visit Steventon and ended by turning up their noses at the Christmas theatricals. If she did indeed behave badly out of sheer impertinence, it is all the more remarkable that her parents took it in their stride: according to Phila the whole family was 'in high spirits and disposed to be pleased with each other'. The parents were to be equally tolerant of the impudence and daring of Jane's early writings.[33]

The party travelled home via London so as to seize the opportunity to visit Eliza and her mother who were packing up to return to France. Their house in Orchard Street was in a predictable state of confusion, for Eliza had made innumerable purchases, including items of furniture, whilst in England. She nevertheless received the visit with real gratification. Unlike Phila, who had reported to her brother that Mr Austen was 'quite white haired' and that Mrs Austen had been made to look old by the loss of several front teeth, Eliza was as delighted as ever with the whole family and especially with her Uncle George, who seemed to her 'more amiable than ever'. For his part, he must surely have been pleased to discover that their relationship had not been impaired by her French marriage. Eliza remained devoted to her mother – the sister George had so often tried to protect; she was still proud to be English, and above all she had remained loyal to her faith and her church. They got on famously. 'What an excellent & pleasing man he is', Eliza wrote, 'I love him most sincerely.'[34]

James and Henry came home from Oxford for the ensuing Christmas vacation, and the usual visit from Edward and Jane Cooper enabled them to stage Isaac Bickerstaffe's new comedy, *The Sultan*, followed by a short farce; but with Eliza now back in France the heart had gone out of the show as far as James was concerned, and no more amateur theatricals were heard of at Steventon. December 1788 would in any case have been a time of mixed feelings in the Austen family, for Frank, who had completed his studies at the Academy six months earlier than the allotted time, joined the frigate HMS *Perseverance* as a volunteer and on 23 December sailed for the East Indies. He had received a glowing report from the Headmaster to send to the Lords of the Admiralty, and there could be little doubt that after a year's practical seamanship he would be successful in becoming a Midshipman. These were matters for pride. Yet Frank was only fourteen years old and life in the navy was tough. There had been anxieties about sending him to the Academy, which had a good academic reputation but was said to be an ill-disciplined place where a boy might be led into drunkenness and riot.[35] Fortunately, his father had been able to write to him frequently with advice, and Frank had not hesitated to seek his counsel.[36]

Communication with a vessel at sea would be more difficult.[37] Frank had shown admirable strength of character so far, but who could tell what difficult circumstances might now arise? Boys under training had no cabins. They messed not with the wardroom officers but with the Midshipmen, sometimes embittered men who had been passed over for Lieutenant and were ready to bully the juniors.[38] George Austen advised his son to write down regular accounts of himself, so that he would have a package ready to send off home whenever an opportunity arose. He assured Frank that among his brothers and sisters there would always be some who would be writing to him. It was equally certain, however, that none of them would see him again for years. The journey to the Cape could take as long as six months, and the rest, through badly charted seas, depended on the season and on the courage and skill of the caption of the vessel. Home leave was a rare occurrence.[39]

Chapter 7

Stories

An intelligent family hidden away in the country must needs provide
its own entertainment. Amateur dramatics were rewarding but required
a great deal of preparation; for impromptu occasions, reading aloud
within the family circle was a better stand-by. Clergymen, on account
of their experience in the pulpit, were expected to take to it readily,
and were often asked, when visiting friends, to oblige the company with
a reading of their own choice from their host's library: in Jane's estimation, it was a black mark against Mr Collins that his choice was
unsuitable.[1] At home, if night after night were available, a whole novel
might be read, with various members of the family taking turns. Such
readings were not only pleasurable at the time; they provided the family
with a fund of common knowledge which could form a topic of conversation and jokes for the future.

For reading on single evenings, or to a mixed age group, a medley
of short pieces was more appropriate than a continuous passage. Jane
began writing pieces for such occasions when she was about eleven.
One of her earliest compositions, a 450-word account of three concur-
rent love affairs conducted by means of letters, was dedicated to her
mother.[2] It may well have been her mother who had introduced Jane
to Samuel Richardson's epistolary novels, since they were thought to
be good for girls on account both of their moral content and their
literary style. Richardson in his early days had eked out a living by
writing letters on behalf of young lovers, and the letters which formed
the text of his novels were often recommended as models of the art.
The publisher Francis Newbery even brought out shilling versions of
Pamela, *Clarissa* and *Grandison* abridged for the purpose.[3] Jane Austen
at the age of eleven had no need of abridgements: she could read the
six or seven volumes of a novel by Richardson with alacrity and enjoyment. This did not prevent her from realising that few young ladies
would be able to emulate his prolix compositions. Reluctant correspondents would be far more likely to make excuses for signing off:

Dear Maud,
          Believe me I'm happy to hear of your Brother's arrival. I have a
thousand things to tell you, but my paper will only permit me to add
that I am y^r Afffec^t Friend
                    Amelia Webster

In the autumn of 1788, Jane's long journey into east Kent, culmin-
ating in an exciting visit to London, put her in mind of other literary
favourites – the novels of Fielding and Smollett. Did not their heroes
and heroines invariably go on adventurous journeys which ended with
plunging them into a vortex of crime, sex and squalor in the capital?
On returning home she decided to prolong the fun of her holiday by
writing a story which cast her sister in the role of a resourceful heroine.[4]
The eponymous heroine of 'The Beautiful Cassandra', only daughter
of a celebrated milliner of Bond Street, puts on one of her mother's
bonnets and sallies forth to seek her fortune. She encounters a handsome Viscount whose attentions she ignores, eats pies at a pastrycook's
and knocks the man down when he asks for payment, drives to Hampstead and back in a hackney coach, then places her bonnet on the
driver's head and runs away. She eventually reaches home by way of
Bloomsbury Square and pronounces the day well spent. The episodes
are recounted in so few words and the sequence of events is so incon-
sequential that, to a modern reader, the impression is reminiscent of
nursery rhyme translated into prose. Collections of nursery rhymes,
containing many lasting favourites, had been available since the middle
of the eighteenth century, but it is not known whether Jane encountered
any until a later date, when she may have sung the musical versions
which appear in one of Cassandra's song books.[5] What is certain is that
she had read *Tom Jones* and knew also that the rest of the family would
recognise her allusions to it. At one level, 'The Beautiful Cassandra' is
a childlike imitation of Fielding's picaresque novel; at another, it is a
clever skit on the entire genre.
     The amorous adventures of Tom Jones would be unlikely nowadays
to seem suitable reading for a boy of nine; yet they had obviously been
enjoyed by Jane's young brother, Charles. The latter was now invited
by Jane to identify himself with one Sir William Mountague, whose
profligate nature leads him to fall in love with three sisters at once.
Escaping from his dilemma by running away to Dover, he becomes
enamoured of a beautiful widow, but deserts her on her wedding day
and flees to Surrey. There he falls in love with a Miss Arundel, kills
her fiancé, marries his victim's sister and settles happily with her in

London, where he hopes to renew his attentions to two other ladies. Charles was said to be so delighted with this 'unfinished performance' that Jane dedicated to him another tale, which recounts an extraordinary journey from Bath to Basingstoke in a chaise and four.[6]

The Evangelical movement within the Church of England eventually caused some of the most popular of eighteenth-century novels to be frowned upon in religious circles. Henry Austen, writing a biographical sketch of his sister Jane shortly after her death, hastened to assure his readers that she had 'recoiled' from the grossness of Fielding.[7] It is true that in her mature works she avoided any temptation she might have had to reproduce coarse language for the sake of verisimilitude. Growing up in the late eighteenth century, however, she took the vulgarity of contemporary speech and manners in her stride and thought it smart to show her familiarity with such habits to her older brothers. 'Sophy will toss off a bumper', and 'Come Girls, let us circulate the Bottle', are among the many references to drink that occur in her early fiction. Ladies breed and bastard children abound. Having been brought up mainly among schoolboys, Jane's stories are full of jokes about unpalatable food, unlikely physical deformities and wild behaviour. An apparent delight in violent death can be attributed either to the insensitivity of youth in face of the barbarity of the times or to a critic's eye for the mechanics of contemporary novel writing, which introduced countless characters only to let them drop out of the story when they had fulfilled their immediate purpose. Sometimes, Jane allowed her characters simply to forget they had wives or offspring.

Shortly after her visit to east Kent, another topic began to absorb conversation at the parsonage: the mawkish sentimentality of the novels which were the stock-in-trade of the circulating libraries and of women's journals. Mrs Austen may have started to subscribe to the *Lady's Magazine* for the benefit of her teenage daughters.[8] Their brothers, naturally, read these publications too, and much fun was had at their expense. This new interest coincided with a new venture of James Austen's. Since returning to St John's in the summer of 1788, James had been planning to produce a weekly magazine devoted to satirical articles on contemporary life as seen at Oxford. Steele's *Tatler* and Addison's *Spectator*, followed by Dr Johnson's *Rambler* and *Idler*, had established the importance of literary periodicals in setting the critical agenda of the times, and James anticipated no difficulty in finding a publisher for a provincial successor to these prestigious London productions. He would himself supply most of the content, with help from his brother Henry, newly arrived in college. There would be occasional items from their cousin Edward Cooper, now up at Queen's, and from other Oxford men such as Benjamin Portal, their neighbour from Steventon. The professed aim of the journal would be 'the exposure of folly and error, and the recommendation of those inferior Virtues, which, though not of the greatest value, are of more frequent currency in Society' – an ambitious programme which makes it hardly surprising that Eliza de Feuillide, visiting Oxford in August 1788, found her 'gallant relatives at St John's' adopting all the airs of men of the world. Whether James was simply having a final fling before resigning himself to the obscurity of clerical office in a country parish (this being the way in which he described the destiny of the majority of Oxford graduates), or whether he was hoping to fulfil his dream of launching himself on a successful literary career, is impossible to say.[9]

The Loiterer appeared for the first time at the end of January 1789, and ran through sixty numbers before ending with a flourish on 20 March 1790. Publication took place in Oxford, but most of the distribution was done by Egerton in London to booksellers in Birmingham, Bath, Reading, Oxford and throughout the capital. Jane read each number eagerly, perhaps hoping that her brothers would be writing about the latest novels. She prided herself on having impressed her brothers when she read out to them her little burlesque, 'Edgar and Emma', in which the heroine, disappointed in her hopes of a visit from her beloved Edgar, trembled, turned pale, sank onto a sofa and dissolved into tears for the rest of her life.[10] The family had laughed, too, at her clever use of sentimental clichés in 'Frederic and Elfrida'.[11] She could not have helped being disappointed when she found that most of the early numbers of *The Loiterer* were devoted to the social affectations and attitudes of university men, about which she knew little. Henry also may have chaffed at the narrow focus of the journal, which allowed him as a newcomer to Oxford very little scope; and it may have been Jane, with Henry's connivance, who wrote a mock serious letter to the editor, published in March 1789:

> Sir, I write to inform you that you are very much out of my good graces, and that, if you do not mend your manners, I shall soon drop your acquaintance. You must know, Sir, I am a great reader and not to mention some hundred volumes of Novels and Plays have, in the last two summers, actually got through all the entertaining papers of our most celebrated periodical writers ...
>
> I assure you my heart beat with joy when I first heard of your publication, which I immediately sent for, and have taken in ever since. I

I am sorry, however, to say it, but really, Sir,
I think it the stupidest work of the kind I ever
saw: not but that some of the papers are well
written; but then your subjects are so badly
chosen, that they never interest one.—Only conceive, in eight papers, not one sentimental story
about love and honour, and all that.—Not one
Eastern Tale full of Bashas and Hermits, Pyramids and Mosques—no, not even an allegory or
dream have yet made their appearance in the
Loiterer. Why, my dear Sir—what do you think
we care about the way in which Oxford men spend
their time and money—we, who have enough to
do to spend our own. For my part, I never, but
once, was at Oxford in my life, and I am sure I
never wish to go there again—They dragged me
through so many dismal chapels, dusty libraries,
and greasy halls, that it gave me the vapours for
two days afterwards. As for your last paper, indeed, the story was good enough, but there was
no love, and no lady in it, at least no young lady;
and I wonder how you could be guilty of such an
omission, especially when it could have been so
easily avoided. Instead of retiring to Yorkshire,
he might have fled into France, and there, you
know, you might have made him fall in love with
a French *Paysanne*, who might have turned out
to be some great person. Or you might have let

K 3   him

No. 9 of the *The Loiterer*: a page of the letter from 'Sophia Sentiment'
thought to have been written by Jane Austen. (*British Library*)

am sorry, however to say it, but really, Sir, I think it the stupidest work of the kind I ever saw: not but that some of the papers are well written; but then the subjects are so badly chosen that they never interest one – only conceive, in eight papers, not one sentimental story about love and honour, and all that – not one Eastern Tale full of Bashas and Hermits, Pyramids and Mosques – no, not even an allegory or dream have yet made their appearance in the *Loiterer*.

In short, you have never yet dedicated any one number to the amusement of our sex, and have taken no more notice of us, than if you thought, like the Turks, we had no souls. From all of which I do conclude, that you are neither more nor less than some old Fellow of a College, who never saw anything of the world beyond the limits of the University, and never conversed with a female except your bed-maker and laundress.

I therefore give you this advice, which you will follow as you value our favour or your own reputation ... get a new set of correspondents, from among the young of both sexes, but particularly ours; and let us see some nice, affecting stories, relating the misfortunes of two lovers, who died suddenly, just as they were going to church. Let the lover be killed in a duel, or lost at sea, or you may make him shoot himself, just as you please; and as for his mistress, she will of course go mad; or if you will, you may kill the lady, and let the lover run mad; only remember, whatever you do, that your hero and heroine must possess a great deal of feeling, and have very pretty names. If you think fit to comply with this injunction, you may expect to hear from me again, and perhaps I may even give you a little assistance – but, if not – may your work be condemned to the pastry-cook's shop and may you always continue a bachelor, and be plagued with a maiden sister to keep house for you.[12]

This cheeky composition was signed 'Sophia Sentiment', a name found in a three-act rhyming comedy by William Hayley entitled *The Mausoleum*.[13] In reply, James affected a stern disapproval of all 'Novels, Eastern Tales and Dreams' as iniquitous in their influence upon young ladies; and thereafter a ruthless dissection of sentimentality in fiction became a major occupation of *The Loiterer*. The cleverest articles were those written by the sixteen-year-old Henry. James could write wittily on subjects dear to his heart, such as the dreary prospect awaiting young ordinands on leaving the delights of the university for a country parish, but when it came to literary criticism it was Henry who showed an insight similar to Jane's into the mechanisms of contemporary fiction. In the preceding few years, Henry had spent more time at home than

James; he and Jane may well have derived mutual benefit from discussion together.

Two months after the demise of *The Loiterer*, the fourteen-year-old Jane delivered a cleverer blow to the cult of sentimentality in fiction than any which had been published in the pages of her brother's journal. Her 'Love and Freindship' is a 10,000-word epistolary novel whose main characters, Laura, Edward, Sophia and Augustus, indulge their emotions to the point at which they become completely self-absorbed.[14] Sophia is so full of 'tender sensibility' that she cannot bear to enquire after the fate of her beloved Augustus, imprisoned for debt. All four members of the quartet are so proud of their sensibility that they condemn as a brute any person who shows the least common sense. The pre-eminence they give to individual feeling (a prime tenet of Romanticism) is demonstrated by an ostentatious rejection of parental advice: Edward, for instance, declares he cannot possibly marry the Lady Dorothea, in spite of being attracted to her, because she is his father's choice of bride for him.

In his articles in *The Loiterer* (from one of which Jane adopted the phrase 'Love and Freindship'), Henry Austen had attributed the birth of sensibility to the writings of 'the great Rousseau' and its excessive growth to 'the voluptuous manners of the present age'. Jane saw equally clearly that sensibility when carried to excess resulted in mere affectation. Gentlemen, she insists, must have auburn hair and have read *The Sorrows of Werther*, whilst for young ladies fainting is *de rigueur* – hence Laura and Sophia 'faint alternately' upon a sofa. As Sophia is dying from a consumption caught by fainting upon the wet grass, she beseeches her beloved Laura:

> Beware of fainting fits. Though at the time they may be refreshing and agreeable yet beleive me they will in the end, if too often repeated and at improper seasons, prove destructive to your Constitution ... One fatal swoon has cost me my Life ... A frenzy fit is not one quarter so pernicious ... Run mad as often as you chuse; but do not faint.[15]

Apart from the saltiness of some of the language, almost the only connection Jane's early writing could be said to have had with the reality of life around her was an occasional reference to the particular interests of the person to whom the piece was addressed. Young Charles, with a boyish fascination for rapid transport, was told of the rich Mr Clifford's many carriages, which included 'a Coach, a Chariot, a Chaise, a Landeau, a Landeaulet, a Phaeton, a Gig, a Whisky, an italian [*sic*] Chair, a Buggy, a Curricle & a wheelbarrow'. James Austen in a short play entitled 'The

Visit' could find repeated allusions to the token props he was obliged to use for his productions on the small stage in his father's barn. Martha Lloyd, the friend at Deane who had been obliging enough to finish making Jane's muslin cloak, was rewarded in 'Frederic and Elfrida' with rapturous approval of her preference for Indian over English muslin. The comparative merits of the two had been hotly debated ever since Crompton's Mule had made the production of a fine cotton thread possible in England, but fashion tended still to favour the Indian product, as Henry Tilney was to discover.[16]

Ostensibly Jane Austen's characters, like Fielding's, were drawn from a cross-section of society. There were landed gentry, clergymen, an army captain, a naval chaplain and daughters of various tradesmen. Seldom, however, did she attempt to fill in their background. Only in 'Edgar and Emma' do we learn that Mr Willmot possessed 'besides his paternal Estate a considerable share in a Lead mine & a ticket in the lottery'. Mining rights and lottery tickets were favourite forms of speculation among the gentry at this time; the Austen family may well have discussed their relative merits. The clergy had no objection to government lotteries, which had often been used for patriotic purposes such as that of financing the American War: when Uncle Francis died in the summer of 1791, leaving his nephew £500, George Austen actually decided to risk £24 on lottery shares – a profitless venture as it turned out.[17] An isolated reference of this kind, however, cannot detract from the overriding impression that Jane's early writing was a response to the books she had read and was, more than anything else, a form of literary criticism. She believed later that she would have been wiser during her girlhood if she had read more and written less.[18] Her father, however, in typical schoolmaster fashion, thought that her writing was useful. His pupils no doubt wrote exercises which they copied into manuscript books to take home. In 1790 he gave Jane a book in which to copy out a selection of her stories: in the course of time she filled three.[19] There was as yet no mention of publication, but there must have been some idea of using the writings in the future, if only as a measure of progress.

At about the same time, Jane began to look for inspiration outside the pages of books and journals. One of the developments which encouraged her to do so was the acquisition of a friend of her own in Martha Lloyd. The previous tenant of the parsonage house at Deane, Samuel Egerton Brydges, had tried to ingratiate himself with the Austen family in order to be able to write prologues for their amateur theatricals, and they had put up with him because he was the brother-in-law of the parson at the neighbouring parish of Ashe; but he was a vain and affected young man whose pretensions as a poet and novelist merely encouraged Jane in her propensity to make fun of inferior literature. Even his interest in genealogy, by which he was later to win fame, seemed ridiculous to Jane, who lampooned the subject in the opening paragraph of her story of Sir William Mountague.[20] Martha Lloyd, who came to live at Deane in 1789, was altogether different. She had no pretensions of any kind. She liked reading and took a great interest in Jane's early writings, but her education, such as it was, had been totally unacademic. Her mother's chief concern had been to arrange for her girls to receive dancing lessons so that they would have 'a good air and carriage' and be able to take part in the opening minuet at local assemblies. She had of course also taught them to sew, and Martha possessed enough skill at making clothes and enough natural taste to dress well: Jane thought her truly elegant. Like Catherine Morland, Jane at fifteen had just begun to 'long for balls' and to delight in finery. She loved discussing such things with the twenty-five-year-old Martha, who soon became a firm friend.[21]

She was less sure of Martha's younger sister, Mary, whose lack of confidence in herself had given her a sharp tongue. Mary's features had been severely scarred by smallpox which had swept through the family when she was young. She had been jealous, even then, of the attention paid to her little brother, who died of the disease; and she was jealous now of her two sisters, the second of whom had married their old friend the Revd Fulwar Fowle. Jane may have learnt a great deal about sibling relationships from the tensions within the Lloyd family.[22]

Her horizons were also widened by Mrs Lefroy at Ashe. When Uncle Francis had succeeded in providing additional income for George Austen by appointing him rector at Deane, he sold his recently-purchased right of presentation at Ashe to a wealthy gentleman of Huguenot descent, Benjamin Langlois, so that ten years later he in turn could provide for a deserving nephew. The Revd Isaac Peter George Lefroy, who took office at Ashe in 1783, was a sophisticated gentleman who liked to live in style: he transformed the parsonage at Ashe from the usual hugger-mugger building into an elegant Georgian residence of beautiful proportions. His wife Anne was a lively and intelligent lady in her thirties; with several children of her own, she still had time and energy to take an interest in Jane when the latter arrived home from school all eagerness to go on reading and learning. Mrs Lefroy loved poetry and could recite to Jane in an expressive voice long passages of Shakespeare, Milton, Pope and Gray. Always generous, she allowed Jane to use the library at Ashe parsonage whenever she liked. It only needed a short scramble up the hanging meadow and across the fields to reach the parsonage, where Jane knew that she would be welcome.

As time went on, Jane also realised that Mrs Lefroy had other interests besides literature. Her husband, it seems, had no need to engage in farming or teaching. As a woman of leisure, intelligence and means, Mrs Lefroy decided to alter the nature of her role as clergyman's wife and become hostess to the neighbourhood. It was the role Mary Crawford was to envisage for herself if she married Edmund Bertram and lived at Mansfield Park: 'commanding the first society in the neighbourhood; looked up to, perhaps, as leading it even more than those of larger fortune'. At Mrs Lefroy's house, local clergy and their wives could meet with members of the gentry on terms of equality; her conversation softened their susceptibilities and charmed them all. Poorer families in the villages were also her concern. She gathered young children together in her drawing-room and taught them to read. Appalled to see so many of them scarred by smallpox, and to learn of brothers and sisters dead of the disease, she persuaded many a parent to allow her to inoculate their offspring with her own hand; over the years she was said to have inoculated hundreds. Because of her stylishness, her fascinating personality and her husband's foreign connections, the neighbourhood called her 'Madam' Lefroy. To Jane during her girlhood she became a model of graciousness and goodness.[23]

Meanwhile Eliza de Feuillide provided Jane with much food for thought. Returning to England with her mother and her little boy in the spring of 1790, Eliza was probably staying at the parsonage when Jane dedicated 'Love and Freindship' to her on 13 June. Little Hastings de Feuillide was now four years old.[24] Eliza's letters had always been full of pride and affection for him: he was her 'wonderful brat', 'most comfortably rude and riotous', who had learnt to double up his fists and box 'quite in the English style' whilst doing his best to chatter in both English and French. If anyone alerted the Austens to the problems he presented it was probably Cousin Phila, who had seen the child when he was two years old and had written to her brother describing the fits he had suffered during teething:

> we all fear very much his faculties are hurt; many people say he has the appearance of a weak head: that his eyes are particular is very certain: our fears are of his being like poor George Austen.[25]

When the party arrived at Steventon, it was clear that Hastings was not a fortunate child. The fits had abated somewhat, but he could neither stand up straight nor walk properly. From Steventon, Eliza took him for the summer to Margate, in the hope that sea bathing would strengthen his limbs. Persuading herself that it was indeed proving beneficial, she stayed there long after the season had ended, and in January 1791 was still braving frost and snow to continue bathing with the boy. Eliza had never really wanted to have a child, but she now proved utterly devoted.[26] Did it cross Jane's mind that her brother George had been treated less lovingly? She never mentions him in her letters, but there is a hint that she showed some concern for him by learning the sign language used for the deaf and dumb.[27]

Eliza finally left Margate and once more set up house in Orchard Street in London's West End, chiefly so that her mother could receive the best possible treatment for a painful illness which had recently struck her. Eliza's sanguine spirits, combined with Mrs Hancock's brave attempts to hide the severity of her suffering from her daughter, manufactured hopes which her Austen relatives must have suspected were false; for as soon as Mrs Austen heard that her sister-in-law was ill she persuaded Edward to post up from Kent to London to find out the truth. Mrs Hancock died of cancer on 26 February 1792 and was buried in the churchyard of St John's at Hampstead, having presumably been receiving treatment from one of the many fashionable doctors in the area.[28]

Phila Walter wondered, rather smugly, how Eliza would manage from now on. Mrs Hancock's misguided kindness, as Phila saw it, had resulted in her daughter being brought up without knowledge of domestic matters. Eliza's 'gay and dissipated life' had not brought her any worthwhile friends: on the contrary, Phila continued, right-minded people had always blamed her conduct and would now wash their hands of her. 'Poor Eliza must be left at last friendless and alone.'[29] But Phila had counted without Uncle George Austen, with whom Eliza and her little boy took shelter for the whole of the ensuing winter. To Eliza, Uncle George was more than a friend. In the gratitude of her heart, she found his likeness to her mother 'stronger than ever'.

> Often do I sit and trace her features in his, till my heart overflows at my eyes. I always tenderly loved my uncle, but I think he is now dearer to me than ever, as being the nearest and best beloved relative of the never to be sufficiently regretted parent I have lost.

She wrote with almost equal warmth of Jane, whose 'kind partiality' to herself required, she believed, 'a return of the same nature'.[30]

It was the duty of a clergyman and his wife to show hospitality whenever they could: in *Mansfield Park* Mrs Norris is criticised because the spare bedrooms in her husband's parsonage were never occupied.[31] Eliza had been at Steventon parsonage scarcely more than a fortnight when another cousin arrived in some distress. Jane Cooper's father had died at his home at Sonning on 27 August 1791. Jane, like Eliza, fled at once to her Austen relatives. She had met them under very different circumstances barely three weeks earlier, when the two families had breakfasted together at the Wheatsheaf Inn on Popham Lane (the name given to to the post road from Winchester as it ran close to Steventon). The Coopers were returning from a holiday in the Isle of Wight. The trip had done nothing to restore Dr Cooper's failing health, for which purpose it had been undertaken; but to his daughter Jane it had brought unlooked for happiness. She had no sooner arrived on the island than she had met, for the first time, Captain Thomas Williams, RN, commander of HMS *Lizard*, and after a whirlwind courtship had returned to the mainland to make arrangements with Aunt and Uncle Austen to be married from their house. In the event, she arrived at Steventon in the autumn not as a bride-to-be but as an orphan, seeking comfort and advice after the death of her father. The wedding was put off for the correct period of three months, then duly celebrated at Steventon Church on 11 December with Cassandra and Jane as witnesses. Eliza had wondered whether she would at all enjoy the event, for she was inclined to think weddings 'a stupid business'. However, the bridegroom in this case was a dashing naval officer, of small fortune at present but with expectations of future preferment. The officiating clergyman invited for the occasion, the Revd Tom Fowle, was George Austen's former pupil, known to Jane Cooper from amateur acting days. He was believed to be attached to Cassandra and may well have chosen this opportunity to arrive at an understanding with her. Eliza (and also Jane) no doubt found much to interest them.[32]

Changes were also taking place in the inner circle of the Austen family. Twelve-year-old Charles – gentle, loving, sweet-tempered Charles – went to the Royal Naval Academy at Portsmouth in July 1791. The reputation of the Academy had gone down since Frank's day and now had only twenty-six out of the available forty places taken up; but as Frank had done well there and was now a Midshipman on board HMS *Perseverance*, there seemed no reason to doubt the advisability of sending Charles after him. His parents and sisters went to Portsmouth to see him installed – an occasion which led Phila Walter to hint that Cassandra might have fallen for some gallant naval officer. The visit is more likely to have given Jane some of the knowledge of the town which surfaced in *Mansfield Park*.³³

James, meanwhile, appeared to have lost some of the interest in literature which had formed his bond with Jane. He had been priested at Oxford in the summer of 1789 but, far from following in his father's footsteps as 'a scholar and a gentleman' as might have been expected, his ambition seemed to be to become a pluralistic parson, hunting, wining and dining with the elite of the neighbourhood. Early in 1790 he became curate at Overton, with the opportunity of moving into its 'very small vicarage house', the vicar being either non-resident in the parish or living in some grander house on the outskirts of the town. James had been interested in sport ever since he was a boy. At Overton he seized the opportunity to hunt the red deer in company with the Prince of Wales in the woods around Kempshott Park. At the same time, a friendship formed with William John Chute, founder of the Vine Hunt, whilst chasing the fox in the woods south of Basingstoke, bore out the satirical comment he had made in *The Loiterer*, that 'a good shot has often brought down a comfortable Vicarage'; for Chute appointed him vicar of Sherborne St John in September, 1791. Some years were to elapse before what Wilberforce called 'the race of buck parsons' was well and truly extinct: Jane could count a number of sporting enthusiasts, including the Revd Fulwar Fowle, among her clergy acquaintances. As late as 1816, she could make it a matter of surprise and regret to Charles Musgrove, the squire's son in *Persuasion*, that his prospective brother-in-law, the studious Charles Hayter, was not the sort of man to appreciate the opportunities offered by his new curacy in the heart of some of the best preserves in the country.³⁴

James could not be expected to live at Sherborne, for the parish was one of the many which had no parsonage house, and the Chutes in the seventeenth century were among the numerous landowners of the time who had appropriated the 'great tithes' (on cereal crops) which would otherwise have formed the major part of the incumbent's income. The remaining 'small tithes' (on commodities such as dairy produce and vegetables) would not have provided an adequate income for a parson, resident or otherwise; but as a supplement to the curate's stipend at Overton they were bound to be welcome. James also had the assurance he had predicted in *The Loiterer* that, when he rode over from Overton to 'do duty' at Sherborne, there would always be 'a knife and fork laid for him at the squire's table'.

It was whilst serving at Overton that he became acquainted with General Edward Mathew, who lived in retirement at Freefolk Priors, the old manor house at Laverstoke. The General, a former equerry to George III, had seen fierce action in the American War of Independence, for which he was rewarded with positions as Commander in Chief of the Windward and Leeward Islands and Governor of Grenada. He had inherited the autocratic temperament of his military forbears, but he was courteous withal, and received the new curate kindly when he arrived to read prayers in the chapel. He and his wife were not too displeased when they saw the romantic young clergyman with the soulful eyes beginning to pay marked attention to their unmarried daughter Anne. A curate could hardly be considered a good match for the granddaughter of a duke (General Mathew had married Lady Jane Bertie, daughter of the 2nd Duke of Ancaster), but Anne was by now thirty-three and this might be her last chance. She was six years older than James, but he had long been susceptible to aristocratic elegance and Anne was tall and slender, with large dark eyes and 'a good deal of nose' (as Jane once put it) to mark her lineage.[35] The marriage took place at Laverstoke on 27 March 1792, with George Austen officiating.

It could hardly have been as spectacular an event as Edward's marriage three months earlier to the daughter of the wealthy Sir Brook Bridges of Goodnestone Park. The bride's father, unlike Sir Brook, was not in a position to provide the couple with a country house. The most the General could afford to do was to provide Anne with an allowance of £100 a year, which proved to be the sum total of her fortune. James's most notable relative on his mother's side, the Honourable Mary Leigh of Stoneleigh Abbey, favoured him with another church appointment, the sinecure living of Cubbington in Warwickshire, but this merely raised his income to about £200. He was nevertheless determined to start married life in style. Leaving the very small parsonage house at Overton, he lived for a year in a grandiose residence, the Court House, near to the church. Meanwhile, he persuaded his father to arrange for the Lloyds to leave Deane so that he could move in and serve as his curate in the parish.[36]

The departure of the Lloyds was a sad day for Jane. Fortunately, they were only moving as far as Ibthorpe, some sixteen miles away, and Jane had hopes of being able to visit Martha there very often. The installation of James as curate at Deane at least exonerated George Austen from the doubts Jane hints at in her novels regarding the propriety of a clergyman holding more than one parish. She firmly believed, as she explains in *Mansfield Park*, that clergy in city churches might dazzle their congregations with brilliant sermons but that the role of the clergyman in a country parish was to set his parishioners an example of godly living. How could he do so if he held parishes in which he was scarcely ever seen? Jane was too practical to think that pluralism could be abolished, for Parliament was not prepared to amalgamate the tiny parishes whilst a great deal of patronage was in private hands. Her solution was for the clergy to appoint curates in the parishes in which they could not themselves reside. Admittedly there would still be problems, for incumbents paid their curates out of their own pockets and some paid very little. There were statutory levels, but whilst there was a glut of ordinands seeking appointments the rules were often ignored. People took it for granted that a curate would be poor: when Mrs Jennings heard that her cousin Lucy Steele was likely to be married to a clergyman, she began to look out her unwanted furniture to give them.[37]

Evidence suggests that James received from his father the statutory £50 a year at least. With Anne's £100 and the emoluments from Sherborne and Cubbington, this ought to have enabled the couple to manage successfully, provided due economy was observed. Unfortunately, James was not cut out for economy. The house at Deane, though not in the same category as Edward's house at Rowling, had been improved considerably by Egerton Brydges, yet James now spent £200 refurbishing it. Anne was provided with her own 'close carriage' for travelling about the neighbourhood, while James prepared to continue in the hunting field by purchasing a pack of harriers. Where such extravagance was to lead could only be conjectured.

With so many changes taking place around her, it is hardly surprising that the literary productions which Jane was now carefully copying into manuscript books were different in character from the earlier pieces. This does not mean that they were autobiographical. Admittedly, three daughters of Sir Brook Bridges had married in a triple ceremony, but Jane would hardly have dedicated to Edward her story of 'The Three Sisters' who fought viciously over a prospective bridegroom if it had borne any serious relationship to his own situation.[38] George Austen was careful to indicate in the third of his daughter's manuscript books that its component stories were 'Effusions of Fancy by a Young Lady', adding, however, that they were 'Tales in a Style entirely new'.[39] In fact, Jane was moving away from parody to criticise individual behaviour in the context of social conventions.

As Jane approached the age of seventeen and could be expected to be thinking seriously of marriage, she began to be aware of the vulnerability of women, often dowerless like herself, and sometimes orphaned. An extreme case had been that of her father's sister, shipped out to

India to find a husband. 'It was ... so opposite to all her ideas of Propriety, so contrary to her Wishes, so repugnant to her feelings, that she would almost have preferred Servitude to it', wrote Jane of one of her early fictional characters similarly placed.⁴⁰ Unless a woman had independent means, like Emma Woodhouse, she must feel it her duty to her parents, and above all to her brothers, to marry if possible. The pressures to accept the first reasonable offer were therefore enormous. To be obliged to remain a spinster was seen, rightly or wrongly, as a humiliation, especially if younger sisters succeeded in marrying and thereby revealed that there were no family hindrances that could be blamed.

Rousseau, however, had argued in the 1760s that a combination of love and mutual respect were the essential ingredients of a satisfactory partnership. His ideas, known to the Austen family through English translations of the work of Madame de Genlis, were adopted by James and Henry in *The Loiterer*: 'Though an Union of *Love* may have some misery, a Marriage of Interest *can* give *no* Happiness', James declared emphatically in No. 52 of the journal. It was easy and natural for Jane, as a young girl, to take the same high moral tone and record with glee, in her story of 'The Three Sisters', the backbiting that went on in a family which she named Stanhope.⁴¹ 'He is extremely disagreeable & I hate him more than anybody else in the world', confesses Mary, the eldest of the three Stanhope daughters, on receiving a proposal of marriage from a wealthy but elderly suitor.

> He has a large fortune and will make great Settlements on me; but then he is very healthy. In short I do not know what to do. If I refuse him he as good as told me that he should offer himself to Sophia and if *she* refused him to Georgiana, & I could not bear to have either of them married before me. If I accept him I know I shall be miserable all the rest of my Life, for he is very ill tempered and peevish ... It will be such a triumph to be married before Sophy, Georgiana & the Duttons; And he promised to have a new Carriage on the occasion, but we almost quarrelled about the colour ... I would refuse him at once if I were certain that neither of my Sisters would accept him, & that if they did not, he would not offer to the Duttons. I cannot run such a risk, so, if he will promise to have the Carriage ordered as I like, I will have him.

Mrs Stanhope rejects indignantly the accusation that she is trying to force Mary to marry the gentleman. 'I only want to know what your resolution is with regard to his Proposals, & to insist upon your making up your mind one way or t'other', she protests – with apparent reasonableness until she adds, '[so] that if *you* don't accept him *Sophy* may ... I am determined not to let such an opportunity escape of settling one of my Daughters so advantageously'.

Closely connected with Jane's views on marriage was her antagonism to the superficial education given to girls. This, too, had been a theme of *The Loiterer*, and Jane had already taken it up in *Jack and Alice*, a tale sent out to Frank on the high seas.[42] Her sole purpose then, however, had been to show the ludicrousness of giving an education which consisted of 'Dancing, Music, Drawing & various Languages' to a tailor's daughter. She now tackled the subject in greater depth in 'Catharine, or The Bower'.[43] The eponymous heroine (known as Kitty throughout the story) has been looking forward to companionship from a visiting relative, Camilla Stanley, only to find that the latter's promising character has been warped by her upbringing, during which

> a period of twelve Years had been dedicated to the acquirement of Accomplishments which were now to be displayed and in a few Years entirely neglected. She was not inelegant in her appearance, rather handsome, and naturally not deficient in Abilities; but those Years which ought to have been spent in the attainment of useful knowledge and Mental Improvement, had been all bestowed in learning Drawing, Italian and Music, more especially the latter, and she now united to these Accomplishments, an Understanding unimproved by reading and a Mind totally devoid either of Taste or Judgement.[44]

The 'useful knowledge' which Jane thought so important for a woman was not to be confined to, nor necessarily even to include, housekeeping concerns: in 'Lesley Castle', she is as critical of Charlotte Luttrell, whose sole thought when her sister's bridegroom is killed on the eve of the wedding is for the 'victuals' she has prepared for the wedding feast, as she is of the bride, who can do nothing but faint.[45] It was to be the kind of knowledge Locke had advocated and which Kitty, like Jane, had acquired for herself: a knowledge of the affairs of the world with a capacity to reflect upon them.

If Jane's attitude seems at times in her early writing to have been unusually detached and condemnatory, it was perhaps only to be expected from a young woman accustomed to receiving applause from her brothers for laughing at other people. She may well have had her own upbringing in mind when at a later date she made Mr Darcy confess to Elizabeth Bennet that he had been encouraged to care for no one beyond his own family circle and 'to think meanly of all the rest of the world'.[46] Gradually, Jane's growing maturity led to a more sympathetic approach. 'Catharine' features a new type of heroine: a humble girl, intelligent and good, discovering the truth about the people she meets. She has been seen as resembling Catherine Morland in *Northanger Abbey* and, on account of her ability to stand her ground, Elizabeth Bennet in *Pride and Prejudice*. Edward Stanley, the attractive young man of doubtful sincerity who appears out of the blue, belongs to the same category as Willoughby and Frank Churchill. Like the former, he disappears without a word of explanation. New characters are about to enter when the writing breaks off, apparently in mid sentence. Had Jane run into problems with the plot? It may suddenly have seemed too late to introduce a Colonel Brandon to rescue Kitty from her sentimental attachment. Or had the sixteen-year-old author simply tired of her formidable undertaking? She had abandoned the epistolary format and attempted for the first time a full-length novel in a more natural, narrative style. Or had other concerns intervened? The family's involvement in political events had certainly become more compelling.

The French Revolution had been under way for three years, yet Jane in her written work had never mentioned it. For that matter *The Loiterer* never mentioned it either, except for a reference in one of James's articles to the iniquities of the *ancien régime*, recently revealed in Linguet's (unreliable) account of the horrors of the Bastille.[47] It is not unlikely that the members of the Austen family joined the majority of England's literate population in approving France's attempt to secure greater freedom and justice. If so, they were to change their minds. Edmund Burke's *Reflections on the Revolution in France*, predicting chaos and dictatorship, appeared in October 1791. Eliza de Feuillide was in England during the ensuing winter, hoping for a visit from her husband; but with the relationship between France and Austria deteriorating the Captain found it difficult to obtain leave of absence from the army. He arrived in England early in 1792, probably just in time for Mrs Hancock's death. If Jane ever met him, it was probably then. In April 1792 France declared war on Austria. M. de Feuillide was informed that he must return to France at once or be considered an émigré, with his property forfeit to the nation. Thus it was that Eliza took refuge at Steventon. Whilst there, she wrote to her cousin Phila on 26 October 1792:

> I can readily believe that the share of sensibility I know you to be possessed of would not suffer you to learn the tragical events of which France has of late been the theatre without being much affected. My

private letters confirm the intelligence afforded by the public prints & assure me that nothing we read there is exaggerated.[48]

With Eliza's husband in Paris, events such as the attack on the Tuileries and the imprisonment of the King and Queen were bound to be discussed in the family circle at Steventon parsonage. Louis XVI had never been a popular figure among England's Protestant clergy, but there was no denying that he was the Lord's anointed and that he had shown admirable loyalty to his religion through years of adversity. The news of his execution in January 1793 aroused widespread revulsion. In less than a month, Britain and France were at war.

The frontispiece to Thomas Wilson's *Companion to the Ballroom* (1816), a manual describing the steps and the etiquette to be followed at balls.

Chapter 8

Dancing

Jane Austen entered upon her adult life at much the same time as her country went to war. In their own small way the preparations for a girl's 'coming out', in families of the nobility and gentry at least, bore some resemblance to the planning of a campaign, the acknowledged objective being to capture a husband. The main theatre of operations was to be the ballroom, since it was the stately dances of the period that allowed a young lady her only formal chance of talking with a gentleman, unchaperoned, for any length of time. As the couples parted and came together again, there was the opportunity to introduce a number of topics and thereby learn a good deal about one's partner, as Elizabeth Bennet attempted to do when dancing with Mr Darcy at the Netherfield Ball.[1] Parents who could not afford to pay for an instructor for their daughters could purchase manuals giving details of the movements and of the etiquette of the ballroom, the latter being regarded as yet another aspect of moral behaviour.[2]

A few preliminary manoeuvres in the coming out process might usefully take the form of allowing a girl who was approaching the critical age of seventeen to attend a few private balls in local gentry houses before launching her into larger gatherings and public assemblies the following year. Hopefully, if she tried out her carefully learnt dance steps with partners she had known since childhood, she would later be successful in combining dancing with conversation when obliged to stand up for half an hour at a time with comparative strangers: no gentleman could be expected to persevere with a young lady who was too shy or too involved in counting out the measures to respond to his civilities. If the worst came to the worst, she could always learn to 'talk by rule', as was done at the Bath assemblies: 'It is your turn to say something now, Mr Darcy', says Elizabeth Bennet provocatively when dancing with him at the Netherfield Ball.

'I talked about the dance, and you ought to make some kind of remark about the size of the room or the number of couples.'

He smiled, and assured her that whatever she wished him to say should be said.

'Very well; that reply will do for the present. Perhaps, by and by, I may observe that private balls are much pleasanter than public ones; but now we may be silent.'

'Do you talk by rule, then, while you are dancing?'[3]

Meanwhile, ball dresses and day dresses sufficient for the rigours of the full season could be acquired and plans made to attract as many invitations as possible. A father with several daughters would need to assess carefully both his financial resources and the number of friends on whose assistance he could call – remembering that younger daughters could not be brought out until the eldest was either engaged or married or had been allowed at least two unsuccessful seasons before being obliged to acknowledge that she had 'failed to take'.

Allusions to the innate cruelties and stupidities of the coming out process are a constant feature of Jane Austen's novels, from Elizabeth Bennet's championship of the rights of younger daughters, who were often deprived of their share of society and amusement 'because the elder may not have the means or inclination to marry early', to Tom Bertram's crude but not unjustified attacks on the behaviour of young ladies themselves – artificially demure before they were 'out' and embarrassingly forward afterwards.[4] Members of the Austen family had long been critical of a set of conventions they could not hope to satisfy in their entirety.[5] Mr Austen could not afford to finance seasons in Bath or London, and no Mr Allen came forward to take Jane under his wing. Preparation of a complete wardrobe would have been out of the question, for the cost of summoning a mantua-maker from Andover or Basingstoke to discuss patterns and take fittings would have been too costly. Jane, like many another young lady similarly placed, usually made her own clothes – picking up ideas about the latest fashions from friends who had visited smart resorts; purchasing the necessary muslins or commissioning friends to purchase them for her on rare visits to a neighbouring town; and buying lace trimmings and ribbons, along with plain cloth for linings and underwear, from itinerant tradesmen. Bonnets and hats, worn out of doors by even the youngest ladies, and headdresses to be worn at balls, were often retrimmed again and again in order to give a new look to a jaded outfit: 'Next week [I] shall begin my operations on my hat, on which You know my principal hopes of happiness depend', Jane wrote, only half playfully, to Cassandra in the autumn of 1798. She had bought Japan ink in the hope that its glossiness when dry would cover up the blemishes in the black straw.[6]

Nevertheless, as the daughter of a clergyman who was thereby accepted into the gentry class, Jane's coming out conformed in a modified way to the accepted pattern. She was lucky in that during the summer of 1792 it became known to family and friends, and apparently to most of the neighbourhood, that her elder sister had promised to become engaged to Tom Fowle as soon as his financial circumstances permitted him to think of marriage. This meant that Jane could dance at local gatherings as soon as the season started in the autumn of her seventeenth year. By late October, Eliza was reporting from Steventon to Phila Walter that their two Austen cousins had already attended an assembly at Basingstoke and a private ball in the neighbourhood, and were now visiting friends at Ibthorpe.[7]

An unexplained access of fortune had enabled the Lloyds to rent an attractive twelve-roomed Georgian house at the edge of this north Hampshire village, and the opportunity for Jane to meet a few new people could not have been better timed. The precise date of the visit may well have been arranged to allow her and Cassandra, accompanied by Martha and Mary Lloyd, to accept an invitation from Anne Mathew's sister, Mrs Dewar, to a private ball at her house, Enham Place. The four young ladies also attended the annual ball given at Hurstbourne Park by the second Earl of Portsmouth – one of the grand county events which members of the nobility were expected to arrange for the benefit of the local gentry and clergy. This was an ambitious venture for a girl of sixteen, even with the twenty-seven-year-old Martha in charge, and would doubtless have been frowned upon by Lady Catherine de Bourgh. However, unless Martha and Mary had been able to secure some male friends to accompany them, they are unlikely to have danced very much: after the formal greeting by their host, they probably sat stiffly against the wall until called into another room for supper. Jane quickly learned to amuse herself in such circumstances by passing judgement on the other guests: her chief memory of this first Hurstbourne Ball was her annoyance at the behaviour of a group of 'fat girls with short noses', whom she afterwards discovered to be the daughters of a local clergyman.[8]

Jane had always admired the determination with which her cousin Eliza conducted her social life in the interests of her own happiness, and she too set out to pursue what she knew to be every woman's task with liveliness and enthusiasm. A neighbouring matron, jealous of her attractions, described her cattily as 'the prettiest, silliest, most affected, husband-hunting butterfly she ever remembered'.[9] She was by no means an accredited beauty – nobody but Eliza would have described her as 'one of the prettiest girls in England' – but her appearance was generally found pleasing.[10] Her face, considered by some to be 'too full', was redeemed by high cheek bones, a small, prettily shaped mouth, a clear, healthy complexion and large, bright, hazel eyes. Her long brown hair was plaited up onto her head, with the shorter strands that were fashionable at the time forming natural curls about her forehead and temples. She had learnt early in life that neatness and propriety, expressed in the high-waisted, narrow-skirted gowns of the late eighteenth century, were the most admired features of a young woman's dress and, being naturally diffident about her appearance, she resigned showier styles without a pang.[11]

She loved being out of doors and could stride along the country lanes without quickly tiring, but she could also sit still for many hours indoors with great patience. Slender and moderately tall, she moved lightly and gracefully, whether walking about the room or traversing the length of a dance floor in a 'longways progressive for as many as you will'. She was an accomplished dancer, and responded with animation to the lights and music and laughter – so much so that Cassandra, secure in her relationship with Tom Fowle, was inclined to criticise Jane's behaviour as giddy and flirtatious. She could converse provocatively with arrogant persons such as the Revd John Calland, rector of Bentworth (who, at a ball, was given to standing at the side of the room with his hat in his hand), and encouragingly with shy young men such as Madam Lefroy's visiting nephew. When paying their courtesy calls at the parsonage, her dancing partners could discover, if they wished, that in spite of her voracious reading she had no pretensions to knowledge or learning of the Blue Stocking variety. Not that she feigned ignorance, as so many women did. She was simply modest by nature and inclined to underestimate her knowledge rather than force it on other people.

Her accomplishments included a more than average skill at needlework but were otherwise comfortably adequate rather than alarmingly impressive. She could draw a little, read French but not converse in it, understand a little Italian and sing simple songs in a small, clear, soprano voice. She had no wish to aspire to the heights of fashion and play the harp, as Eliza did, but she was at last learning to play the piano. This was widely believed to be an important skill to acquire, for ladies were often called upon to play at evening parties whilst the gentlemen listened and displayed their appreciation (or otherwise) of

13. Cottages at Steventon, straggling along a lane. From a sketch by Anna Austen (later Lefroy). (*Private Collection*)

both the music and the performer by the degree of attention they paid them. Jane's parents had managed to procure, perhaps at second hand, a reasonably good instrument by Ganor of Soho in a Sheraton-type case, and she was receiving lessons on it from the talented George William Chard, whom her father knew as assistant organist at Winchester Cathedral. Chard was merely in the early stages of what proved to be a successful career as a musician, and willingly added Steventon parsonage to his itinerary as a teacher, especially when he found he was taking on a pupil who was learning by her own choice. He was a handsome man some ten years older than Jane, with a lively manner and a sense of humour. Jane soon became eager to practise a little each day, if only to please him. Like Elizabeth Bennet, she believed that her technique would be improved thereby, but she was anxious not to overestimate her own talent, and above all not to appear to be doing so. Hence, although she attempted some technically demanding pieces such as the Rondo from Steibel's Grand Concerto (pencilling some of the fingering into her copy), she preferred to stick to popular airs and to sets of dances and variations by minor British composers of the period. Many of these she copied out laboriously in her own neat hand. Her taste was not impeccable, but at least she was unlikely to make ill-judged demands upon her listeners, as Mary Bennet was to do when she played (albeit with some skill) an overlong concerto at a modest supper party.[12]

The village of Steventon, like Catherine Morland's village of Fullerton, offered few opportunities to a young lady eager to launch herself into society.[13] A single row of cottages scattered intermittently for about half a mile along a lane, a couple of outlying farms and a few isolated homesteads did not promise much. There was no inn to bring travellers, no lawyer, doctor, teacher or apothecary to be invited to swell an evening party after the main guests had dined. Apart from the Austens, the Digweeds at the Manor House were still the only 'family' in the village. Of the four sons born to Hugh Digweed and his wife Ruth, the eldest, John, had moved away to manage the family's estates elsewhere, leaving three brothers at home. Harry, James and William, aged twenty, seventeen and fifteen at the time of Jane's coming out, were promising young men in their way: James was at university, aiming to take Holy Orders, whilst Harry and William were destined to take over their father's property. As a family, however, they seem to have had none of the cultural interests Jane had been brought up to expect. She was fond of 'dear Harry' (her Aunt Leigh-Perrot got the idea that she had formed a serious attachment to him, and for some obscure reason disapproved), but in fact it was difficult for her to think of either him or his brothers as anything other than childhood playmates. The two families met frequently for an evening of card games, and a noisy time was had by all.[14]

Not much in the way of social life was to be expected from the Austen's nearest neighbour in the next village either. Of the two young Holder brothers who had so delighted Mrs Austen when they first arrived as tenants at Ashe Park, one had married and gone away; the other, James, was now a staid, middle-aged bachelor, kind and courteous but hardly lively. Without a wife or a sister to act as hostess he could not be expected to give balls, and he himself never danced. Even his card parties were not always a success, his guests having a habit of crying off. His conversation was not especially entertaining either. Jane liked to amuse Cassandra by pretending that she was in danger of receiving amorous advances when alone with him, but in reality she regarded him as a safe, avuncular figure. After being out on a nasty wet day, she could appreciate a quiet evening at his house, sitting before a blazing log fire in his large, bow-windowed drawing-room and chatting effortlessly.[15]

George Austen perhaps hoped that Jane, like Cassandra, would find a partner among his former pupils, who were always welcome at the parsonage during the holidays. At twenty she showed a flickering interest in John Willing Warren, an Oxford graduate who had been sufficiently close to her brothers to contribute occasionally to *The Loiterer*. Destined for the Bar, he was kicking his heels as a Fellow of Oriel College whilst awaiting entrance to the Inner Temple. He was not good looking, but Jane found him sufficiently 'agreeable' to stand up with him twice at a local ball and to confess to missing his company when he left for town. Mary Lloyd, who as Jane's companion-in-arms in the husband-hunting campaign kept an eye on her prospects, thought that John was a distinct possibility, but Jane soon realised that he wanted to be nothing more than another elder brother.[16]

Fortunately George Austen's position as a clergyman assured his family of an entrée to the neighbourhood at large – in other words to the small group of families recognised as forming the social elite of the area. He and his wife, with their limited income, had never aspired to a leading role such as the Lefroys had secured for themselves, but they had ensured that their children were well known and well liked. In a country neighbourhood, where travel along muddy roads was hazardous and genteel families few and far between, hostesses often had difficulty in finding enough guests for dinner parties; even an

energetic organiser like Sir John Middleton, who readily galloped about
the neighbourhood for a whole morning in his efforts to drum up a
sufficient number of young couples for a ball, sometimes had to admit
defeat because families had already committed themselves to visit elsewhere whilst the moon was full.[17] A set of fine sons and accomplished
daughters, such as Parson Austen had to offer, were always likely to be
considered an asset at social events.

In theory, Jane knew that her lack of a dowry would be a drawback.
She also knew that her father's status as a property owner was not quite
the same as that of others into whose circles he was admitted. Unlike
them, he had neither house nor land to bequeath to his offspring. A
clergyman's property was his freehold: he could let his house to a tenant
or lease his land to a neighbouring farmer; but at the end of his ministry
in the parish he must hand on both house and land intact to the next
incumbent. To hard-bitten persons like Lady Denham, this was not
'real Property': a clergyman had 'an Income, perhaps, but no Property'.
In practice, Jane gave little thought to these matters in the first few
years after her coming out. She believed that personal relationships
should count for more than worldly considerations and, with the optimism of youth, she was sure that she could make them so. She knew,
too, that in her own neighbourhood she would be among friends and
need have no fear of meeting with snubs. Hampshire had a number
of great landowners – the Portals, Dorchesters and Boltons with whom
a clergyman's daughter was privileged to shake hands on formal occasions; but the gentry around Steventon were not on this level. Nor were
they in the same category as the landowners who surrounded her
brother Edward in Kent – a county at the height of its prosperity and
well known for being rich in baronets. When Elizabeth Bennet visited
the Revd Mr Collins and his wife in their parsonage near Westerham,
Kent, she found them leading a comparatively secluded life, dependent
for entertainment on an occasional summons from Lady Catherine de
Bourgh to fill up her card table. 'Their other engagements were few',
we are told, 'for the style of living of the neighbourhood in general,
was beyond the Collinses' reach.' The residents of manor houses near
Steventon were more like Mr Knightley: a gentleman farmer with broad
acres but little money to waste on cutting a fine figure.[18]

The most prominent family in the Steventon area was the Harwoods
at Deane House (a long, low, red-brick building backed by tall trees
and fronted by a wide, sweeping lawn). The family had owned most of
the land in the parish of Deane since the time of Charles I, and
successive John Harwoods had grown accustomed to the role of squire.

Jane never quite liked the present holder of the title. Had she known at the time that he was mortgaging his property and squandering the money on gambling, she would probably have disliked him even more, for she tended to think that all property-owners should regard themselves as trustees for the future, as her father did. His iniquities, however, were not revealed until his death. Meanwhile Jane appreciated his hospitality, especially at his occasional dances. The rooms at Deane House were not large, but this hardly mattered when a dozen couples were considered enough to make a satisfactory set, with a few hired fiddlers to supply the music. Of the three Harwood sons, Charles was still a boy and Earle a somewhat wild young man whom the family considered a problem. The eldest, another John, often stood up with Jane for a couple of dances at local balls, but she knew him to be deeply in love with one of her friends, Elizabeth Bigg of Manydown. As a mere curate, he had no prospect of being able to support her in her accustomed state and in 1799 he saw her married to a wealthier suitor. This might be supposed to have given Jane a chance, and she did indeed begin to think that John 'took to her rather more than he used to', but she never supplanted his lost love.[19]

Elizabeth Bigg was one of the younger daughters of Mr Lovelace Bigg-Wither of Manydown Park, Wootton St Lawrence. This courtly gentleman had added the name of his distant relatives, the Withers, to his patronym when in 1789 he inherited the estate they had held for centuries. He entertained lavishly, for as Deputy Lieutenant of Hampshire he had a duty to make himself available to any of the local gentry who might aspire to the magistracy. His house, 'with all its rights of Court-Leet and Court-Baron', was a heavy pile such as might have inspired Fanny Price's comment on first seeing Sotherton Court: 'a sort of building which she could not look at but with respect'. Its rooms, like those which Mr Rushworth had recently acquired, were doubtless lined with family portraits 'no longer anything to anybody'. At Manydown Park, however, the warmth of the family's hospitality made up for any lack of comfort in the surroundings. Jane and Cassandra were often invited to stay there for the night, not only when a ball was to be held in the large drawing-room but when they were engaged to accompany Elizabeth and her younger sisters, Catherine and Alethea, to assemblies at Basingstoke. Catherine Bigg, 'a nice, composed-looking girl', became a particular friend of Jane when Cassandra's preoccupation with Tom Fowle drew her away a little from her sister.[20]

An equally large but more attractive house in the neighbourhood was The Vyne, the home of William John Chute, Member of Parliament for Hampshire. Knights of the Shire were generally supposed to be in close touch with the gentry who had elected them. Chute was certainly well known to those who shared his interest in fox hunting; but, having wrested his seat from the Whigs in 1790, he seems to have been secure enough for many years to be able to do without courting his constituents to any great extent. In the House of Commons he had the reputation of being more interested in dining and wining his neighbours at The Vyne than in taking a part in political manoeuvres, but local experience hardly bore this out. His wife Elizabeth, whom he married in October 1793, was a shy woman. She and her husband were quietly hospitable to James Austen, as vicar of the parish of Sherborne St John in which their house was situated, but on a larger scale they gave only two or three dinner parties a year. Jane dined there in 1799, and may also have attended a dance held in one of the drawing-rooms, refurbished with crimson damask and overlooking the lake. The Strawberry Hill style of Gothick in which Horace Walpole had decorated the famous ante-chapel was probably a disappointment to her compared with the Romantic edifices described in Ann Radcliffe's novels. Moreover, she had no love of politicians, and was not prepared to follow her brother's lead in courting William Chute. Whenever the latter had the courtesy to call on her father, she suspected him of wanting something – either political support, or permission to hunt over the Steventon manor. She nevertheless had a friend in the family – a younger brother, Tom, three years older than herself and a student at Cambridge, where he intended to qualify for Holy Orders. She met Tom at card parties, and often danced with him at local balls.[21]

Nearer to home were the Terrys of Dummer and the Wither Bramstons of Oakley. The Terrys, whose large neo-classical house, not yet mellowed by time, stood out starkly from the wooded hillside, were according to Jane a noisy family. Of the thirteen children, Stephen and Michael were closest to her in age and the other eleven younger. She was often critical of them, but could rely on Stephen to partner her at dances.[22] Wither Bramston and his wife Mary (a sister of William John Chute) had an even starker house, Oakley Hall, built in 1789 on the edge of the parish of Deane. They had plenty of money to spend on the latest attractions: it was Mrs Bramston who proudly showed Jane a set of transparencies during their brief vogue at the end of the century. (By the time *Mansfield Park* was written, these translucent prints of abbeys, caves and moonlit lakes had been pushed away into attics, to be rescued, if they were lucky, by sentimental and less affluent young ladies such as Fanny Price.) It was probably from Mrs Bramston that Jane was able to borrow Mrs

Radcliffe's novels when they first came out, for they are known to have formed part of the library at Oakley Hall. The Bramstons, having no children of their own, took a great liking to Jane and Cassandra. In private Jane sometimes commented sharply on their lack of intelligence, but she saw, too, that Mrs Bramston was a generous and kind-hearted if insensitive woman – almost pleased that the Austens had no carriage and she could offer her own little 'moveable apartment', as Jane called it, to convey them to events in the neighbourhood. Her officious attentions may have provided a model for similar behaviour on the part of Mrs Jennings in *Sense and Sensibility*.[23]

In the eyes of the gentry, the lack of a carriage was such an obvious sign of deprivation that Jane sometimes found herself embarrassed by offers of transport. 'Did you think of our Ball on thursday evening, and did you suppose me at it?' she asked Cassandra in a letter of November 1800.

> You might very safely, for there I was. On wednesday morning it was settled that Mrs Harwood, Mary & I should go together, & shortly afterwards a very civil note came from Mrs Bramston, who wrote I beleive as soon as she knew of the Ball. I might likewise have gone with Mrs Lefroy, & therefore with three methods of going, I must have been more at the Ball than anybody else.

The occasion was one of the assemblies held frequently in the Town Hall at Basingstoke, which Mrs Bramston could have seen advertised in the *Reading Mercury*. They were public events, which might be attended by a wide variety of people from the gentry, professional and trading classes, although the nucleus was expected to come from annual subscribers. They were occasions for enjoyment rather than parade, and for some of the light-hearted country dances rather than the more stately court measures danced at superior gatherings. Members of the local aristocracy were nevertheless expected to put in an appearance, even if they arrived late and left early like the Osbornes of Osborne Castle. 'It was a pleasant Ball', Jane reported, '& still more good than pleasant, for there were nearly 60 people, & sometimes we had 17 couple – The Portsmouths, Dorchesters, Boltons, Portals & Clerks were there, & all the meaner &c. &cs.' Anyone like Mr Darcy, whose manner was so 'high' that he could not bring himself to dance with a lady outside his own circle of friends, would have been very much frowned upon.[24]

Jane was always sorry if an engagement away from the neighbourhood caused her to miss a Basingstoke assembly. If such a catastrophe occurred, she made sure friends would be there to tell her who danced with whom and what the ladies wore. She enjoyed the assemblies far more than the grander occasions such as the annual Hurstbourne Balls, which created excitements but also problems. It would not do to turn up to such a ball in simple country attire, and how was one to obtain anything more elaborate? ('Mary said that I looked well last night. I wore my Aunt's gown & handkercheif, & my hair was at least tidy, which was all my ambition.') In her later years at Steventon, Jane could at least rely on getting through the opening reception with credit, for in 1797 the second Earl of Portsmouth was succeeded by his son. This was none other than the poor little Lord Lymington who as a child had been a pupil at Steventon Rectory. Mrs Austen, realising that he was mentally retarded, had treated him with great kindness, and he always remembered it. His condition had deteriorated over the years, but under the supervision of his formidable mother he was able for a time to carry out his social duties without causing embarrassment, and an innate courtesy prompted him to be particularly welcoming to the less privileged of his guests such as Jane.[25]

There were other grand occasions: at Kempshott Park, where the joy of dancing on a crowded floor made up, as far as Jane was concerned, for the shortage of chairs and the predictableness of the food served at supper; and Hackwood Park, where the black sheep of Lord Bolton's family, the affable but foolish Charles Powlett, tried to steal a kiss from her. Such balls started at 10 o'clock in the evening and went on until the small hours of the morning. On one such occasion she deliberately sat out for a couple of dances rather than partner Lord Bolton's eldest son, 'who danced too ill to be endured'. More often, however, she danced with as many partners as she could find and prided herself on being able to dance without fatigue 'for a week together'.[26]

Chapter 9

War

When Jane first plunged into the whirl of activity which accompanied her 'coming out', Britain was witnessing across the Channel the beginning of a chain of events that was to lead inexorably to war. French armies, which had been unsuccessful in the early stages of their campaign against Austria and Prussia, saw the tide turn in their favour: exhilarated by the revolutionary fervour that followed the attack on the Tuileries and the imprisonment of the King, they swept into Belgium. Regarding themselves as destined to liberate Europe, they declared the River Scheldt, which rose in France, ran through Belgium and reached the sea at the border between Belgium and Holland, open to the ships of all nations 'by natural law'. Since navigation of the river had previously been confined by international agreement to the Dutch, the threat to the latter was clear. By mid November 1792, the French were threatening to overrun the whole of the Netherlands.

The Prime Minister, William Pitt the Younger, had until then set his face resolutely against war. George III might think that Britain ought to fight to restore the French monarchy, but in Pitt's view ideological warfare was not acceptable: no civilised nation should interfere with the internal affairs of another unless its own security was threatened. Edmund Burke might declare that France's revolutionary ideas, if not destroyed at source, would soon spread to Britain, but Pitt believed that the best way to prevent the British people from harbouring sedition was to increase the nation's prosperity through economy, efficiency and trade. Up to now there had been many that agreed with him, but French arrogance in opening up the Scheldt aroused the wrath of people and politicians alike. While loyal addresses poured into government offices, MPs voted by a large majority to increase the armed forces. Pitt, too, could not stomach the unilateral abrogation of solemn treaties and he feared that Britain, as Holland's chief ally, would now have to fight. He was nevertheless still trying desperately to bring about some form of European mediation when on 21 January 1793 the French guillotined their King. The British Court went into mourning and, on 1 February, France's republican government declared war on Britain and Holland. In his cold, accomplished voice, the Prime Minister announced to a candlelit House of Commons on the evening of 12 February that diplomacy was no longer an option:

> It now remains to be seen whether, under Providence, the efforts of a free, brave, loyal and happy people, aided by their allies, will not be successful in checking the progress of a system, the principles of which, if not opposed, threaten the most fatal consequences to the tranquillity of this country, the security of the allies, the good order of every European government and the happiness of the whole human race.[1]

He believed it would be a short war, since France's economy was already in ruins. 'No, sir', said Burke, 'it will be a long war, and a dangerous war.' It was to last, with two very short intervals, for more than twenty years.

Jane Austen's persistent neglect of the war as a main theme or background for a novel has often been attributed to a lack of knowledge on her part concerning it. Historians, at one time, imagined that a conflict whose battles were fought either on the Continent or at sea could have had little effect on Britain's population as a whole: the fact that a talented writer, who prided herself on her realism, could produce six major novels with no more than incidental references to it seemed proof of the slightness of its impact. Even the threat of invasion, it was argued, could not have been taken seriously, for fashionable society continued to flock to Brighton, and holiday resorts proliferated along the south coast, in spite of their proximity to France. A fuller picture of Britain's war effort, however, makes such a view untenable.[2]

At the outbreak of hostilities, Britain, with a population of only ten million, was called upon to increase her army from 45,000 men to 100,000 and her navy from 16,000 to 130,000. The death toll was high from the start. The army served in a number of costly efforts to deprive France of her colonies, before being employed spectacularly in the Peninsular War. The navy was continually engaged in dangerous convoy duties both before and after the Battle of Trafalgar. There was a constant struggle, not only to replace the dead and wounded but to find ever increasing numbers of men for new theatres of war. The cherished freedom of British citizens forbade conscription to the army but did not deter either the government or captains of ships from sending out press gangs, especially in seafaring counties such as Hampshire, to capture unwary merchant seamen as crew for naval vessels.

MASSACRE OF THE FRENCH KING!

VIEW OF

La Guillotine;

OR THE

MODERN

Beheading Machine,

AT PARIS.

By which the unfortunate LOUIS XVI. (late King of France) suffered on the Scaffold, January 21st, 1793:

The execution of Louis XVI, from a contemporary English broadside

Recruitment for the army demanded relentless propaganda, along with expedients such as bounties, which were costly to the taxpayer. The militia, which normally met for a mere two or three weeks a year to train for defence purposes, was now embodied on a longer-term basis. It continued to be regarded as a volunteer force, but all civilian males other than clergy were obliged to make themselves available for enrolment, and increasing numbers were taken into the ranks during the early years of the war. Other men, partly to avoid enrolment in the militia and partly out of a genuine desire to defend their home ground, joined independent forces known as Volunteers. Threats of invasion across the Channel were intermittent, but they were nevertheless serious when they occurred and much effort went into organising Sea Fencibles – a volunteer force capable of manning small craft to keep a look-out among creeks and inlets along the coast. The possibility of invasion from Ireland was a more continuous threat, and large numbers of troops had to be kept there when they could better have been employed elsewhere. The Irish militia, recruited from 1793 to defend its own shores, was widely, if often wrongly, distrusted because it was mainly Catholic.

During the nine years of warfare against Revolutionary France, eight of which Jane spent at Steventon, she had two brothers in the navy and a third in the militia. Many of her friends and neighbours were engaged in either the regular forces or the Volunteers. Her father, too, was required to play his part. The clergy were on more than one occasion called upon to supply information to the authorities regarding the resources and needs of their parishes in the event of invasion. More important still was their role in strengthening people's resolve to support the burdens of the war. Hitherto, wars had been merely an extension of diplomacy, fought by comparatively small numbers of soldiers and sailors who looked upon fighting as a part of their chosen occupation. This time, the entire population was involved in one way or another. Rising food prices at times of bad harvest were exacerbated by the need to supply the troops; lack of purchasing power caused businesses to go bankrupt and threw their employees out of work. To the cost of maintaining an unprecedentedly large military establishment was added that of huge subsidies to foreign powers. Taxes multiplied at an alarming rate. It was essential to forge Britain into a previously unknown weapon: a nation at war. The church, through its prayers, petitions, fast days and thanksgivings, was a major instrument for doing so.

The explanation for Jane Austen's reticence must therefore be sought elsewhere than in a lack of knowledge or concern. She has been severely criticised by feminists for backing away from a topic which could be regarded as a male preserve, and it is indeed not unlikely that, if it ever crossed her mind to write a novel centred upon the war, she rejected the idea on the grounds that she could not reproduce conversations between officers in camp or on board ship: she once declined to write a novel featuring a high-ranking clergyman on the grounds that she lacked the learning to represent such a person's academic interests.[3]

In fact there is no evidence that she ever considered the possibility of writing a novel about the war, even though, like many novelists, she tried continually to find new topics and worried over whether she had written herself out. A most probable explanation for her avoidance of the subject is that, like most people who have to live through a war, she kept it as much as possible in the background of her life and got on with her own affairs as best she could. After reading *Pride and Prejudice* in print for the first time, she suggested to Cassandra (merely as a joke) that it might suitably have contained a passage on Buonaparte as a contrast to its general playfulness.[4] She wrote her novels primarily to entertain her readers. To make them worthwhile, she took the opportunity to pillory characters who promoted what she believed to be the major faults of upper-class society, namely, selfishness and materialism. The war would not have served as a subject of entertainment, and she had no fundamental criticism to make of her country's conduct in regard to it.

She nevertheless could not help bringing aspects of the wartime situation into her novels. Though her main theme is always connected with life among the gentry, insights into the effects of war can claim to play a supporting role, of considerable importance in that some of them are not easily found elsewhere. *Sense and Sensibility* signals a growing respect for the clergy: only women such as Mrs Ferrars and her daughter Fanny think that soldiers and sailors are more important to the nation than clergymen. *Pride and Prejudice* illustrates the role a militia regiment could play in the life of a country community. *Mansfield Park* describes the worries undergone by a young Midshipman who despairs of obtaining patronage as a means of promotion. *Persuasion*, written during the brief period of peace in 1814, has a number of naval characters who look back upon their years of warfare at sea with apparent regret that they are over. Even *Emma*, which scarcely moves beyond the confines of the village of Highbury and may seem at first to have nothing to do with the war, is imbued with the particular kind of patriotism, consisting of a nostalgic devotion to England's countryside, England's manor houses and England's supposedly caring gentry, which developed during the conflict and which the church did much to promote.

Patriotism created problems for a Christian church dedicated to universal benevolence and the overwhelming emotion which it engendered in wartime, was unlikely to appeal to mainstream members of the Church of England, who prided themselves on their rationalism. Jane Austen loved her country but was not prepared to praise the nation's heroes uncritically. She remained aloof from the mindless adulation of Nelson which gripped the country after the latter's death at Trafalgar, and refused to admire the patriotic words General Sir John Moore was reported to have uttered when dying at Corunna ('I always wished to die like this. It is a great satisfaction to know we have beaten the French'): at so solemn a moment he should have 'united something of the Christian with the Hero', she thought. Like the clergy of the Church of England, she seems eventually to have adopted the arguments which Burke had supplied in his *Reflections on the Revolution in France*. Love of country, Burke argues, arises from a natural attachment to one's own neighbourhood: the only open profession of patriotism in Jane Austen's novels is made by Frank Churchill with reference to his native village. Extended to one's country as a whole, the sentiment is justifiable if one's country is truly lovable. England was worth fighting for because it was religious and because its religion was Protestant.[5] In 1813, with victory in sight, Jane shared the widely held view that God must have been on England's side. Despite their faults, England's ruling classes must have been more moral, more caring, more mindful of the community than their counterparts in France.

In *Emma*, Jane Austen describes a rural community which many people at the time liked to regard as traditionally English. Its leading landowner, Mr Knightley, presides over the neighbourhood with courtesy, sensitivity and generosity – characteristics which he regards as typically English compared with Frank Churchill's superficial, French-like charm. She gives a glowing description of Mr Knightley's rambling old manor house, which stands for English traditions of hospitality, reliability and unpretentious comfort. This is followed by an ecstatic description of the surrounding countryside – the farm, the old mill, and the cattle grazing by the bend in the river.

> It was a sweet view – sweet to the eye and the mind. English verdure, English culture, English comfort, seen under a sun bright, without being oppressive.[6]

Jane shared her father's wish of keeping in close touch with the sailor brothers and went to a great deal of trouble to do so. Her letters to

Frank often took a month to reach him, and his own ill-spelt replies were subject to the uncertain movement of ships casually encountered and thought (sometimes wrongly) to be on their way home.[7] Tirelessly, Jane sought out navy lists and newspapers, and even wrote to officials of the Admiralty in search of information. Neither Frank nor Charles was married during the family's residence at Steventon: their contact with England was through letters to and from Cassandra and Jane. Later, though loyalty and affection remained firm on both sides, the priority for the two brothers was necessarily to communicate with their wives. It is hardly surprising, therefore, that when Jane, in her novels, wrote of the sea, she employed most often the knowledge obtained from Frank and Charles during these years of war against Revolutionary France.

William Price, as he appears in *Mansfield Park*, is an eager young man in the early stages of his career, proud of the dangers he has survived, though modest in talking about them. William has not been trained at the Royal Naval Academy like Jane's brothers. He has entered the navy by the only route open to youngsters without education: that of finding a Captain willing to take him on board at the age of eleven as an apprentice officer. His family could not have afforded to buy his uniform or supply the £30 a year required as an assurance that a young man training to be an officer could support a gentlemanly style of living during the three years that he received no pay. It was his rich Uncle Thomas who had 'done most for his support and encouragement', and William has now come to Mansfield Park to persuade his benefactor that he has not wasted his money. Jane's brothers had doubtless told her that the tough training given to apprentice seamen was the best way of producing good officers, this being the common opinion at the time: she admires William, whom she says has 'a right to be listened to', and she clearly disapproves of Mrs Norris for interrupting his narrative by fussing about her sewing.[8] William is keen on dancing – an important accomplishment for an officer, since officers were supposed to be gentlemen, and gentlemen danced.[9] Jane's brothers had learnt to dance at the Naval Academy, where Charles, more than Frank, became an addict: Jane often relied on her younger brother to get superseded for a day when in dock at Portsmouth and escort her to a ball.[10] William has learnt to dance on board ship, where the men danced with each other. He is looking forward to proper partners whilst on leave, but the girls at Portsmouth refuse to look at him because he is only a Midshipman. 'One might as well be nothing as a midshipman', he tells his sister Fanny.

One *is* nothing, indeed. You remember the Gregorys? They are grown up amazing fine girls, but they will hardly speak to *me*, because Lucy is courted by a lieutenant.[11]

He is worried that he may never get promotion because he can think of no friends who might recommend him to the Admiralty: the method by which he eventually succeeds is an important part of the plot of the novel. By the time she wrote *Persuasion*, Jane realised that a young man could *sometimes* get on without patronage, as Captain Wentworth showed; nevertheless, she admits that Lady Russell was right to doubt the possibility. Even patrons were not always helpful. At the outset of the Napoleonic phase of the wars the Austen family had great hopes for Charles, on account of his friendship with the younger brother of the influential William Paget, later Marquess of Anglesey; but the connection merely resulted in Charles being transferred from European waters to the western Atlantic, where he saw no action and took no prizes, returning home in 1811 a comparatively poor man. 'I hate all the race of Pagets', Jane once wrote.[12]

In *Persuasion* Captain Wentworth, like Frank Austen, has distinguished himself in the action off St Domingo in 1806, yet it is mostly his early years at sea that he talks about. Like Frank, he commanded a battered old ship, but she was *his* ship and he was proud of her: 'she was a dear old *Asp* to me', he says. 'She did all I wanted. I knew she would.'[13] Jane remembered other things Frank had told her, too: how captains sometimes stole each other's men to make up their own crews (a practice which Admiral Croft condemns in *Persuasion*); how the Admiralty 'entertained themselves now and again' by sending men to sea in rotten ships (a practice which Captain Wentworth thinks might easily have been the death of him); and how senior officers sometimes abused their position and took to buggery (a piece of information Mary Crawford hints at vulgarly in conversation at Mansfield Park: 'Certainly, my home at my uncle's brought me acquainted with a circle of Admirals. Of *Rears*, and *Vices*, I saw enough. Now, do not be suspecting me of a pun, I entreat.') A significant factor in the wars, and one which emerges clearly from Jane Austen's letters and novels, is that, despite Nelson's emphasis on destroying the enemy fleet in battle, many officers were equally if not more concerned to capture individual ships and thereby obtain prize money. 'Ah, those were pleasant days when I had the *Laconia*', sighs Wentworth. 'How fast I made money in her.'[14]

It may have been in part a result of Frank's prejudices that Jane cast Fanny Price's feckless father as a Lieutenant of Marines, with 'no curiosity, and no information beyond his profession'.

He read only the newspaper and the navy-list; he talked only of the dockyard, the harbour, Spithead and the Motherbank; he swore and he drank, he was dirty and gross.[15]

Sailors often spoke disparagingly of marines, for the simple reason that marines were virtually passengers when on board ship and often appeared ignorant in the presence of skilled seamen. Jane also, however, visited Portsmouth on a number of occasions, and knew the dockyard area and the back streets of the town, with their slovenly womenfolk and rowdy children, tolerably well. A great many lower-ranking officers in the Marines came from families of poverty-stricken tradesmen and clerks, long resident in tall, narrow, thin-walled and jerry-built houses such as Jane describes in *Mansfield Park*.[16]

Unlike militia officers, few soldiers of the regular army appear in Jane's novels – understandably, since she seems to have known only a few and none intimately. In October 1793 James Austen's father-in-law, General Mathew, purchased for him the position of chaplain to one of the new regiments hastily formed for overseas service; but James – a married man with a six-month-old baby – had no wish to take up active service, nor did General Mathew expect him to do so. Almost all army chaplains hired substitutes and pocketed the surplus pay. In James's case, any hope of making money by this method was thwarted by inefficiency in the army's record-keeping. He never so much as told his family about the appointment.[17]

The army had the advantage that it could be entered at any time, whereas the navy required training to begin no later than at the age of twelve: Edward Ferrars, fighting off his family's attempts to make him join a 'smart' profession, was saved from having to consider the navy by being too old (he was eighteen) when the subject was first thought of. Nevertheless, proximity to the great naval base at Portsmouth had always made the sea an obvious choice of career for Hampshire men. When called upon to sing in local drawing-rooms, Jane was accustomed to alter the words of Dibdin's 'The Soldier's Adieu' to refer instead to sailors. Later in life, she was to refer to Captain Pasley, whose delightful *Essay on the Military Policy and Institutions of the British Empire* she very much enjoyed, as 'the first soldier I ever sighed for'. Shortly before then, she had written tongue-in-cheek to Cassandra about the marriage of Lady Sondes of Nackington to General Montresor: 'I like his rank very much – & always affix the ideas of strong sense, & highly elegant Manners, to a General.'[18] Thanks to an age-old fear of armies as a potential weapon of despotism, soldiers were far less respected than sailors by the public at large: early readers of Jane's novels are unlikely to have objected to the deplorable character given to General Tilney and his son, Captain Frederick Tilney, in *Northanger Abbey*. Nor would they have been surprised to learn that a commission in the regular army failed to deter Wickham, in *Pride and Prejudice*, from running into debt: army regiments, even when 'banished to the North', were moved about, like the militia, from town to town.[19]

The only honourable soldier in Jane Austen's fiction is Colonel Brandon, whose service in the East Indies has helped to give him a knowledge of the world which Elinor Dashwood admires.[20] Travel, in the days of the Grand Tour, was regarded as an essential means of broadening a man's mind, though women might make do with travel books describing strange creatures encountered in unknown climes. Brandon, however, has sold out of the army, before *Sense and Sensibility* starts, in order to run the family estate on the death of his elder brother; we therefore see him at his best. The role of a landowner was considered as being of vital importance to the country: no one would have expected Mr Darcy to buy an ensigncy for himself as he does for Wickham.

The Austen family's involvement in the war began almost at once. Although there seemed at the beginning to be little danger of the French mounting an invasion, a nation at war must look to its defences. For this purpose, Britain traditionally relied on the navy and the militia. Little more than a dozen of Britain's 115 ships of the line were ready for service, but a few weeks sufficed to bring a further fifty-four into commission. Many an officer on half-pay (including Nelson) saw signs of getting a ship at last. The Austens could look forward to seeing Frank back in European waters, with better chances of promotion than sailors had had since the ending of the American War. Jane soon learnt that sailors cannot be expected to long for peace. The only character in *Persuasion* who fears a renewal of war is Anne Elliot, engaged to Captain Wentworth; and Jane Austen's only comfort for her is that she will have to consider the alarms and anxieties of war as the price she has to pay for the honour of marrying into so noble a profession.[21]

The size of the militia was voted annually by Parliament, after which it was the duty of each Lord Lieutenant to organise a ballot of the able-bodied men between the ages of eighteen and forty-five to produce the quota for his county. With 19,000 extra men called for at the beginning of the war, and the regiments embodied for full-time service, more officers were required. Among the young gentlemen who hastened to answer the country's call was Henry Austen, who had graduated at Oxford the previous summer and was now enjoying a Fellowship at

St John's whilst awaiting the age at which he could be ordained. Discovering that the defence of Britain's shores would not require him to resign his Fellowship, and that the recommendation of relatives and friends would serve in lieu of the statutory property qualification, he took a commission as Lieutenant in the Oxfordshire Militia in the spring of 1793 and joined the regiment at Southampton in readiness to guard the coast.[22]

If he had had the purchase money he would have preferred a commission in the regular army, as being more permanent. The militia provided an income only when the regiments were embodied. News was already arriving of the French undergoing reversals once more: the war seemed likely to be over in no time and the militia disbanded. Until that day should come, however, it provided young men like Henry with pocket money and plenty of social opportunities. Its officers were billeted in comfort upon local inns. Like those of the regular armed forces, they were admitted to the houses of the gentry, where they made a welcome addition to the small local clientele available for dances and card parties. Parents of marriageable daughters might look a little warily upon dashing young blades who had broken free from the restraints of neighbourhood and family to move in circles where their antecedents were unknown and their stay likely to be short, but their scarlet uniforms made them attractive to many a young lady bored with life in a small village or county town. The regiments could not be sent abroad, and the officers had plenty of leave: Henry was often at liberty to visit friends and relatives in Oxford, London and Kent and to spend time at home. He was over six feet tall and endowed with a good deal of charm and address. Eliza had found it necessary some little time ago to put an end to his boyish admiration of her and establish 'proper relationlike terms'.[23]

Towards the end of the year 1793 the family joyfully received Frank back home after nearly five years of service in the Eastern Seas. He had left England as a boy of fourteen and returned as a weather-beaten young man of nineteen. He had much to tell his favourite sister of his experiences, and also of his 'hopes and fears, plans, and solicitudes respecting that long thought of, dearly earned, and justly valued blessing of promotion'. Unlike William Price, of whom these words were to be written, Frank had already been made a Lieutenant, but there was still far to go, and everything would depend on what happened to him during the next few years. His interest lay in being near the centre of action. Frank was a career sailor, for whom there was no point in being squeamish about fighting. He was to be bitterly disappointed at narrowly missing the Trafalgar action, Nelson having sent him to Genoa at the crucial time to collect supplies.[24]

Meanwhile, he had a few months leave and, since it behoved him to remind the naval authorities as often as possible of his availability, he readily undertook to escort Jane, this time with Cassandra, on a visit to their cousin at Southampton. Elizabeth-Matilda Austen had married John Butler Harrison, who was an important figure in the town. As a candidate for the mayoralty, Harrison was expected to attend, with his guests, at local functions; hence Jane and Casssandra danced at a public ball at the Dolphin Inn and perhaps at other balls too. Cassandra returned home early, but Jane had become enough of a favourite to be asked to stay on with the Harrisons over Christmas and stand as godmother to their newly-born third child. She had had some experience of handling babies since the arrival, in April, of her niece Anna at Deane.

With their brother as escort, the sisters may well have travelled to Southampton by stagecoach, waiting with their trunks at the Wheatsheaf Inn for the coach to arrive from Basingstoke on its way to Winchester. Passengers on routes from London to the south coast were predominantly sailors, and others hoping to board at intermediate stages often found that, in spite of early booking, their places had been taken and the coach was full on arrival. Even if inside seats were successfully obtained, the journey could be uncomfortable – stuffy in summer and cold in winter, with the extra hazard in wet weather of outside passengers, soaked to the skin, squeezing in alongside. But at least, with Frank present, Jane and Cassandra would not have been besieged alarmingly by beggars when the coach halted, or bullied by dishonest coachmen into giving up their inside seats and sitting on top. On the longer journey which they made by themselves the following summer, to visit Edward in Kent, they probably travelled post – Edward's in-laws being too awesomely wealthy to be expected to receive guests who travelled by stagecoach. There was always the risk, even then, of having to wait for several hours at a posting inn because all the horses had been taken out (an eventuality that could only be avoided by people wealthy enough to keep their own horses at the major posthouses).

Edward was proud of his connection with the Bridges family, whose imposing, lavishly fenestrated house, Goodnestone, was only a mile across the park from his own house, Rowling. During his sisters' stay, he went out of his way to introduce them to his new relatives and to friends in the area. There may have been impromptu dances at Goodnestone, for there were several unmarried daughters at home and

Edward's wife was usually happy to play the required tunes on the piano. Eighteen-year-old Jane had an exciting time, and returned to Steventon imagining herself in love with the nineteen-year-old Edward Taylor, whose 'beautiful dark eyes' and large manor house of Bifrons she viewed with equal rapture.[25]

That same summer, the Austen family struggled to assimilate the garbled accounts that reached them of the fate of Eliza's husband. Eliza had always said that M. de Feuillide was a Royalist, in sympathy with the Princes who had fled abroad to foster counter-revolution. Like many Frenchmen on the fringes of the nobility, he had probably been more stridently aristocratic in his opinions than greater men needed to be. He certainly flaunted aristocratic connections longer than was safe. When his friend the Marquise de Marboeuf was accused, on pettifogging evidence, of conspiracy against the Republic, he unwisely if quixotically tried to bribe one of the secretaries to the Committee of Public Safety to intervene on her behalf. The man encouraged him, then denounced him. He was arrested at his lodgings, brought to trial before the dreaded Revolutionary Tribunal on 22 February 1794, and guillotined the same day. The Tribunal having more to do than communicate with the relatives of traitors, Eliza received no definite news and may still have been refusing to believe rumours of her husband's death as late as July, when she was staying with friends in Durham.

To her relatives at Steventon the story must have been almost beyond belief – fit only for a melodrama. Events in Paris had long had an air of unreality to outsiders. Jane Austen copied into her songbook Storace's plaintive air, 'The Lamentation of Queen Marie-Antoinette on the Morning of her Execution', but renamed it 'Queen Mary's Lamentation', since the Scottish Queen still meant more to her than the frivolous Austrian woman. Marie-Antoinette was pitied in her misfortune, but the British public, in spite of Burke's championship, had never had much admiration for her. Nor could the family at Steventon deeply mourn the loss of M. de Feuillide. They knew that Eliza had never loved him. They may have known, as she most certainly did, that he kept a mistress in Paris. He had continued to the end to run up debts in his wife's name. Yet when the reality of his death finally sank in, the violence of it could not fail to shock. It was one more justification for hating the French, with whom Britain had been at war for much of the past century.[26]

The Jacobin government had by now fallen in its turn, but not before its ferocious idealism had transformed France's military situation. A concentric assault across her frontiers by Austrian, Prussian, Spanish and Sardinian forces, aided by a British expeditionary force to Flanders, was beaten off and French armies once more took to the offensive. By May 1795 all of Britain's allies except Austria had made peace with the enemy, and France was in control of the entire Channel coastline from Brest to Hamburg. Invasion of Britain became a real possibility for the first time. Many shared the fears Parson Woodforde, in his Norfolk village, committed to his diary: 'Dread and terrible times appear to be at hand.'[27]

Chapter 10

Love and Tragedy

In December 1794, perhaps as a present for Jane's nineteenth birthday, her father bought her a mahogany writing desk with a drawer and a glass inkstand.[1] It was a very small desk, hardly big enough, one would have thought, to use when writing letters; but Jane not long afterwards sat down at it and started to write a novel. She always wrote on small pieces of paper, and the drawer was useful to keep them in. The novel, originally called 'Elinor and Marianne', was to lie there a long time before it appeared in print as *Sense and Sensibility*.

At just what point in her life Jane Austen decided she might actually publish a novel is uncertain. There was nothing unusual in a woman hoping to do so. By the mid eighteenth century, Richardson, Fielding, Sterne and Smollett had made novels so popular that circulating libraries were demanding more and more titles. The libraries catered mainly for women's leisure hours, and women were supposed to enjoy reading books written from their own point of view. Women writers had therefore hastened to take advantage of a genre which had no classical precedents and no learned tradition, and which was believed to be undemanding in that it relied a great deal on ordinary powers of observation. The epistolary style, used so effectively by Richardson, was an especial attraction to them.

The only barrier they encountered was the conventional view of womanly behaviour. Women were not supposed to thrust themselves into the public view. They might be excused for exposing themselves in print only if, like Hannah More, they were driven to do so by some overriding moral purpose, or if they needed to do so as their sole means of support (though they might then find themselves accused of hack writing). No woman who wished to be thought womanly could write for public recognition. The obvious solution, however, was simply to publish anonymously. In time the author's identity would become an open secret, but convention would be satisfied if an outward pretence of anonymity, or a show of dismay at having had one's name discovered, were maintained. Sarah Fielding, Charlotte Lennox, Charlotte Smith and Fanny Burney were already well known. By 1773 the *Monthly Review* could declare that the business of writing novels (and it had indeed become very much a business) was 'almost entirely engrossed by the Ladies'.[2]

Jane Austen, however, had her own inhibitions. Her critical intelligence had made her so aware of the second-rate quality of most of the novel writers appearing since mid century that she needed to aim at the highest standard in order to satisfy herself. She was a fierce admirer of Fanny Burney, whose professed aim in her novels was to portray human nature; but at the age of nineteen Jane was probably too diffident to do more than dream that she might one day emulate her. Fortunately, she had a father who both understood her diffidence and admired her talents. As a firm believer in goodness receiving its just reward, he encouraged her when he thought the time had come. In this respect she was luckier than Fanny Burney, who wrote her first novel during the night, crouched over a candle in a cold room, for fear lest her father should discover what she was about.[3]

In searching for a theme for her novel, it seems that Jane was not as yet prepared to break away from her reading and rely solely on experience. The war which her country had been waging for the past two years was having its effect on her family and on others around her. Charles Austen had followed his brother to sea; William Fowle had taken a commission as an army doctor and had sailed for the West Indies; his brother Charles Fowle had succumbed to the drumming and trumpeting of one of the many recruiting parties which paraded England's county towns and joined the Hungerford Volunteers; Mr Holder at Ashe Park had become captain of the Steventon force; the Harwoods' second son, Earle, having failed in his attempt to make quick profits as a coal merchant when the price of fuel rose astronomically during the severe winter of 1794, had joined the Royal Marines; but neither personal involvement nor the national crisis caused by low wages, high prices and a steep rise in taxes were to Jane topics that she cared to bring within the compass of a novel.

The theme she ultimately chose was one which had been discussed in literary and philosophical journals for several decades – namely, the rival merits of different approaches to the role of feeling. Disagreement raged over whether emotion should be checked in the interests of caution, decorum and consideration for others, or whether it should be allowed free rein for the sake of spontaneity, individuality, generosity and enthusiasm. Adherents of the former opinion could invoke the value long attached to discrimination and 'taste', but their view could easily be made to appear cold and worldly. Adherents of the cult of 'sensibility' quoted Shaftesbury in believing that human beings were endowed with an instinct for right judgement, and that this should be heeded in preference to the corrupting influences of civilisation; their views, however, could easily be shown to be at best impractical and at worst dangerous. Jane set out to illustrate these conflicting positions by attributing them to two sisters, Elinor and Marianne, whose names were to form the title of the novel.

The topic was not without relevance to everyday life, for advocates of sensibility questioned social conventions and unsatisfactory personal relationships which had long been accepted, thereby making them less easy to endure. For instance, they condemned loveless marriages, yet many women felt they were forced into such arrangements by economic and social pressures. They poured scorn on second attachments, on the assumption that a first love is irreplaceable and no other grounds for union are valid; yet the incidence of early deaths placed many young women under the necessity of finding protection where they could. Public criticism cannot have helped the victims of such circumstances, especially since it was echoed by people who were not necessarily keen advocates of sensibility. Jane Austen herself, for instance, greeted the news of a local woman's plans to remarry very shortly after her first husband's premature death with the caustic comment:

> Mrs John Lyford is so much pleased with the state of widowhood as to be going to put in for being a widow again; she is to marry a Mr Fendall, a banker in Gloucester, a man of very good fortune, but considerably older than herself & with three little children.[4]

Tension was rife in other areas, too. Rules governing entry into gentlemanly circles, though unwritten, were so rigid as to startle foreign visitors expecting to find England a land where there was perfect freedom of social intercourse.[5] Men who had risen in the world by making money were afraid of exposure by lapses in behaviour, or by association with persons of lower rank. In the tight little communities of rural England, neighbourhood opinion could be harsh and inexorable, as Jane Austen well knew: she once confessed to feeling sorry for the newly married Mrs John Butler of Ibthorpe, obliged 'to stand the gaze of the neighbourhood as the Bride of such a pink-faced, simple young man'.[6] Nor should the sheer boredom of life in a country house be underestimated. However energetically the social round was pursued, there were likely to be long periods of time during which visiting was restricted by dark nights and muddy lanes. Charlotte Brontë's first comment on reading Jane Austen's novels was, 'I should hardly like to live with her ladies and gentlemen in their elegant but confined houses'.[7]

Social pressures were such that there had for some time been a marked increase in nervous disorders, described by George Cheyne in a popular medical work of the early eighteenth century as 'the English malady'. Cheyne attributed the spread of the disease to increasing wealth and leisure among the middle classes; others, equally censorious, ascribed it to a self-indulgent nurturing of personal responses and emotions, to which women were said to be particularly prone. From here, it was a short step to the melancholia and female hysteria beloved of novel writers. Since both states were a protest against circumstances over which the sufferer felt he or she had no control, they were condemned by conduct writers as particularly deplorable in women – submissiveness being the only proper female response.[8]

The writing of Jane's novel was interrupted by tragedy. On 3 May 1795 her brother James's wife Anne, after dining with her husband in apparent health, collapsed in his arms and died a few hours later. James was distraught. His two-year-old daughter, Anna, bewildered and lost, wandered around the house asking for 'Mamma'. To help James in the only way that was possible, it was agreed that Anna should be brought to Steventon to stay for as long as seemed necessary with her grandparents. Mrs Austen had helped to bring her into the world, and loved her as she loved all young things; and, with Cassandra and Jane at hand, the little child it was hoped would soon settle down. Her father rode over to see her at least once a day, and sometimes twice. Her maternal grandfather, fierce old General Mathew, doted on her, and transferred to her the £100 a year he had formerly paid to Anna. If Jane afterwards used his frightening demeanour to help her portray General Tilney, she had reason to know that in Edward Mathew's case there was genuine kindness under the surface.

In spite of the disturbance which the arrival of a young child must inevitably have created, Jane finished her novel within the year. The manuscript of 'Elinor and Marianne' no longer exists, and its contents can only be deduced from what appear to be survivals of it in the text later published as *Sense and Sensibility*. The family must have commended it to some degree when it was read out to them, or Jane would not have persevered with it to the extent of rewriting it the following year, but it cannot have been wholly successful. It was written in the epistolary style which Jane had used effectively in her story of Lady Susan but which was likely to have exaggerated the dichotomy between

SENSE

AND

SENSIBILITY:

A NOVEL.

IN THREE VOLUMES.

BY A LADY.

VOL. I.

𝔏𝔬𝔫𝔡𝔬𝔫:

PRINTED FOR THE AUTHOR,

By C. Roworth, Bell-yard, Temple-bar;

AND PUBLISHED BY T. EGERTON, WHITEHALL.

1811.

Title page to the first edition of *Sense and Sensibility.*

'sense' and 'sensibility' to an extent that practical persons such as Mrs
Austen found unacceptable. A certain amount of priggishness clings to
Elinor Dashwood even in the published version of the novel: it is
possible that in the original version her dampening comments were as
unfeeling and hence as ludicrous as those of Charlotte Luttrell in Jane's
juvenile story, 'Lesley Castle'.[9] Some elements of comedy are present
even in the later, published version; in the original draft they may have
overwhelmed the characterisation of the two sisters.

The main message conveyed by the plot must nevertheless have been
clear – namely, the need to subdue an eager young woman such as
Marianne in a world in which unscrupulous people were only too eager
to take advantage of her innocence. Disaster results when Marianne
bestows her affections wholeheartedly and at once on an attractive but
immoral young man, whose common decency in helping her home
after an accident she interprets as heroism and whose soulful appreciation of Shakespeare's sonnets she accepts as proof of genuine feeling.
No hope is held out of her falling in love a second time, with someone
equally romantic but more worthwhile: she must find happiness of a
soberer kind with a man for whom she feels 'no sentiment superior to
strong esteem and lively friendship'.[10] It was a sad and even cynical
message to emerge from an author not yet twenty. Jane was to learn
by it in time, but she cannot immediately have taken it to heart, for
she showed no intention of putting it into practice. After laying 'Elinor
and Marianne' aside for future consideration, she plunged recklessly
into her first love affair.[11]

Tom Lefroy was a charming young Irishman, very near to Jane in
age, who had recently graduated from Trinity College, Dublin, and was
now taking a well-earned holiday with his aunt and uncle at Ashe
Rectory before beginning further studies for the Bar. Jane first met
him at a ball – perhaps an assembly at Basingstoke. Madam Lefroy
had no doubt primed the neighbourhood with such an impressive
catalogue of his achievements that everybody was on the look-out for
him. He had won three gold medals in college debates and had left
with such glowing reports of his abilities that his family could be assured
of his advancement to the very top of his profession. Far from being
the bumptious young man that some may have feared, he turned out
to be shy when confronted by so many strangers, all of whom knew
each other. Jane had some idea of what it was like to be an outsider:
Tom soon began to take refuge in her company. They talked of their
likes and dislikes. Jane learnt that he read novels – always a point in
a man's favour. They met again at a ball given by the Harwoods at

Deane House. Here they discovered that they both liked dancing – 'a certain step towards falling in love'. When they were not dancing they were sitting out together – something that was always equally noticed by the neighbourhood.[12]

Tom knew that on the morning after the ball he should have called on Jane at Steventon, but his uncle and aunt teased him so much that he did not dare. When Jane and her mother called on Mrs Lefroy he 'ran away'. Jane also got teased, and was rather pleased about it. John Warren even suggested that an engagement was in the offing, by drawing a picture of Tom for Jane to keep.

On Friday, 8 January, there was to be a third ball, this time at Manydown. Jane had spent all the money she could afford on the white elbow-length gloves required for a dance and on 'pink persian', a thin silk material with which she probably made a new underslip for a muslin dress. Manydown was warm and welcoming, and its greenhouse elegantly lit for the supper. Jane knew very well that it was considered imprudent – even improper – to dance more than two dances with the same gentleman, but she decided she did not care.

Next morning, she sat down to write a full account to Cassandra. So-and-so had danced with so-and-so. Elizabeth Bigg had danced twice with her wealthy suitor, Mr Heathcote, 'but *they* do not know how to be particular. I flatter myself, however, that they will profit by the three successive lessons I have given them'. As she wrote these words, she was handed a letter that had just arrived from Cassandra. Someone had reported to Cassandra – or perhaps she had inferred from previous ecstatic letters from Jane – that her twenty-year-old sister was behaving rashly, and she wrote to remonstrate. But Jane was unrepentant, telling Cassandra that she was welcome to imagine that there had been 'everything most profligate and shocking in the way of dancing and sitting down together' during the ball at Manydown. She tried to divert Cassandra's attention with other matters, but could not help returning to Tom with every other sentence. 'He is a very gentlemanlike, good-looking, pleasant young man, I assure you.' If only Charles Fowle had been at the ball, as he had promised, he would have been able to give Cassandra a description of Tom, and Jane was sure she must be impatient to hear what he was like. Cassandra had no need to worry, because there would be only one more opportunity for her to 'expose herself': Mrs Lefroy had decided to give a ball the following Friday, after which Tom would be leaving the neighbourhood.

This news was calculated to make Cassandra worry even more. The formidable etiquette surrounding balls and courtship was designed to safeguard women from the pain of becoming attached to men who were not serious in their intentions and from becoming laughing-stocks by allowing themselves to be taken in. Jane seemed to be set on exactly such a course. True, she was protecting her pride by adopting the reckless language she had so frequently used in her early stories. She was looking forward to the ball at Ashe, 'as I rather expect to receive an offer from my friend in the course of the evening. I shall refuse him, however, unless he promises to give away his white Coat' (the light-coloured Irish tweed coat in which he was conspicuous in an English country neighbourhood).

> Tell Mary [Lloyd] that I make over Mr Heartley & all his estate to her for her sole benefit in future, & not only him, but all my other Admirers into the bargain wherever she can find them, even the kiss which C. Powlett wanted to give me, as I mean to confine myself in future to Mr Tom Lefroy, for whom I donot [*sic*] care sixpence.[13]

On the morning of the ball itself, she wrote with forced playfulness:

> At length the Day is come on which I am to flirt my last with Tom Lefroy, & when you receive this it will be over – My tears flow as I write, at the melancholy idea.

What exactly did happen at the ball on Friday 15 January 1796?[14] Jane cannot seriously have been expecting a proposal of marriage after so short an acquaintance, but she perhaps hoped that that there would be some indication of Tom's intending to pursue the attachment. He was to be in London for the next two years, living with his Great Uncle Benjamin whilst studying for the Bar; there would be opportunities for visits to Steventon. It seems she received no such assurance. Perhaps there was less opportunity than she had hoped. Mrs Lefroy, faced with the task of entertaining a number of other young people who were visiting relatives in the area, decided that they should draw for partners – a common practice at informal dances. Tom left the neighbourhood almost immediately afterwards.

Tradition on the Irish side of the family has it that Madam Lefroy, afraid of Tom forming an imprudent attachment which would displease Great Uncle Benjamin, had packed him off to London as soon as possible; but if this were the case why had she apparently encouraged the friendship in the first place and why had she risked giving a final ball? And could Tom reasonably have taken more time away from his studies? Her two sons, George and Edward, told a different story. They remembered that their mother, and their father too when he thought of it, was angry with Tom for flirting with Jane when he had no intention of entering into a serious relationship. He may even have had an attachment already, for as soon as he returned to Ireland from his two-year course of study in London he married an Irish girl he had known in former times. When he was a very old man, and Jane Austen's novels were famous, he was proud to claim that he had loved her, but said that it was 'a boyish love', by which he presumably meant that it ought not to have been taken seriously.

The Thomas Langlois Lefroy who visited Ashe for a Christmas holiday was a very ambitious young man. It was the trait his Great Uncle Benjamin admired in him, and the reason why he had paid for his university education. Benjamin Langlois was a descendant of one Peter Langlois who, in the early decades of the eighteenth century, had allied with the fellow Huguenot Lefroys both in business and marriage. The business had since collapsed, leaving the Lefroys without much money. Benjamin Langlois, by contrast, had had a successful career in diplomacy and politics and, having no children of his own, had been pleased to establish two Lefroy nephews in promising situations. The Revd I.P. George Lefroy he had established at Ashe by buying the presentation to the living, whilst for George's brother Anthony Peter he had bought a commission in an army regiment stationed in Ireland. George had done well, but Anthony Peter, instead of concentrating on his career, had married at an early age an Irish lady of little if any fortune and saddled himself with eleven children. Tom was the eldest son, and Benjamin hoped that he would rise in the world and 'haul up the rest'. Clearly, he would not have been pleased if Tom had at once married a portionless girl, but he could have had no objection to a continued acquaintance and perhaps, in time, to an unofficial engagement such as Cassandra had entered into. Egerton Brydges, who met him in the 1780s, found him 'fatiguingly ceremonious' but 'a good and benevolent old man'. The Austens were on friendly enough terms with him for Jane to stay at his house in London the following summer on her way to Edward's. Neither he nor Madam Lefroy can reasonably be blamed for the nephew's behaviour. Nor can Jane's lack of a dowry have been decisive: the woman Tom married on completing his studies had no prospect, at the time, of the fortune she later inherited through the untimely death of her elder brother. Great Uncle Benjamin does not seem to have regarded the marriage as a hindrance to Tom's rise in the legal profession; nor did it prove to be so, for he eventually became Lord Chief Justice of Ireland.

Jane was to ponder for a long time over her own behaviour. Had she frightened the young man away by appearing to force the pace? Cassandra had criticised her behaviour as indiscreet, but if a woman did not show her partiality for a man, how was he to know that his attentions would be welcome? The problem is presented in a number of the novels and never wholly resolved. In *Sense and Sensibility*, Marianne is proved to have been unwise in giving too much encouragement to Willoughby; but in *Pride and Prejudice* is Charlotte Lucas wrong in believing that Jane Bennet should show more attachment to Bingley? Elizabeth Bennet insists that any man is bound to realise when a woman is in love with him, however reticent she may be; but Charlotte's view is that time is often too short for comprehension to dawn. In the course of the novel, however, it is Darcy, not Bingley, who has doubts about Jane; and Darcy is no great judge in such matters. In *Northanger Abbey* the hero comes to love the heroine because he has gradually realised that she first loved him. On the other hand, in *Mansfield Park*, Edmund Bertram has to discover that he loves Fanny before she feels she can confess to her long-standing regard for him. Unfortunately, Jane Austen does not tell us if this was one of the reasons why her mother thought Fanny 'insipid'.[15]

Tom Lefroy, it seems, came once more to Ashe in November 1798. Jane waited for him to visit the parsonage but he never appeared. Mrs Lefroy called eventually, and Jane managed to secure a little time alone with her, but Madam never mentioned her nephew and Jane was 'too proud to make any enquiries'. Jane's father, coming into the room later, asked outright where Tom was. Mrs Lefroy replied sheepishly that he had returned to London on his way to Ireland, where he was to be called to the Bar.[16] It was a blow to Jane, although she had tried for some time to tell herself that it was all over. Fortunately, she was young, and resilient enough to recover. Meanwhile she would have been ashamed to draw attention to her hurt when the vicissitudes of war had brought Cassandra a much deeper cause for sorrow.

Pitt the Younger had never had a great deal of faith in Britain's ability to fight successfully on the Continent of Europe. Her role ought rather to be to subsidise such continental states as were prepared to fight, and to use her incomparable sea power to weaken France's economy by depriving her of her colonies. His favourite scheme all along had been to launch an attack from Britain's positions in the West Indies on the islands held by the French. An expedition sent out for this purpose at the end of December 1793 came to grief, but, nothing daunted, another was planned for the autumn of 1795. The prime target on both occasions was St Domingo, where slaves, provided by British slave traders, enabled the French to produce more sugar than

Britain in all her colonies put together, thereby seriously undercutting British exports of sugar to the European Continent.

Frank Austen, like most sailors, looked forward to this renewal of the 'Blue Water' policy. Frank's hopes of advancement in the navy as a result of the war against France had so far been unfulfilled. In March 1794 he had been assigned to a sloop, a lightly-armed vessel in which he had spent most of his time patrolling in the North Sea. There had been hardships, as in the arctic winter of 1794–95, when he had accompanied the convoy evacuating British troops from Holland, but there had been little chance of his being engaged in any action or of taking prizes. His ambition was to be transferred to a bigger ship – a frigate or a ship of the line. His father assumed, as any clergyman was likely to have done, that the way forward lay in securing patronage. Frank warned him that appointments in the navy were entirely in the hands of the First Lord of the Admiralty, but he was not to be put off. The Earl of Chatham, as First Lord, was notoriously disinclined to exert his own authority in the matter of appointments and there might therefore be scope for outside interference. In November 1794 George Austen wrote to the family's old friend, Warren Hastings, to ask him what he could do. Hastings, in spite of his long years of trial before the House of Lords for alleged mismanagement in India, had retained his influence with some of the members of Pitt's party, including Admiral Affleck, a senior member of the Admiralty Board with whom he had served in the East India Company as a young man. The Admiral promised to press Frank's case, as did a Mr Pybus, another member of the Board whom George Austen had managed to contact. As a result either of the efforts of these two men, or of the pressing need to secure reliable officers for major tasks, Frank was transferred from ship to ship until he found himself posted to HMS *Glory*, a 98-gun battleship destined to help escort a force of 19,000 men under General Sir Ralph Abercromby to Barbados.[17]

With service in the army unpopular and conscription unthinkable, raising this number of troops was far from easy. Senior commissions were promised to anybody who, by offering bounties, could add sizeable numbers to an existing battalion or raise a private company. Among the individuals fired with military enthusiasm by these opportunities was Lord Craven, who secured a lieutenant-colonelcy in the 3rd Regiment of Foot ('The Buffs') and prepared to leave for the West Indies. Learning that army chaplains had one and all refused to accompany the expedition, Craven decided to appoint a private chaplain and offered the position to his young protégé, Tom Fowle.

Two generations of Tom's family had owed their clerical preferment to patronage by the Craven family, with whom they were connected by marriage. Tom himself had been promised another of Lord Craven's livings to add to his small parish of Allington as soon as one became vacant, a prospect on which all his hopes of marriage with Cassandra Austen rested. Not daring to offend the fighting mad baron, he accepted the offer of the chaplaincy. It was one of the drawbacks to patronage that patrons had to be kept sweet.[18]

Reading between the lines of the newspaper handed on to them regularly by Mr Holder at Ashe Park, it was not difficult for the family at Steventon parsonage to envisage the fate that was likely to befall any British troops sent to the islands. The climate was so iniquitous to white men that a quarter of the force regularly garrisoning the islands died annually of disease. During the attack on Martinique, St Lucia and Guadeloupe in 1794, 12,000 men had died of Yellow Fever.[19] To add to this problem, the slaves all over the British West Indies were rising on behalf of the French, who had proclaimed emancipation. By contrast, the British government, swayed by the planters and by the West Indian lobby at Westminster, had refused even to raise an army from among the natives lest it should give them ambitions. The British had for many years declared themselves bitterly opposed to the slave trade, which supplied the French planters with 40,000 slaves a year: Jane Austen had been informed long ago, in the pages of the otherwise deplorable *Mentoria*, that commerce in human flesh was 'repugnant to human nature and an unjustifiable infringement of the privileges granted by Providence to every class of human creatures'. Yet the freeing of existing slaves formed no part of Britain's programme. Tender-hearted Fanny Price, like most of the British public, seems to have been unaware of the paradox when she questioned her uncle eagerly about conditions on his plantations.[20]

Realising that he may well have signed his own death warrant by agreeing to go to the West Indies, Tom Fowle hastily made a will leaving his small savings to Cassandra and then determined to spend as much time as possible with her before sailing. The pair were spending a tense Christmas season with Tom's parents at Kintbury when Jane lost her heart to Tom Lefroy.

Frank Austen, who had sailed with the fleet in November 1795, twice found himself battling with severe gales in the Channel. Casualties among ships and men were so great that the expedition twice had to put back into port and did not reach Barbados until March. Tom Fowle at least missed these hazards, since he was not due to sail until January

1796, when he accompanied Lord Craven in his private yacht. He wrote to Jane the day before he left Falmouth, and she kept an eye open for weather reports in order to calculate the day of his arrival at Barbados.[21]

Throughout the summer, whilst Jane copied Irish airs into her song book and hoped that Tom Lefroy would return to Ashe, Cassandra went on calmly preparing her trousseau and placed what faith she could in newspaper reports of Abercromby's successes. In October, Jane began to write another novel, about two sisters who lost their lovers but found them again in the end. In real life, things were to turn out differently. Tom Lefroy came no more to Steventon. Tom Fowle was expected to return early in 1797, but instead there arrived news that in February that year he had died of Yellow Fever off St Domingo and had been buried at sea.

Chapter 11

Publishing

On 7 July 1795, whilst Jane Austen was at work on 'Elinor and Marianne', an announcement in the *Morning Chronicle* invited subscriptions of one guinea each towards the publication of a new novel by 'the author of *Evelina* and *Cecilia*'. Jane's father probably supplied the necessary sum, and in July 1796 the five volumes of Fanny Burney's *Camilla*, their uncut pages held between plain boards, arrived at Steventon parsonage. Jane could proudly display her name in the list of subscribers, along with those of Warren Hastings, Hannah More, Humphry Repton and other notable personages.[1] Reviewers proved to be mixed in their opinions of the novel, but Jane was determined to like it, and for some time afterwards she referred to it in and out of season. Neither its reliance on absurd coincidences and unlikely misunderstandings nor its irrelevant passages of comedy put her off. The novel confirmed the view of sentimentality she was herself expressing in 'Elinor and Marianne', for Camilla's excessive tearfulness is portrayed as foolish and harmful. Jane continued to regard Fanny Burney as one of the best of women writers, and viewed with favour any new acquaintances who said they liked *Camilla*.[2]

It was about this time, too, that Jane's father provided her with more privacy than she had had in the past. With his sons off his hands, there was less need for him to supplement his income by taking in pupils; their numbers had been allowed to decline ever since 1791, when Charles entered the Royal Naval Academy, until by 1796 the last set had left.[3] Their departure made the house less crowded. The girls, as their father continued to call them,[4] were allowed to move from the bedroom they had previously occupied into one which communicated with another room recently vacated. Two beds with blue check and lace trimmings were purchased at Ring Brothers' Emporium in Basingstoke for the bedroom, whilst the adjoining room was fitted up to form what Jane and Cassandra liked to call their dressing-room – a private drawing-room to which they could retreat and in which they could receive their guests.[5] The decade, as reported in the newspaper press, was one of mounting suspicion regarding the prevalence of deviant sex, but the Austen sisters, if they were aware of contemporary scandals, took no notice of them.[6] Like many other young women of their time, they were prepared to go on sharing a bedroom in order to be able to follow the latest fashion in household arrangements and acquire a dressing-room.

Their new sanctum could hardly be said to compare in elegance with the much talked of dressing-room which their cousin Edward Cooper had set up for his bride (a former Powys) in his parsonage house at Harpsden.[7] Jane's niece, Anna, remembered 'the common-looking carpet with its chocolate ground' and the painted chest of drawers with shelves above it for books.[8] The room could never have been said to belong entirely to Cassandra and Jane either, for Mrs Austen was not one to await an invitation to use it. Jane nevertheless made the best of it in both respects. 'We live entirely in the dressing-room now, which I like very much', she reported to Cassandra in December 1798. 'I always feel so much more elegant in it than in the parlour.'[9] Against a stylish (if reasonably priced) blue wall-paper and blue-and-white striped curtains, the room contained some of her most important personal possessions. Anna remembered seeing Jane's piano there but made no mention of her desk. How much writing Jane did in the dressing-room is a matter for conjecture, but the fact that she could now escape, if she wished, from family conversation in the common parlour meant that she was better off than many women novelists of her day. Eliza Fenwick, for instance, was obliged to write whilst surrounded by half a dozen small children whom she was paid to mind.[10]

Having put aside 'Elinor and Marianne' for the time being, Jane at once embarked on a new novel, 'First Impressions', published many years later under the title *Pride and Prejudice*. Again, the manuscript of the original version no longer exists, but it is reasonable to assume that the characters and the plot that were later to become familiar to readers were already in place. The Revd Mr Collins belongs indubitably to the 1790s, when the Evangelical movement within the Church of England was in its infancy and its adherents (like its leader, Wilberforce) could play cards at family parties and make a distinction between dancing at public assemblies, which was frowned upon, and at a private ball such as the one given by Mr Bingley at Netherfield, which was unlikely to have any 'evil tendencies'.[11] Mr Wickham and his fellow officers can likewise only have belonged to the early years of the Revolutionary Wars, when the shortage of barracks caused the militia to be billeted on civilians for the winter months. Although camps continued to be held at Brighton, it was the gathering of large numbers of men – as many as 7000 – in 1795 and 1796 which created a public sensation.[12] Jane Austen tells us that she 'lop't and crop't' her work for publication in 1813. The months and days of the week were changed to fit the calendar for that year, and it seems likely that much of the writing was also revised; but although *Pride and Prejudice* is clearly the work of a mature woman it retains much of the optimism and piquancy of a young lady of twenty.[13]

The title 'First Impressions' indicates that Jane was still involved in the debate over reason and sensibility, in which the validity of first impressions was an important issue. Adherents of sensibility argued that love at first sight is the only true love, since it occurs at one of the rare moments in life when human beings foresee eternity. Jane took more kindly to the view, originated by Locke and current in the Enlightenment teaching of her father's generation, that impressions are important not as revelations of truth but as material for the mind to work on. The mutual attraction between Darcy and Elizabeth Bennet is clear from the start, but the sexual nature of their relationship, compounded of love and hate, has to be transformed into the true understanding which comes from self knowledge. 'First Impressions', though less intriguing, would have been more accurate as a title than *Pride and Prejudice*, since there is no monopoly of pride on Darcy's part and prejudice on Elizabeth's, but rather an equal misunderstanding.

Because the novel in its published form contains a great many letters, it has been suggested that 'First Impressions', like 'Elinor and Marianne', was written in epistolary form. It seems more likely, however, that Jane would have tried to emulate the narrative skill displayed by Fanny Burney in *Camilla* rather than persist with a style abandoned by an author she so much admired. The new novel was to differ from 'Elinor and Marianne' in a number of respects, not least by relying on a plot which featured a significant aspect of the country's wartime situation.

The importance attached to the militia had increased since the outbreak of war in 1793. With the British Navy recklessly extended from the West to the East Indies, and facing single-handed the combined fleets of France, Spain and Holland, the threat of invasion was by 1795 seen to be acute. Regiments were increased in size and moved around the coastal areas to be ready for instant deployment: in Hampshire a voluntary subscription was raised so that recruits could be encouraged with the offer of bounties.[14] Jane grew accustomed to the appearance of red coats against the prevailing green of the countryside, as first the South Devon Regiment and then the Oxfords and the Derbyshires marched into the county to take up winter quarters in towns surrounding Steventon. Her brother Henry, whose regiment was involved for a time in guarding the largest prisoner of war camp in the country at Portchester Castle, was in frequent touch with the family. In 1794 his integrity and abilities were recognised by his appointment as acting paymaster, a position in which he handled all the financial transactions of the Oxfordshire Regiment until he left the service in 1801. He was on leave when the men rioted in 1795 over the rising price of food, which they had to buy for themselves out of their pay; but, on his return to duty, he was obliged to witness the execution of two of the leaders by firing squad at Brighton.[15]

It was not such doings as these, however, which were of immediate concern to Jane. For the purposes of her novel, which was set in a country house environment, she needed an attractive stranger to arrive from elsewhere, as Willoughby had done, and wreak havoc among the young ladies. Where better to find one than in a militia regiment? The officers could claim to be gentlemen, since even a Lieutenant was supposed to be possessed of land to the value of £50 a year, and the requirement was larger still for senior officers; yet who could really be said to know anything about them? Some were married men and brought their wives with them; others were known sprigs of the nobility; but a few were bound to be merely footloose young men who had escaped from the restraints of family and neighbourhood and were out to enjoy themselves. Young ladies bored with life in the country found them exciting; hostesses seeking guests for dinner parties and balls were delighted to entertain them; fathers of daughters were dutifully hospitable but regarded them with suspicion. Jane was fully prepared to indulge such prejudices, widespread among the gentry whom she perhaps imagined would be reading her novel one day. Twenty years later, when she had published three novels and was writing a fourth (*Emma*), she decided to give a militia background to the engaging but slightly unreliable Mr Weston (who cannot keep a secret). She placed him in the Surrey Militia and arranged for him to have married his first wife at an early age, when the regiment was stationed in Yorkshire – a county to which the Surreys were indeed 'exiled' in 1795 as a punishment for misconduct.[16]

Until 1796, when barracks were made available, militia officers spent the winter months in the inns and taverns of England's small towns, whilst their men crowded into the livery stables and outhouses of the place. As they were to remain only a short time in any one locality, there was an obvious temptation for them to run up bills and leave without paying. Innkeepers and tradesmen disliked them; there were frequent petitions against having a regiment quartered upon the town or even passing through it.[17] Wickham's conduct at Meryton would come as no surprise to readers.

In summer the regiments went into camp, where a certain amount of training could be carried out. Camps were located at intervals along the southern and eastern coasts, the largest being at Brighton, which was itself the largest and most popular of England's seaside resorts. In 1794 Brighton's 5700 inhabitants received an influx of 4300 visitors, some of whom no doubt were attracted, like Lydia Bennet, by the thought of 'the streets of that gay bathing place covered with officers'. Jane Austen may have visited her brother there in August 1793, and seen for herself

> all the glories of the camp; its tents stretched forth in beauteous uniformity of lines, crowded with the young and the gay, and dazzling with scarlet.

To the usual entertainments of a watering place, Brighton added the dissipated pleasures encouraged by the presence of the Prince of Wales, who had visited it annually since 1783. The transference of Mr Wickham's regiment from Meryton to Brighton would provide a perfect setting for a scandalous climax to the novel.[18]

In addition to this topical interest, 'First Impressions' was to differ from 'Elinor and Marianne' by being altogether more romantic. Neither the diffident Edward Ferrars, pushed around by his female relations, nor the melancholy Colonel Brandon, comparatively middle-aged and murmuring of flannel waistcoats, can be relied upon to cause female hearts to flutter; but Darcy, tall and handsome, wealthy, disdainful, and driven by desire into a proposal of marriage against his every judgement, is a hero Byron might have invented. His station in life precludes Jane Austen from having been more than distantly acquainted with anybody like him, for neither the gentry around Steventon nor her brother's neighbours in Kent were in the same category as the nephew of an Earl. Elizabeth Bennet is horrified when her clergyman-cousin, Mr Collins, approaches Mr Darcy conversationally at the Netherfield Ball: like Jane after her formal reception at the Earl of Portsmouth's ball, Mr Collins should have realised that any further notice on either side was entirely at the discretion of a person so vastly superior in consequence.[19] Darcy is a young girl's dream. His house in Derbyshire (a part of the country Jane had read about but never seen) is equally dreamlike.[20] The houses Jane visited in Hampshire and in Kent, including the mansion her brother Edward was shortly to inherit at Godmersham, dated for the most part from the early Georgian period and were heavier in style than the elegant structure conjured into mind by the vague and ecstatic terms in which she describes Pemberley.[21]

The erudite Annabella Milbanke, Lord Byron's future wife, nevertheless judged *Pride and Prejudice* to be 'the *most probable* fiction' she had ever read when it appeared in 1813. To a perceptive reader, Darcy need appear neither as a demon lover nor as a hero of romance but as an ordinary, if rich, young man, overawed by his duty to his family, inexperienced in dealings with women, fallible and vulnerable in spite of his apparent haughtiness. Jane's honest recognition of the impact of economic circumstances on marriage could also be appreciated by serious readers, although it was not yet popular with those scanning the shelves of circulating libraries in search of entertaining literature. The account of young ladies in the vicinity of Netherfield on the look out for a wealthy bachelor, and of Charlotte Lucas calmly accepting her need to marry any man who could provide her with a respectable home, was startling to readers accustomed to reading novels in which their everyday sentiments were ennobled and their problems dramatised. To some, it even appeared crude. Time was to elapse before the reading public was prepared to accept a novel which not only rejected sentimental escapism but moved on from Fanny Burney's descriptions of fashionable behaviour to scrutinise personal conduct in the face of worldly pressures.[22]

The most scathing condemnation in the novel is directed at the behaviour of Mr Collins, 'a conceited, pompous, narrow-minded, silly man', and of his arrogant and domineering patroness, Lady Catherine de Bourgh. Subsequent readers have imagined that by her portrayal of this appalling pair Jane Austen was attacking the system of patronage which could place the Church of England in such despicable hands. Jane, however, would have known that, if her novel should succeed in being published, its contemporary readers would have no such suspicions. Patronage was a form of property, defensible in the law courts; with the example of the French Revolution fresh in people's minds, only the most rabid of radicals would have dreamt of attacking it. Lady Catherine and Mr Collins were invented primarily for entertainment. They were known stereotypes, of which a similar pair, Lord Grondale and the sycophantic Dr Blick, appeared in Robert Bage's novel *Hermsprong* that same year. Jane imagined her novel being read by gentry families of the kind she knew in Hampshire. The gentry always thought of the aristocracy as proud and tyrannical; they would be delighted with Lady Catherine de Bourgh. They were always on the look-out, too, for any collusion between the great landowners, to whom many of them paid rent, and the clergy, to whom they paid tithe; they would therefore be even more delighted with Lady Catherine in partnership with Mr Collins. The pair were bogeys and could be enjoyed as such; for in fact a conspiracy between landowner and parson directed at grinding down the faces of the hard-working farmers would have been difficult to achieve, as Cobbett, who liked to suggest such a possibility, was obliged to admit.[23]

Although Jane Austen wished to entertain her readers, she also wanted her novel to have a moral purpose. The much-admired Dr Johnson had said that a novel must either entertain or improve its readers and a good novel would do both. Jane Austen was not interested in reforming institutions, either in the church or elsewhere; she was concerned only about the way people behaved within them. The lesson to be learnt from Lady Catherine is that her position as patron of a living gave her no right to treat the incumbent as a lackey or to dictate his wife's mode of housekeeping: Elizabeth Bennet discovers with both astonishment and disapproval that Lady Catherine de Bourgh

> enquired into Charlotte's domestic concerns familiarly and minutely, and gave her a great deal of advice as to the management of them all; told her how everything ought to be regulated in so small a family as her's, and instructed her as to the care of her cows and poultry.

As for Mr Collins, there was no need for him to sit at the card table 'agreeing to everything her Ladyship said, thanking her for every fish he won, and apologising if he thought he won too many'. The respect due to his patron did not require obsequiousness. He was at liberty to show a manly independence, for Lady Catherine, once she had presented him to the living of Hunsford, could not in any circumstances dismiss him. His position as rector, of which he is rightly proud, does not justify his giving advice, unsolicited, to persons not under his pastoral care, in circumstances of which he can know little. His duty to collect tithes should not be rated as the paramount task of a parish priest, in the way that he suggests to the company at the Netherfield ball. The christenings, weddings and burials he ostentatiously pronounces himself 'ever ready to perform' are minimal requirements of his office, not great favours bestowed on his parishioners. His obligation to relieve the poor and needy does not mean that he should spy on the villagers, reporting their 'minutest concerns' to Lady Catherine, so that whenever any of them were 'disposed to be quarrelsome, discontented or too poor' she can 'sally forth into the village to settle their difference, silence their complaints, and scold them into harmony and plenty'.[24]

In every particular, Mr Collins either overdoes or overrates what is required of him – the reason being that he lacks the discrimination, known at the time as 'sense' or 'taste', which was the hallmark of a gentleman. 'Can he be a sensible man, sir?' enquires Elizabeth Bennet of her father, on hearing him read out the letter in which Mr Collins announces his intention of visiting his relatives at Longbourn. Mr Bennet, who delights in watching people make fools of themselves, replies promptly: 'No, my dear, I think not. I have great hopes of finding him quite the reverse. There is a mixture of servility and self-importance in his letter which promises well. I am impatient to see him.' In the course of the novel Mr Collins more than fulfils such expectations, for he proves to have a totally false sense of values. He judges Lady Catherine's greatness by the number of carriages she keeps, describes the beauty of her park at Rosings by the number of trees in each group (trees being valuable for timber), and assesses the elegance of her mansion in accordance with the amount of money it must have cost Sir Lewis de Bourgh to glaze the main front. He is comfortably situated at Hunsford, as he is fond of telling people; yet he continues to attend Lady Catherine's ghastly dinner parties in the hope that she will bestow further parishes upon him and thereby increase his consequence. Mr Bennet has summed him up well when he advises him sarcastically on the line to take in the quarrel between Lady Catherine and Mr Darcy: 'If I were you I would stand by the nephew. He has more to give.'[25]

The members of Jane Austen's family who were privileged to have 'First Impressions' read out to them whilst it was in progress (including her father and her eldest brother, James – clergymen both) heard it with great enjoyment. They were sworn to secrecy, for Jane had no wish to set neighbourhood tongues wagging with the news that she 'wrote novels'. When it was discovered that James's three-year old Anna was listening wide-eyed to the readings, it was decided to defer subsequent instalments to times when she was in bed.[26] Cassandra was entrusted with the manuscript, which she read again and again.[27] Martha Lloyd was allowed one perusal, to which she responded with the same enthusiasm that she had shown for Jane's simpler compositions in the past.[28] 'I would not let Martha read *First Impressions* again on any account', Jane wrote jokingly to Cassandra:

She is very cunning, but I see through her design; – she means to publish it from Memory, & one more perusal must enable her to do it.

George Austen did in fact think in terms of publication. Having decided that the novel deserved to be seen in print, he showed a surprisingly good grasp of the means by which he ought to proceed.[29] Fanny Burney had published *Camilla* by subscription, but this method was feasible only because 'the author of *Evelina* and *Clarissa*', as she described herself, was well known. It was in any case a tiresome proceeding, which required the author to collect subscriptions and then employ a publisher to bring out the book. Fanny Burney collected £1000, but this was an unprecedented sum; readers were becoming chary of sending money in advance for books, some of which took years to appear, and in consequence authors sometimes had to withdraw from publication and return the subscriptions they had received.

The two most popular methods of publication were 'on commission' and by 'sale of copyright'. Later in life, Jane Austen was to publish *Sense and Sensibility*, *Mansfield Park* and *Emma* by the former method and *Pride and Prejudice* by the latter. Publication on commission was sometimes referred to as publishing at the author's risk, for any losses that were sustained had to be carried by the author. In addition, the author could be asked to supply an advance to the publisher for the initial costs of production. More often, however, the publisher brought out the work and recouped himself for the costs of printing, binding, advertising and distributing the copies from the proceeds of the early sales, before taking a commission of 10 per cent on all further copies sold. A drawback to the method was that the publisher had no incentive to push forward with the work: manuscripts for which he had laid out money to purchase the copyright might take precedence.

Although publishing on commission was considered perfectly respectable, female writers usually preferred to sell the copyright of their works and retire gracefully from any further concern in the business. The money was paid by the publisher in a lump sum either on acceptance of the manuscript or within a year of publication of the book. No further communication need take place between him and the author until the end of the fourteen or twenty-eight years for which the copyright had been purchased. Publishers stood to gain a great deal of money by this method, but the risk was entirely at their door. They were often unwilling to purchase a manuscript from a first-time author, however cheaply the latter was prepared to sell.

George Austen was anxious for his daughter's book to be published by a respectable firm so that it would be reviewed as a serious work. His choice fell upon Cadell and Davies, possibly because they had published Charlotte Smith's *Emmeline* (1788) and *Ethelinde* (1789), which the Austen family had enjoyed; or perhaps because he had received Jane's copy of *Camilla* from them only a year ago. On 1 November 1797 he wrote to the firm:

> Sirs
>
> I have in my possession a Manuscript Novel, comprised in three Vols. about the length of Miss Burney's Evelina. As I am well aware of what consequence it is that a work of this sort should make its' first appearance under a respectable name I apply to you. Shall be much obliged therefore if you will inform me whether you chuse to be concerned in it; what will be the expense of publishing at the Author's risk; & what you will advance for the Property of it, if on Perusal it is approved of?
>
> Should you give me encouragement I will send you the work.
>
> I am, Sirs, Yr. obt. hble Servt:
>
> Geo Austen
>
> Steventon near Overton
> Hants

At the publishing house in the Strand the letter was endorsed 'declined by Return of Post'.[30]

Jane was not as crushed by this summary rejection as one might expect. She probably knew that it was very unlikely that a publisher would consider purchasing copyright from an unknown author acting through an unknown agent. There had been more chance of success with the request to publish on commission, and by mentioning the approximate length of the novel George Austen had given the inform-ation that would be needed for an estimate of the cost; but on reflection he could hardly have expected a publisher to accept a work, even on these no risk terms, without setting eyes on it. The manuscript might have turned out to be illegible, the topic (not mentioned) unsuitable, and the style (which from the reference to *Evelina* might be thought to have been epistolary) unacceptable. For George Austen to have travelled to London to present the manuscript to the publisher would unfortunately have taken a good deal of time and would also have involved him in a good deal of expense; all possibly to no avail, since he had no influence with Cadell and Davies or any other publisher.

A little courage, and perhaps the acquisition of a friend who had connections with the publishing trade, would be needed in order to try again. Meanwhile, for a compulsive writer, there was much that could declined by Return of Post.

Sir

 I have in my possession a Manuscript Novel, comprised in three Vol! about the length of Miss Burney's Evelina. As I am well aware of what consequence it is that a work of this sort should make its first Appearance under a respec:table name I apply to you. I shall be much obliged therefore if you will inform me, whether you chuse to be concerned in it; what will be the expence of publishing at the Author's risk; & what you will venture to advance for the Property of it, if on a perusal it is approved of.

 Should your answer give me encouragement I will send you the work.

    I am, Sir, y.^r ob.^t hble Servt

     Geo Austen.

Steventon near Overton
  Hants
 1.st Novr 1797.

'First Impressions' (*Pride and Prejudice*), rejected by the publishers Cadell and Davies. (*St John's College, Oxford*) be done. 'Elinor and Marianne' had already been brought out of the drawer, and Jane had begun on the difficult task of rethinking the story in more realistic terms and relating it in narrative form. In the course of the following year she laboriously wrote out the whole of the three-volume novel again by hand, with a quill pen dipped in ink, possibly of the kind that had to be mixed from powder ground from a solid cake. The paper, which was handmade, cost her a good deal of her spare money and had to be obtained from stationers at Overton or Basingstoke. Members of her family later gave the impression that Jane wrote her novels in odd moments, rising from her needlework and jotting down a sentence or two whenever an amusing thought occurred to her.[31] When she was seen behaving in this way she is more likely to have been writing one of her letters to Cassandra, which sometimes lay open for several days and often give the impression of having been written disjointedly. The writing of the novels could not have been accomplished in anything but a dedicated manner.

With a few minor insertions and amendments, made in 1809, the novel as Jane now wrote it in 1797 was the version that was published in 1811 as *Sense and Sensibility*. The new title was adopted almost as soon as the rewriting was finished – perhaps as a result of seeing the phrase used as a title for a series of essays in the *Monthly Museum*, a new journal to which Mrs Austen may have subscribed. Elinor and Marianne were now credible human beings, Elinor with strong feelings hidden under her apparent composure, and Marianne combining a good deal of perception with her all too headstrong emotions. In *Sense and Sensibility* Jane Austen does not condemn a sensitive approach to life, which can be charming even in the middle-aged Mrs Dashwood and can bring an element of chivalry and mystery to the otherwise dull and reliable Colonel Brandon. She makes the reader aware of how tiresome emotional behaviour such as Marianne's can be to others who are having to get on with the daily routine, and how impossible social intercourse would become if everybody flouted the harmless hypocrisies of life as Marianne did, but she reserves her total condemnation for the self-destruction wilfully brought on by emotion carried to the point of hysteria. Marianne gratifies her own feelings to the extent of living in a world of her own devising: when this collapses she takes refuge in illness which borders on suicide. Heroines had been warned of such consequences from the time of Richardson onwards; Jane Austen's contribution was to bring Marianne to see that her conduct was unjust-ifiable in God's sight; and that to make atonement she must regulate her emotions not only by reason and self-discipline but by 'religion'.

Marianne's thoughts as she contemplates her previous behaviour ('Whenever I looked towards the past, I saw some duty neglected, or some failing indulged. Everybody seemed injured by me') are in line with the words of a prayer Jane wrote later: 'Have we neglected any known duty, or willingly given pain to any human being? Incline us to ask our hearts these questions oh! God.' [32]

Sense and Sensibility became, in 1811, the first of Jane Austen's novels to be published. Her brother Henry had by then left the militia and become a banker of some repute, established in London. He was in frequent touch with Jane, and it was possibly his idea to take the manuscript to Thomas Egerton of Whitehall, whose firm, more than twenty years earlier, had distributed *The Loiterer*. Egerton did not usually publish novels, but may have taken *Sense and Sensibility* out of respect for Henry. It seems that the latter may actually have advanced money for the costs – an unusual but not unknown proceeding – although Jane also insisted on putting aside a small sum of money from her meagre savings to bear any losses.[33] As in most arrangements by commission, Henry Austen had to nag the publisher to get on with the work. When it eventually appeared, probably in the usual-sized edition of 750 copies, the novel was an immediate if modest success.[34] Its subject was by then a safer one than it might have been earlier, for intellectual opinion had settled in favour of restraint in women: a generation was to elapse before Emily Brontë, in *Wuthering Heights*, could safely describe unreasoning emotion as a kind of fate from which, for good or ill, there was no escape. In 1811 the Prince Regent's impulsive daughter, Charlotte, was pleased to liken her own imprudence to that of Marianne, but other readers preferred to applaud Elinor as a model of female behaviour. Jane Austen had been aware of this change of opinion, to the extent of fearing that her theme might at any time be forestalled by some other writer. She was naturally worried about the impression the novel would make on such readers as Mrs Knight, whose opinion she valued; but of one thing she felt certain: 'She will like my Elinor.' [35]

If Elinor Dashwood was by 1811 a fairly conventional heroine, Jane had reason to doubt whether Elizabeth Bennet would 'take'. This may have been why she decided to keep back *Pride and Prejudice* until Henry could commend it to the publisher as a further novel 'by the author of *Sense and Sensibility*'. The title 'First Impressions' had been discarded sometime after 1800, when a novel of the same name was published by the Minerva Press. 'Pride and Prejudice' was a phrase often found with reference to the social distinctions of the age; Fanny Burney used it three times in quick succession in *Camilla*, and Robert Bage twice in one sentence in *Hermsprong*, a novel of which Jane Austen also possessed a copy.[36] For a second work by a trusted author, Egerton was willing to purchase the copyright, but at a lower figure than the one currently offered by other publishers for manuscripts of the same length. Unfortunately, too, neither Jane nor Henry was sufficiently experienced to stipulate for a further sum should the work run to a second edition. Hence the lion's share of the profits from Jane Austen's most popular novel, which sold between two and three thousand copies, went mainly to the publisher.[37]

Jane need have had no qualms about her heroine, for with a few exceptions such as Mary Russell Mitford, who deplored 'the entire want of taste which could produce so pert, so worldly a heroine as the beloved of such a man as Darcy', readers found Elizabeth Bennet as engaging as did the author herself. 'I must confess that I think her as delightful a creature as ever appeared in print', Jane wrote. The success of *Pride and Prejudice* gave her the confidence to produce three more novels, *Mansfield Park, Emma* and *Persuasion*, though the last was not published until after her death. It also made her authorship an open secret within literary coteries in London and Edinburgh: from then on, anonymity was more of a convention than a reality.[38]

Chapter 12

Marriage and Money

During the two years that Tom Lefroy spent on his legal studies in London, his aunt was by no means idle in the marriage market. Marrying people off was a favourite female occupation at the time, since it gave women an outlet for their managerial talents and an interest outside the narrowly domestic. Mrs Jennings in *Sense and Sensibility* and Mrs Grant in *Mansfield Park* are typical of many women who took to match-making for their young friends and relatives because they had nothing else to do. Mrs Lefroy, with her many social interests and family duties, was hardly in this category, but she could not be expected to forego the attractions of an occupation in which parsons' wives were generally supposed to have advantages. Among her circle of clergy acquaintances there were bound to be some who were eligible for matrimony. Moreover, Madam Lefroy was not one of those mothers who kept all other young women at a safe distance until her own offspring were settled in life. Her daughter Lucy had reached the crucial age of seventeen, but Madam was generous – or, as some might have said, meddlesome – enough to continue to take an interest in the matrimonial prospects of Jane Austen, her protégée at Steventon.[1]

The Revd Samuel Blackall was invited to stay at Ashe parsonage during the winter of 1797. At the age of twenty-six he was large of stature and overbearing in manner, thoroughly pleased with himself and as pompous as Mr Collins. As a Fellow of Emmanuel College, Cambridge, he was not immediately in need of a wife, but he spoke grandly of the day when he would be offered one of the livings in the gift of the college; and when such a day came he would wish to marry without delay. In fact, college livings were not easily acquired: both Jane's father and her brother James had spent many years at St John's without acquiring one. Vacancies could lead to intense rivalry, involving costly elections among competing Fellows in college halls. However, Blackall was not the man to underestimate his chances; and Mrs Lefroy saw no harm in his preparing for the future by inspecting suitable young ladies in her neighbourhood.

It was soon discovered that, whilst giddy little Lucy Lefroy might have satisfied his more boisterous avuncular instincts, Jane Austen provided him with an ideal audience before which to pontificate on matters great and small. She listened to him in stunned silence, which he misinterpreted as awe and reported in gratified terms to his friends at Ashe. He had a large appetite for good food, which Mrs Austen's competent housekeeping enabled him to indulge with gusto. He enjoyed himself so much that, when he was obliged to leave Ashe for the start of the college term, he gave broad hints of visiting again the following Christmas.

Madam Lefroy did her best to fan his ardour by keeping him in touch with events at Steventon. Writing in the autumn of 1798 to solicit his interest in a young acquaintance recently entered at his college, she took the opportunity to report that Jane had done good service in nursing her mother through a distressing illness. The response was not what she had hoped for. 'I am sorry to hear of Mrs Austen's illness', Blackall wrote. 'It would give me particular pleasure to have an opportunity of improving my acquaintance with that family – with a hope of creating to myself a nearer interest. But at present I cannot indulge any expectation of it.'

Jane was less surprised by his withdrawal than she had been by his sudden advances. His letter, she told Cassandra, was 'rational enough'.

> There is less love and more sense in it than sometimes appeared before, and I am very well satisfied. It will all go on exceedingly well, and decline away in a very reasonable manner. There seems no likelihood of his coming into Hampshire this Christmas, and it is therefore most probable that our indifference will soon be mutual, unless his regard, which appeared to spring from knowing nothing of me at first, is best supported by never seeing me.

In fact she heard nothing more about him until, some fourteen years later, she read in a Hampshire newspaper a report of his induction to the college living of Great Cadbury in Somerset. This was followed shortly afterwards by a notice of his marriage with a Miss Lewis of Clifton. Jane mentioned the news to Frank, who had obviously heard of the egregious Mr Blackall and may even have been at Steventon on leave during the inept courtship. Jane confessed to being curious as to what the bride was like. Remembering Mr Blackall's 'noisy Perfection' and personal preferences, she hoped that Miss Lewis would be 'of a silent turn & rather ignorant, but naturally intelligent & wishing to learn – fond of cold veal pies, green tea in the afternoon, & a green window blind at night'.[2]

Mrs Lefroy sheepishly reported his defection at the same time as being obliged to report Tom Lefroy's indifference. Jane's real hurt over the latter made it easier for her to laugh away any harm done by the former. Mr Blackall had clearly not been in love with her, though he probably imagined himself to be so; what he had really wanted was a housekeeper and companion for the long winter evenings in his forth-coming country parish. On his return to Cambridge he had either been disappointed in his immediate hopes of preferment or he had decided to wait until the well-endowed Somersetshire parish he most coveted became available – a distant prospect, since the incumbent currently in office was a man in the prime of life. In the former case, Jane would have understood his predicament, for he would have been obliged to resign his college Fellowship on marriage and would have had nothing to live on. If, on the other hand, he had turned down offers of livings which would have enabled him to marry but were less lucrative than Great Cadbury, she was faced with the lowering thought that her attractions were inferior to those of a handsome parsonage, extensive glebeland and productive tithes.

She cannot have been altogether sorry that he had cried off, but it would have been a blow to any woman's pride, and it presents clearly the problems Jane faced in trying to find a husband. Clergymen's daughters, brought up as gentlewomen but with neither the money to marry impecunious gentlemen nor the status to marry wealthy ones, were to be found leading spinster lives in vicarages everywhere. The Revd Peter Debary, James Austen's friend at Hurstbourne Tarrant, had four unmarried sisters: 'the Endless Debaries', Jane Austen called them.[3] In a moment of dejection over her matrimonial prospects, Elizabeth Bennet thinks that all she can hope for is to meet with 'another Mr Collins'.[4] Jane could be fairly sure of meeting with other clergymen, since they were every hostess's best bet as guests at parties and balls. Unfortunately the younger ones that were most likely to attend such events were also likely to be poor. Few were as lucky as Mr Collins, who had obtained the living of Hunsford at the age of twenty-five and was in a position to ignore straitened circumstances in a prospective bride. Jane would not have wanted to be a burden to her husband, but she had no money other than the £50 Thomas Knight had left her when he died in 1794 and no income other than the £20 a year her father managed to allow her (in quarterly instalments) as spending money. This may have been why she deliberately avoided dancing or conversing with John Lyford when she met him at public assemblies. Lyford was the son of her family doctor at Basingstoke and a friend of her cousin Edward Cooper. Having only recently been ordained, he was still enjoying a Fellowship at the Queen's College, Oxford; but on marriage he would be reduced to reliance upon a meagre curacy at Basing, which was all he had so far managed to acquire. It indeed turned out that he was in dire straits when in 1799 he married a Miss Lodge – even though the lady had £800 of her own. He proposed to take in pupils to make ends meet, but there was no very large supply of them in rural Hampshire, as Jane well knew.[5] The problem was compounded for Jane in that the acute powers of observation which enabled her to describe in her novels the subtle social distinctions operating in tiny communities such as Highbury made her all too aware of her own position. She knew that neighbourhood opinion could be biting and cruel. She would not have wanted to be classed with 'such young Ladies as may be met with, in at least one family out of three, throughout the Kingdom', whose sole object in life was 'to captivate some Man of much better fortune than their own'.[6]

It was during her trips to Kent that she found it hardest to forget her poverty and lack of social standing. For her second visit to Edward at Rowling in the summer of 1796 she had bought a new gown. Anxiously, she asked the servants to handle it carefully, but found to her dismay that the colours washed out of its cheap material at the first laundering. As the time drew near for her to leave, she realised that she had no idea how much she ought to tip the chambermaid.[7] Edward was still her kind brother, but he had never been a sensitive man and he seems to have been unaware that Jane was not entirely happy in his house. She could never feel at ease with his wife, although as a Christian she admired her domestic virtues and tried to love her for Edward's sake.[8] Elizabeth Bridges was an affectionate wife and mother, but outside her immediate family circle she treated everybody with the smooth, gracious, carefully practised manner she had learnt, under the heading of 'Decorum', at her expensive boarding school in Queen Square, Bloomsbury. She was not quite two years older than Jane, but the latter, on account of her comparatively lowly status as a parson's daughter, qualified for the particular 'suavity' the school syllabus had prescribed for 'the humblest individual present'. Elizabeth was without doubt well-meaning, but Jane was acutely sensitive to condescension. There were other barriers too. Elizabeth had married at eighteen and after less than five years of matrimony was already the mother of three children. This placed her in the superior position

Godmersham House, home of Jane Austen's brother Edward and his wife
Elizabeth. From Edward Hasted, *The History and Topographical Survey of the County
of Kent* (1778–99).

mothers sometimes enjoy at the expense of women who have not yet had children; Jane was allowed to hold little George in her arms just once during her visit. It soon became apparent that Elizabeth's one interest in life was her children. She suckled her babies until they were nine months old and was desolate when they had to be weaned; as infants she kissed and cuddled them constantly; and nothing pleased her more than to float around the house with a flock of young ones hovering around her. Their number increased every year or two until she died, at the age of thirty-five, a fortnight after the birth of the eleventh child.

To be fair to Elizabeth, she was probably as frightened of Jane's wit and intelligence as Jane was of her sophistication. She had learnt all the right things, but she was not naturally intelligent. She had reached the height of fashionable achievement on the piano by learning to play 'The Battle of Prague' (a flamboyant sonata by Kotzwara), but her comments on music were confined to criticism of Jane's notation when copying out pieces into her music book. When there were no parties to be presided over, Elizabeth spent her evenings sewing whilst someone read to her and Edward slept by the fire.[9] During her visits to Kent, Jane was gratified to find that when it came to making shirts for Edward she was more proficient than Elizabeth; but, in spite of filling some of her days with practising her piano lesson for Mr Chard, she was soon bored and longed to go home. Another sign of her dependence, however, was that she could not come and go as she pleased. Her father had no carriage and coachman to send for her; she had to wait until one of her brothers could accompany her. She would have liked sometimes to travel alone by stagecoach, whose dangers for women, as we learn from Catherine Morland's experience in travelling home by herself from Northanger, Jane believed to be more imagined than real; but her family would not hear of it. To that extent, they were determined to keep up appearances.[10]

In 1798 Jane visited Edward and his wife in unexpected circumstances. Since the death of Thomas Knight in 1794, his widow had lived alone at Godmersham Park, supported by a retinue of servants. It was thought that she would soon remarry, for she was handsome, rich and little more than forty.[11] Far from doing so, she decided in 1797 that she was going to retire to Whitefriars, near Canterbury, and leave Godmersham to her adopted son. Her husband had named Edward his heir, but had intended his estates to remain with his wife until her death. Mrs Knight, however, had come to believe that it would be better for the neighbourhood to have a man in charge, and that

Edward was eminently suited for the role of squire.[12] He did his best
to dissuade her but she was determined, and in 1797 the deed was
signed. There was never any intention that Edward should return to
Hampshire; he left Steventon Manor in the hands of the Digweeds and
continued to let out the Great House at Chawton on short-term leases
to a succession of gentlemen in need of a country residence. In the
early summer of 1798 he left his house at Rowling and moved back
into the mansion at Godmersham which he had first entered as a boy.
There in August his parents and his two sisters arrived to visit him.

The parents, it seems, were not in the least overawed, either by the
house or by seeing their son exalted to the position of a great landowner.
The pair wandered happily through the many rooms, leaving their
possessions here and there and forgetting where they had put them.
Mrs Austen was soon in her element advising Edward on the building
of a henhouse, whilst his father tried to get him to take a special interest
in the pigs.[13] For Cassandra and Jane, this was to be the first of many
visits. Cassandra was always welcome. Her quiet cheerfulness, good
sense and self-effacing usefulness were much appreciated by Elizabeth
while nursing her through her confinements and looking after the
children during the period of lying in. Sometimes Cassandra was prevailed on to stay so long – four or five months at a time – that Jane
grew a little jealous of the family's hold over her.[14] She herself liked
best to visit when one or more of her brothers could be there too, to
enjoy riding about the estate with Edward and shooting birds in his
well-stocked woods. Their good spirits, and confident air as men of the
world, dispelled the feeling that they were the poor relations.[15]

Jane never at any time expressed admiration for the appearance of the
house – a plain building of seven central bays dating from the previous
reign, with two flanking wings of five bays added later. Whenever in her
novels she wishes the reader to picture an elegant house, she suggests
that it is of much more recent origin – 'a spacious, modern built house'
(Cleveland in *Sense and Sensibility*), 'a handsome house, modern built'
(Mansfield Park in the novel of that name). These were vague phrases
of the kind she might have picked up from compilations such as W.
Watts's *Seats of the Nobility and Gentry* (1779) or W. Angus's book of the
same title published in 1787. Assuming Jane to have seen Godmersham
on one of her earlier visits to Kent, the sight of it standing on the lower
slopes of a hillside framed in trees might have inspired the setting of
Darcy's Pemberley, 'on the opposite side of a valley' and 'standing well
on rising ground'; but this, too, was the kind of setting favoured by
writers on the Picturesque and could easily have come from them.[16]

At Godmersham House, Jane eventually became familiar with a daily routine which gave the inmates the use of vast alternative spaces: breakfast parlour, drawing-room, dining-room, billiards room, library; and, upstairs, the Hall chamber, the Yellow room, the Chintz room, the White room, and so on. She was faintly disapproving. Ensconced in the Yellow room in 1800 she wrote to Cassandra, 'It seems odd to me to have such a great place all to myself'. On another occasion, she described herself as 'alone in the Library, Mistress of all I survey', and believed she could recite the whole of Cowper's poem if she wished, and nobody be any the wiser. Sitting in one of the drawing-rooms during her final visit, she reported to Cassandra: 'At this present time I have five Tables, Eight and twenty Chairs & two fires all to myself.' She appreciated the privacy available to her by sitting in her room for two or three hours after breakfast with nobody enquiring where she was or what she was doing, but she also sometimes found the routine restricting: 'I did not mean to eat, but Johncock [the butler] has brought in the Tray, so I must.' She could enjoy for a short while the 'Elegance & Ease & Luxury' of Godmersham, where French wine was served instead of home-made drinks, and she could be 'above Vulgar Economy'; but before long she was ready to go home to 'the pleasures of Friendship, of unreserved Conversation, of similarity of Taste & Opinions'.[17]

Many years after Jane's death, Edward's eldest daughter, Fanny, saw fit to inform her own daughter that

the Aunts (Cass & Jane) were brought up in the most complete ignorance of the World & its ways (I mean as to fashion &c) & if it had not been for Papa's marriage which brought them into Kent ... they would have been, tho' not less clever and agreeable in themselves, very much below par as to good Society and its ways.

It was a snobbish comment, coming from a niece who had once been proud to enjoy Jane's friendship and affection, but there was some truth in it. Jane's visits to Godmersham undoubtedly gave her the knowledge of the daily routine of a great house, which she used effectively in *Mansfield Park*. She could nevertheless still make mistakes. After her first visit to Godmersham, she wrote to Cassandra, who had been left behind to nurse Elizabeth through her fifth confinement, 'We dine now at half after Three, and have done dinner I suppose before you begin ... I am afraid you will despise us'. Yet when she revised *Pride and Prejudice* for publication, in 1811, she failed to notice that she had allowed Mrs Bennet to arrange a dinner party at Longbourn at so early an hour that there would have been time for supper later.[18]

Edward soon reached the distinction of being a magistrate and High Sheriff of the county, in which capacity he once took Jane on a visit to a prison. On the whole, however, her days at Godmersham were spent, like Elizabeth's, in receiving visits and paying calls. 'In this House there is a constant succession of small events, somebody is always coming or going', she wrote disparagingly in 1813. She did, however, admit that it 'extended her Lights'.[19] She visited large numbers of great houses – Chilham Castle with its park landscaped by Capability Brown at his best; Mersham-le-Hatch by Robert Adam in his early days; Mystole, then an unadorned cube of a building; Eastwell Park with its ridiculously impressive entrance; and many others Cassandra did not need her to name. Jane was not particularly interested in architecture, for in her novels she could evoke the atmosphere of a dwelling in a few carefully chosen words, without need for elaborate detail. She was more interested in the people she met. Amongst them, she liked those who were courteous and modest, and she could regard with tolerant amusement the harmlessly eccentric. It was in Kent, however, that she also encountered, on the one hand, the peculiarly rude, silent stare of the well bred and, on the other, the boring conversation of people whose pretensions outran their intelligence. For the benefit of Cassandra, and to exorcise her feeling of inferiority, she described them with devastating succinctness:

Mrs Britton called here on Saturday. I never saw her before. She is a large, ungenteel Woman, with self-satisfied & would-be elegant manners.

George Hatton called yesterday ... I discerned nothing extraordinary. I should speak of him as Gentlemanlike young Man – eh! bien tout est dit.

Mr W. is about 5 or 6 & 20, not ill-looking & not agreable [*sic*] ... A sort of cool, gentlemanlike manner, but very silent ... We have got rid of Mr Mascall, however. I did not like *him* either. He talks too much & is conceited.[20]

During her later years, when she was known to be a novelist, an ill-natured acquaintance described her as sitting making mental notes of people's idiosyncracies and shortcomings. Like Elizabeth Bennet, she hoped that she never ridiculed the wise and good, but she was certainly aware of the temptation to be over-critical of 'foibles and nonsense, whims and inconsistencies' and prayed earnestly that God would incline her to judge others only as she would wish them to judge her.[21]

To her own surprise, she was happier with Edward's in-laws than with him and his wife. Her niece Anna believed that the in-laws, too, were overawed by Jane: 'A little learning went a long way with the Goodneston Bridgeses of that day, and much must have gone a long way too far', she wrote.²² Jane herself was pleasantly surprised by the warmth of greeting she received from the eldest of the daughters, Fanny Cage, when she arrived in Kent in 1796, and honoured at being asked to lead the dance with their brother Edward at an impromptu ball held at his mother's house. As the years went by, she became genuinely fond of the three younger sisters, especially Harriot. Meanwhile, her friendship with Edward Bridges grew into a mutual regard, though when he seemed about to propose marriage to her in 1805 she discouraged him. His mother, the Dowager Lady Bridges, had always been hospitable; Jane liked her, and could not have brought herself to repay her kindness by encouraging her son to make so unequal a marriage. Everybody would have thought that she had 'drawn him in' (to use Lady Catherine de Bourgh's vulgar phrase), and that she was marrying purely for security and consequence.²³

Long before then, Jane had realised that a happy marriage was not easily achieved. Cousin Eliza, after recovering from the news of her husband's violent death, took great delight in advertising to all and sundry the pleasures of independence. During the winter of 1796–97 she was to be found enjoying the social round in London, holding what she described as a *levée* each morning and boasting of having attracted 'a reasonable quantity of Beaux – the present hard times considered'. James Austen, tired of a lonely widower's existence, was not the only man who aspired vainly to marry her. She vowed she would not give up 'dear Liberty, & yet dearer flirtation' for any man, even the importunate 'Lord S-'. She preferred to devote herself to the care of her stricken son, spending some time each morning in an attempt to teach him to read and write, pleased sometimes to think that he was improving in health and cast down whenever he succumbed to increasingly serious bouts of illness.²⁴

Henry Austen fluttered around her like a moth around a flame until, finding no encouragement, he entered on a lightning courtship of a lady reputed to be 'a pretty wicked-looking girl with bright black eyes', the daughter of Captain Sir Richard Pearson, one of the officers of the Hospital for Seamen at Greenwich where the militia regiment was stationed. At Henry's request, Jane called on Mary Pearson on her way to Rowling that year, and thought that she was less pretty than her portrait had led the family to expect; but it hardly mattered, since she broke off the engagement shortly afterwards. Eliza, who saw Henry in town, thought he looked 'thin and ill' and promptly condemned Miss

Pearson as a flighty piece who had put on airs to catch him. Her sympathy for the poor young man made her kinder to him, and Phila Walter predicted that she would soon succumb to his worship of her.[25]

Their marriage on the last day of the year 1797 nevertheless came as a shock to Henry's family at Steventon. George Austen fulfilled his role as adoptive father of the bride by sending £40 to Henry's regiment to celebrate the wedding, but he must have known that the financial prospects of the couple were not bright. Eliza was ten years older than Henry. He had been prepared to offer her the earth, and had generously agreed that all her money should be signed over to her son, Hastings. Eliza was proud of Henry's position as a militia officer. She took up married quarters at Ipswich, where the regiment was stationed, and enjoyed herself hugely, driving around the countryside at Henry's daredevil speed and flirting outrageously with his fellow officers at a continual round of parties and balls. She had always rigidly refused to gamble and was meticulous in avoiding debt, but she made no provision for the fact that Henry's present income, which she described as 'comfortable', would last only as long as the war.[26]

Henry had toyed only a few years earlier with returning to the family's ambition for him and entering the church, Thomas Knight having declared in his will that Henry was to be given the living of Chawton should another relative, John Rawstorne Papillon, refuse it. Jane Austen knew enough about the clergy to realise that there was good sense in an attitude which made ordination dependent on the prospect of obtaining a living, although it seemed cynical to outsiders. In *Mansfield Park*, Edmund Bertram explains patiently to the critical Mary Crawford that it would be madness for anyone to enter the church without such a prospect. He himself has been lucky enough to have a family living lined up for him since birth, and he admits that this has influenced his choice of a profession; but he sees 'no reason why a man should make a worse clergyman for knowing that he will have a competence early in life'. Unfortunately, John Rawstorne Papillon had no intention of refusing the living of Chawton when it became available, and Edward Austen, acting for his brother, failed to reach an agreement on terms to buy him out.[27]

Meanwhile James Austen, cold-shouldered by Eliza and discouraged in a brief courtship of Alethea Bigg, had met with more success in lowlier sections of the marriage market. Having taken steps to improve his dancing, he became the life and soul of local gatherings and soon had two clergymen's daughters dangling after him. Jane waited with interest to see 'which of the two Marys [Mary Lloyd at Ibthorpe and

Mary Harrison at Overton] would carry the day'.[28] Mary Lloyd eventually triumphed over her rival and married James at the church at
Hurstbourne Tarrant on a bright, cold morning in January 1797. Mrs
Austen was delighted to welcome her into the family, believing that she
would be a second mother to little Anna. Jane professed to be pleased,
too; but, if she was genuinely so, the feeling soon wore off.[29] Mary's
lack of self-confidence resulted in a nagging jealousy of the memory
of James's first wife. She insisted on using the whole of her small fortune
to pay off the debts James had accrued whilst married to Anne and,
although she accepted of necessity the £100 a year General Mathew
continued to contribute towards his granddaughter's upbringing, she
could never like either him or the child.

Anna now had to be sent back to live at the parsonage at Deane. She
remembered long afterwards how her two aunts would trudge in their
pattens along the muddy lane from Steventon so that Jane could read
to her another instalment of the tale she was writing for her. Mary was
not eager to return their visits and resented James's habit of riding
over to Steventon every day to see his mother. He took no notice, and
sometimes appeared at the parsonage twice a day;[30] but in other respects
he gave in to his wife far too much, Jane thought. He was content in
his marriage, and came in time to think that he was ideally happy, but
he purchased his peace of mind by paying very little attention to his
daughter Anna and ceasing, in the end, to love her. He and Mary were
not well off in their early days together. Fortunately, Mary was a good
housekeeper, but her efforts to equal her predecessor's style of living
whilst at the same time struggling to make ends meet made her bossy
and irritable. Jane soon found that she derived little pleasure from
visiting her.[31]

The birth of a son to Mary and James, in November 1798, did not
improve matters. Jane had always disliked the idea of childbirth – not
altogether unreasonably, for its hazards were enormous. Obstetric practices had improved during the century, but inadequate knowledge of
hygiene on the part of midwives, especially in country districts, caused
infection to carry off large numbers of women: at the end of the
eighteenth century, nine in every thousand births still proved fatal to
the mother.[32] Jane was prone to fending off her fears by making tasteless
jokes on the subject, as in the notorious remark:

> Mrs Hall of Sherbourn was brought to bed yesterday of a dead child,
> some weeks before she expected, owing to a fright. I suppose she
> happened unawares to look at her husband.

Her phobias were not allayed by the news which reached her shortly before Mary went into labour that two ladies in the neighbourhood had died in childbed, or by the attitude of Mrs Austen, who had become paranoid about childbirth as soon as she had given up having children herself and refused to be told anything about Mary's confinement until it was all over. Mary was delivered safely of a fine boy, but Jane's distaste for the whole process was exacerbated by the sight of the mother some two weeks later: 'Mary does not manage matters in such a way as to make me want to lie in myself', she wrote.

> She is not tidy enough in her appearance; she has no dressing-gown to sit up in; her curtains are all too thin, and things are not in that comfort and style about her which are necessary to make such a situation an enviable one.

Normally, Jane might have found that one of the hardest things to bear about her other sister-in-law, Elizabeth Bridges, was that she always looked so beautiful, with her milky complexion, deep-set eyes, and hair dressed in the latest 'natural' style; but after visiting Mary, who looked alarmingly pale and haggard, she remembered gratefully the sight of Elizabeth, sitting up in bed after her fifth confinement in six years, 'with her nice clean cap put on so tidily and her dress so uniformly white and orderly'. Continual child-bearing did not seem to age Elizabeth, as Jane saw it age other women.[33]

The marriage service, at which Jane had so often acted as witness, gave as the primary purpose of marriage in the eyes of the church 'the procreation of children, to be brought up in the fear and nurture of the Lord, and to the praise of his holy Name'. Jane did not dote upon babies as a matter of course. Her novels, unlike those of Charles Dickens, do not end sentimentally with the patter of tiny feet. She connected young children with 'dirt and litter'.[34] In the ongoing debate about how to discipline them she did not subscribe to the view, apparently favoured by Lady Middleton, that they should be allowed to do as they liked and suffer only the consequences. As a Christian she knew that one must be kind to children, and respect their feelings, but she did not find them interesting. In *Sense and Sensibility* she wrote scathingly of women who could devote a lengthy conversation to comparing their children's height; and when, in later life, her niece Anna sent her some chapters of a novel she was writing, her comment was: 'You are but *now* coming to the heart & beauty of your book; till the heroine grows up, the fun must be imperfect.'[35] Children did not always like her, even when they listened with interest to the stories she told. Yet when any of them took to her – as did James's Anna and, for a time, Edward's little George – she was almost pathetically gratified and went to a great deal of trouble over them. Children were not so tiresome to her as to have formed a barrier to marriage with a man of her choice, but she was not prepared to dwindle into a loveless marriage for the sake of having them.

At the same time, she was aware that her prospects if she remained unmarried were bleak. 'Single Women have a dreadful propensity for being poor', she told her niece Fanny many years later.[36] The only profession open to gentlewomen was that of teaching in a school or as a governess in a private family. Neither she nor Cassandra had the qualifications often asked for in such appointments: skill in the use of the globes, or the ability to play the harp. In any case, such a course of action would have brought shame on their brothers, who would have been criticised for allowing them to expose themselves to possible exploitation and unhappiness. Jane writes in *Emma* of a school in which the teachers were well treated and of a household in which the governess, Miss Taylor, became a friend of the family; but there were schools in which the teaching was drudgery and households in which the governess was despised by adults and pupils alike: Miss Lee's position at Mansfield Park cannot have been altogether enviable; and in *Emma* Jane Fairfax faces her forthcoming employment as governess with trepidation as a form of slavery, devoid of 'all the pleasures of life, of rational intercourse, equal society, peace and hope'.[37] Jane Austen might by now have nourished a hope that she would one day earn a little money by writing, but she could not reasonably expect much. Fanny Burney had made £2000 from *Camilla*, but this was exceptional. During the 1790s a generous publisher might offer £50 a volume for the copyright of a novel by a known author such as Charlotte Smith, but for a beginner £10 to £15 was more likely – and this at a time when £50 a year as stipend for a curate was considered only just enough to live on.[38]

Elizabeth Bennet, and by inference her creator, can understand Charlotte Lucas's reasons for marrying Mr Collins. He is a reputable man and can give her a comfortable home. Her younger sisters will not be hindered in their chances of matrimony, and her brothers will be relieved of the fear of having to look after her into old age. Yet Elizabeth cannot regard these reasons as sufficient to acquit Charlotte of 'sacrificing every better feeling to worldly advantage'. Jane makes it clear, in both *Sense and Sensibility* and *Pride and Prejudice*, that she does not demand romantic love as a basis for marriage. 'Esteem' is her favourite word for the kind of love which should exist between man and wife: Charlotte is at fault in marrying Mr Collins not because she cannot adore him but because, as an intelligent woman, she cannot possibly respect him.[39] Jane's view of matrimony was attuned to the times in not expecting too much. Yet she required a change in attitude on the part of many men and women. Men should cease to look upon women simply as alluring creatures, or as unpaid housekeepers, and value them as rational beings – a phrase she had adapted from one of the female characters in *Sir Charles Grandison*.[40] Women, for their part, should cease to underestimate themselves. Jane was not a feminist in the sense later given to the term: she was not concerned about legal rights for women or for opportunities for them to compete in public life or in the professions. She was simply concerned that women, when taking a husband, should value the contribution they could make 'to the mutual society, help, and comfort that the one ought to have of the other', and prepare themselves to be true helpmeets as the church ordained.

THE

MYSTERIES OF UDOLPHO,

A

R O M A N C E;

INTERSPERSED WITH SOME PIECES OF POETRY.

BY

ANN RADCLIFFE,

AUTHOR OF THE ROMANCE OF THE FOREST, ETC.

IN FOUR VOLUMES.

Fate fits on thefe dark battlements, and frowns,
And, as the portals open to receive me,
Her voice, in fullen echoes through the courts,
Tells of a namelefs deed.

VOL. I.

LONDON:
PRINTED FOR G. G. AND J. ROBINSON,
PATERNOSTER-ROW.
1794.

Title page to Mrs Radcliffe, *The Mysteries of Udolpho,* the novel which enthralled
Catherine Morland during her visit to Bath.

Chapter 13

Classical Scenes and Gothic Novels

Catherine Morland, a parson's daughter living in a tiny village, has 'reached the age of seventeen without having seen one amiable youth to call forth her sensibility' and 'without having inspired one real passion'. She has always been happy in the country, but she is obliged to confess that there is very little for a young lady to do there. 'One day in the country is exactly like any other'. However,

> when a young lady is to be a heroine, the perverseness of forty sur-
> rounding families cannot prevent her. Something must and will happen
> to throw a hero in her way ... Mr Allen, who owned the chief of the
> property about Fullerton, the village in Wiltshire where the Morlands
> lived, was ordered to Bath for the benefit of a gouty constitution; – and
> his lady, a good-humoured woman, fond of Miss Morland, ... invited
> her to go with them.

By the grace of wealthy connections, Jane Austen too was able to visit Bath, in her case at least twice, whilst living at Steventon. Although it did not provide her personally with a hero, it probably produced a model for Henry Tilney, as well as furnishing a delightful setting for the opening chapters of her third novel.[1]

Jane had heard a great deal about Bath from her childhood onwards. Her juvenile writings contain more than one reference to it, including (in 'Evelyn') mention of a particular address, Westgate Buildings, which she was later to realise lay in a socially inferior part of the town and could therefore be selected as a location for the despised and impoverished widow, Mrs Smith, in *Persuasion*.[2] It is just possible that Jane was taken to Bath as a child when her Aunt and Uncle Cooper lived there. Her first recorded visit, however, was towards the end of 1797, when she went with her mother and sister to spend a month or more as guests of her Uncle and Aunt Leigh-Perrot, who every winter left their house in Berkshire and took up residence at No. 1, the Paragon. It was probably in the summer following this visit that Jane began to draft the novel which for many years was to be known as 'Susan', until the heroine's name was changed to Catherine and the novel finally became *Northanger Abbey*. She may have finished it after her second visit in the spring of 1799. On this latter occasion, she and her mother accompanied Edward and his wife and their two eldest children and stayed with them for six weeks in lodgings at No. 13, Queen Square. The Bath that Jane came to know and enjoy during these visits was essentially an eighteenth-century creation: the Royal Crescent was begun in 1775, the year of her birth; and Pulteney Street was less then ten years old when she established Catherine Morland with the Allens in 'comfortable lodgings' there.[3] It was barely fifty years since John Wood had set out to reproduce the classical environment which had delighted wealthy citizens in the first century A.D. and which eighteenth-century Englishmen saw as epitomising the virtues of honesty, simplicity, freedom and decorum they so much wished to achieve in their own time. His son inherited both his skill and his ambition, with the result that within half a century the father's dream had materialised in a series of terraces, squares and crescents, rising up the south-facing slopes overlooking the Roman site of Aquae Sulis. By the 1790s Bath was one of the architectural wonders of western Europe. Visitors who knew what they were about would pause as they approached the city over Kingsdown Hill and view the honey-coloured spectacle before them with suitable rapture. Jane could not help but be impressed, even though her arrival on both her early visits took place in rain.

She was later to discover that the mood of the viewer was important. In 1801, when she arrived under sadder circumstances, a reluctant exile from her native Steventon, she found the prospect less enticing: 'My first view of Bath in fine weather does not answer my expectations', she wrote.

> I think I see more distinctly through rain. The sun was got behind everything, and the appearance of the place from the top of Kingsdown was all vapour, shadow, smoke and confusion.[4]

It was a mood she later transferred to Anne Elliot, the heroine of *Persuasion*, also uprooted from her home. In the earlier years, Jane, like Catherine Morland, 'was come to be happy', and no doubt as the coach clattered towards the centre of the city 'she felt happy already'.[5] The very different impressions of Bath which are given in *Northanger Abbey* and *Persuasion* are often regarded as evidence of changes in society during Jane Austen's lifetime, but they could equally have been experienced at one and the same time by different persons approaching the city under different circumstances.

Even in her happiest days, Jane's imperviousness to architecture was such that she paid no attention to the elegance of Bath's Palladian structures. The graceful curve of the Paragon meant nothing to her. Remembering the muddy lanes around the parsonage at Steventon, she appreciated most the smoothly paved streets, which could recover quickly from the 'dirtiness' caused by wet weather and become 'white' again in no time. Visually, her main interest at this time was in the Picturesque. The centre of Queen Square being at that time devoid of trees, the principal windows of No. 13 gave an uninterrupted view of the magnificent terrace forming the north side, but Jane was too much occupied with Gilpin to give much thought to John Wood the Elder's neoclassical masterpiece. 'The prospect from the Drawing room window at which I now write is rather picturesque,' she informed Cassandra, 'as it commands a perspective view of the left side of Brock Street, broken by three Lombardy Poplars in the Garden of the last house in Queen's Parade.' The celebrated view over the city from Beechen Cliff merely provided her with material for Henry Tilney to lecture Catherine Morland on the application of Gilpin's principles. By the time he had finished his discourse on 'fore-grounds, distances, and second distances – side screens and perspectives – lights and shades', his awe-stricken pupil was prepared to reject the whole city of Bath as 'unworthy to make part of a landscape'.[6]

No. 13, Queen Square met with Jane's modified approval, mainly because from a domestic point of view it bore comparison with Steventon parsonage.[7] She and her mother had 'two very nice sized rooms'.

> I have the outward & larger apartment, as I ought to have; which is quite as large as our bed room, & my Mother's is not materially less. The Beds are both as large as any at Steventon; & I have a very nice chest of Drawers & Closet full of shelves.

She pronounced the Square to be 'more cheerful' than the Paragon, but her opinion of houses (in life as in her novels) tended to be coloured by her feelings about the inmates. She did not like staying with her Aunt and Uncle Leigh-Perrot, and even avoided it when she could. She can have had no objection to her uncle, who was by all accounts a gentle, cultivated, witty companion. He was wealthy enough to have amassed a library worthy of a gentleman of the Enlightenment, and generous enough to hand on to his niece a number of expensively bound, multi–volume works: David Hume's *History of England* (mentioned respectfully in *Northanger Abbey*); John Bell's *Travels from St Petersburg in Russia to Diverse Parts of Asia*; Oliver Goldsmith's *An History of the Earth*; Ariosto's *Orlando Furioso*; *The Works of James Thomson*; and probably others lost to her when her collection had to be sold on leaving Steventon.[8] Unfortunately, his wife Jane was a formidable woman, domineering and aggressive even in her offers of hospitality. Increasing deafness made her more and more difficult to withstand. Although she was never short of money, she had a sharp eye for prices and was known at times to be downright mean. She was useful in putting Jane in the way of cheap shops in Walcot Street, but unfortunately she also seems to have been in the habit of bargaining with shopkeepers over prices. There were even rumours abroad to the effect that, if she did not get her own way, she was not averse to helping herself to the goods.

On 14 August 1799, a few months after Jane's second visit to Bath, her aunt was arrested on a charge of stealing a card of white lace from a shop at the corner of Bath Street and Stall Street and committed to the county gaol at Ilchester. She was lodged in privileged but nevertheless squalid conditions in the Governor's quarters, her devoted husband remaining with her there for the whole of the seven months during which she awaited trial. Mrs Austen offered to send either Jane or Cassandra or both to join her, but to Mrs Leigh-Perrot's credit she refused to submit them to so dreadful an ordeal. The penalty she faced was tranportation to Botany Bay. At the trial at Taunton Assizes on 29 March 1800 her lawyer was not allowed to speak in her defence, but by cross-examination of prosecution witnesses it was made clear that the shop assistants may have planted the lace on their victim for purposes of blackmail. Mrs Leigh-Perrot was triumphantly acquitted; but doubts remained in some quarters, and subsequent evidence suggests that the lady may in fact have suffered from sporadic fits of kleptomania. Jane's views on the terrible affair are unknown; her attitude towards her aunt remained as ever, dutiful but without affection.[9]

The venom displayed by Mrs Leigh-Perrot's accusers arose from the fact that the shop whose management they represented was in the hands of receivers. The building boom of the 1770s and 1780s was halted by the war; the City Bank failed and many builders went bankrupt. Increasing taxation reduced spending capacity and crime rose as depression set in. Even Marshall's, the fashionable circulating library in Milsom Street, found the number of its subscribers dwindling. However, large parts of Bath had long resembled building sites; the piles of bricks and rubble that now lay abandoned were not at first much noticed. In the centre of the city, life could appear to go on much as usual, and a young woman who suddenly found herself able to be there for a season could enjoy herself without much thought for hidden problems.

With 147 coaches running weekly from London alone, there seemed to be no end to the number of visitors flocking to Bath. They came for a variety of reasons, of which the most publicised was the hope of finding a cure for ailments real and imagined by sampling the waters. Three thermal springs, rising under pressure through faults in the rock at temperatures between 104° and 120° F, and collected into the King's Bath, the Cross Bath and the Hot Bath, had been the raison d'être of the town since the middle ages. In the seventeenth century, an emphasis by the medical profession on imbibing mineral water rather than bathing in it had given rise to a number of purely 'drinking spas', such as Tunbridge Wells, but at Bath it was possible to do both. Each of the three baths had a pump attached to it. The finest Pump Room was the one associated with the King's Bath, built in 1706 and remodelled some eighty years later; patients recommended by their doctors to use one of the other locations because of its supposed efficacy for a particular condition would usually frequent the Pump Room at the King's Bath as well. Serious sufferers from arthritis or rheumatism, like Mrs Smith in *Persuasion*, were lowered into the baths by attendants for such periods of time as they could endure the heat, whilst gentlemen suffering from gout (a complaint which seems to have affected males especially, although female victims were by no means unknown), hobbled to the Pump Room and drank glasses of water once or twice a day. A total of two or three pints was usual, and four or five was not unknown. Doctors recommended that the water should be drunk hot from the pump, but patients who were confined to the house, their swollen feet bound in flannel bandages, were obliged to get what benefit they could from having the water conveyed to their lodgings. A chronic sufferer was Jane Austen's Uncle Leigh-Perrot, who became so dependent on Bath water that by 1798 he had taken a permanent lease on the house in the Paragon so that he would not have the anxiety of looking for lodgings each winter.[10] Whatever benefit he derived from the waters was to some extent offset, however, by the fact that he very often 'overwalked himself' on the steeply sloping streets of the town and was then confined to the house until his agony had abated sufficiently for him to take a Bath Chair.[11]

Invalids and health fanatics (for the active pursuit of health by apparently healthy people was one of the new obsessions of the eighteenth century) brought their families with them for the season, and entertainments had to be arranged to keep them there. The leisure industry became so highly organised that for many people it became the main purpose of their visit. Jane Austen had already made use of Bath as a recognisable setting for Willoughby's unbridled pleasure-seeking and she was to use it again, in *Mansfield Park*, as one of Henry Crawford's dissolute haunts.[12]

Bath was also well known for attracting social climbers and money-makers, like General Tilney, hopeful of striking up a profitable acquaintance with the titled or rich. The variety of social classes frequenting the spa had been seen as a problem in late Stuart times, when members of the aristocracy found that their presence attracted country gentry who did not always know how to behave in polite company. This particular problem was solved by the enterprising Richard 'Beau' Nash, who invented the largely informal but increasingly influential position of Master of Ceremonies. By the end of the eighteenth century, he and his successors, assisted by the city council, had created in Bath a ritualised society unparalleled anywhere else in the country outside the Royal Court. From mid century, the aristocracy gradually deserted the resort in favour of other spas and watering places (Tunbridge Wells, more easily reached from London; or Brighton, popularised by the Prince of Wales), leaving gentry and professional families to enjoy an experience which made them feel privileged, genteel and secure. Entrance to the baths and to balls, to assemblies, and to most concerts was by subscription only, paid in advance. Strict codes of behaviour operated not only at public gatherings but among chairmen carrying passengers through the streets. Dancing and card-playing finished strictly at 11 p.m., when the watch took over the lamplit streets and reassuringly called the hours till daybreak. For many a young man or woman, a season at Bath became a preliminary to entry into the more alarming world of London.

'Every morning now brought its regular duties', Catherine Morland found when she had been in Bath a few days.[13] Persons drinking the waters were advised by local guides to do so between 6 and 10 a.m., to allow the beneficial draught to pass through the stomach before breakfast. Thereafter they could repair to the card room, or read the newspapers, or join their companions in strolling up and down the Pump Room to see and be seen whilst listening to music by the town band. Newcomers were expected to sign a book and give their address in Bath, so that their friends could look out for them and the Master of Ceremonies call on them. After breakfast, walking could continue along the Parades or in Sydney Gardens; riding could be practised in the small ring on the common known as Hyde Park or, more strenu-ously, up the surrounding heights; carriage drives could be taken to beauty spots outside the city; or shops and circulating libraries (which displayed artists' work and sold useful items such as parasols as well as lending books) could be visited. A further session in the Pump Room, or tea-drinking in the Assembly Rooms, brought the time to three or four in the afternoon when it was necessary to return to one's lodgings and prepare for the evening's entertainment. Two 'dress' balls and two 'fancy' or 'cotillion' balls were held every week during the eight-month season from October to May, alternating between the Upper and Lower Rooms so as never to coincide. Concerts and theatre performances filled most other evenings except Sundays, when church-going, followed on fine days by strolling on the green slope below the Royal Crescent, formed a major part of the week's ritual.

Henry Tilney, introduced to Catherine Morland at the Lower Rooms by Mr King (Master of Ceremonies in the 1790s) asks his partner during the dancing if she has 'yet honoured the Upper Rooms?'

> 'Yes, sir, I was there last Monday.'
> 'Have you been to the theatre?'
> 'Yes, sir, I was at the play on Tuesday.'
> 'To the concert?'
> 'Yes, sir, on Wednesday.'

The nonchalant attitudes which became increasingly fashionable with the onset of the Romantic movement demanded a pretence at boredom with so rigid a regime: when Catherine, at the end of a fortnight, continues to express delight with her stay at Bath, Henry issues a facetious warning: 'Take care, or you will forget to be tired of it at the proper time. You ought to be tired at the end of six weeks.' Catherine does not think she would be tired if she stayed six months. The pleasure-loving Eliza de Feuillide, hearing of Bath long before she visited it, felt equally sure she would find it a place after her own heart.[14]

The visit of the Austen family to Bath in 1799 was partly for health reasons and partly for pleasure. Edward, since his marriage, had become subject to bouts of nausea which Jane could not believe to be due to any serious physical cause. She admitted he seemed 'fagged' by the journey to Bath, but was convinced that 'the bustle of sending out for Tea, Coffee & Sugar &c, & going out to taste a cheese himself would do him good'.[15] (Like most wealthy visitors, Edward had taken a fur-nished house, or 'lodgings', rather than stay in a boarding house, and the family was catering for itself. A team of servants saw to most of the requirements, but beverages and cheeses were too expensive and too individual a taste to be left to hirelings.) Edward had also arranged, before leaving Godmersham, to put himself in the hands of one of the most fashionable consultants in Bath: Dr Fellowes, Physician Extraordinary to the Prince of Wales, who advised him to drink at the Hetling Pump and occasionally to bathe in the Hot Bath to which the pump was attached. He continued to have good days and bad days, but his relatives hoped that, since he could apparently take the waters without incurring stomach or bowel upsets, they would actually benefit him in the end. 'Everybody encourages us in this expectation,' Jane wrote, 'for they all say that the effect of the Waters cannot be negative, & many are the instances in which the benefit is felt afterwards more than on the spot.' Edward nevertheless persuaded Dr Fellowes to let him try the new electrical treatment recommended for circulatory disorders. This apparently had little success, for he soon began to complain of a variety of symptoms which convinced him he might be getting the gout ('perhaps a fit of it might cure him', Jane wrote enigmatically). His family began to be sorry he had 'tied himself' to Dr Fellowes, for they had heard better reports of one Dr Mapleton, with whom the Leigh-Perrots were on friendly terms. Fortunately an apothecary (dispensing chemist) in Queen Square ('a sensible, intelligent man', Jane decided), assured him that his 'little feverish disposition' was due to something he had eaten, and that 'the occasional particular glow in his hands and feet', which was the main cause of his worries, was due to better circulation as a result of taking the waters. Encouraged by these wise words, the party returned home in time for Edward to supervise the quarterly rent day on his estates. Jane was by then ready to leave. Like Catherine Morland, she could enjoy an interval of pleasure without becoming addicted to it.[16]

Edward's mother is likely to have encouraged him, both in his undue concern for his own health and in his determination to try the Bath waters, for she was herself a hypochondriac and at the same time a believer that there was no place on earth more efficacious for health than the town in which she had been happy in her younger days. Like many another parson's wife, Mrs Austen found her country rectory dull once her children had grown up. Her spirits had been raised considerably by her visit in 1797 (although the improvement did not last). There is no evidence that on her next visit she took part in any of the formal entertainments on offer, but she got herself up-to-date on the pros and cons of the various housing developments in Bath, and became so enamoured of Queen Square that she began to hanker after living there.

The twenty-three-year-old Jane, meanwhile, seized every opportunity to enjoy herself. On the day of her arrival, she learnt from the newspaper that there was a public breakfast every morning in Sydney Gardens; and with Edward's two children aged five and six to entertain it seems more than likely that she attended once or twice, family tickets being available. Better still, she learnt when she had been in Bath a fortnight that there was to be a 'grand gala' in the Gardens one Tuesday evening – 'a Concert, with illuminations and fireworks'. The city's Director of Music, Signor Rauzzini, was a celebrated impresario, and the chance to hear good music, professionally played, was for many visitors from the country one of the greatest attractions of Bath.[17] Jane was no great lover of concerts, but an outdoor performance appealed to her more than the subscription concerts held every Wednesday in the Upper Rooms, on the grounds that she would be too far away to hear much of the music; and the rest of the evening's entertainment she looked forward to enormously. In the event, the party arrived almost too late for the music but in very good time for the fireworks, which Jane pronounced even better than she had expected. The illuminations, too, she found 'very pretty'.[18]

Sydney Gardens had been opened in May 1795, to rival London's Vauxhall. With their groves, vistas, serpentine walks, cascades and ornamental bridges, they attracted Jane as much by day as by night. As one who loved walking, she also took advantage of the beautiful walks outside Bath, across fields to the villages of Charlcombe and Weston.[19] Like most female visitors, she came to Bath armed with queries about the latest fashions and with plans for purchases from the city's haberdashers, costumiers, drapers and milliners. Material could be bought and made up quickly, and it was not long before Jane was reporting to Cassandra:

> My Cloak is come home, & here follows the pattern of its lace [drawing]. If you do not think it wide enough, I can give 3d a yard more for yours, & not go beyond the two Guineas, for my Cloak altogether does not cost quite two pounds. I like it very much ... I saw some Gauzes in a shop in Bath street yesterday at only 4s a yard, but they were not so good or so pretty as mine. Flowers are very much worn, & Fruit is still more the thing. Eliz: has a bunch of Strawberries, & I have seen Grapes, Cherries, Plums & Apricots. A plumb or green gage would cost three shillings, Cherries & Grapes about 5 I believe – but this is at some of the dearest Shops.

She had probably seen the fruit whilst window-gazing in Milsom Street, where Isabella Thorpe saw a hat with coquelicot ribbons and longed to buy it. She was disappointed to find that the cheap shop to which her aunt directed her did not stock fruit; she seemed inclined to settle for flowers, arguing facetiously that it was more natural to have flowers than fruit growing out of one's head.[20]

Edward, meanwhile, bought a pair of small black coach horses, price sixty guineas. Such a purchase was not unusual: many men came to Bath especially to trade a horse, there being five dealers in the town. John Thorpe in *Northanger Abbey* is forever talking about buying and selling horses; his comment on first setting eyes on Henry Tilney is 'A good figure of a man; well put together. Does he want a horse?' Edward, however, made his purchase on the more reliable recommendation of his Kentish friend Mr Evelyn, now living in Bath – a noted expert and whip, who was later to give Jane the excitement of riding in his 'bewitching Phaeton & four'.[21]

Jane was as interested in assessing the merits of professional acting as in analysing those of its amateur counterpart. The small theatre in Orchard Street was a touring venue for most of the London companies, and Edward booked seats for 19 June when, as usual, two pieces were performed: a lavishly staged pantomime (*Bluebeard*) and a new comedy called *The Birthday Day* by Kotzebue (famed for his *Lovers' Vows* performed at Mansfield Park). Theatres, like every other rendezvous in Bath, were places in which to be seen as much as to see. It was not unusual for habitués of the boxes to arrive half way through the performance, as Henry Tilney and his father do; or for others, like Catherine Morland, to spend more time looking for friends in the candlelit audience than watching the play.[22] In addition to mentioning these theatre-going habits, Jane was able, in *Northanger Abbey*, to write with insight of the mixed feelings of nervousness and excitement experienced by a young girl attending balls in the Upper and Lower Rooms. In her letters she makes no mention of attending balls in either set of rooms herself during her stay in Queen Square, but if she failed to do so it can only have been because she lacked a chaperon, Elizabeth being as staid in her habits as Edward. On her previous visit, she may have been escorted either by her mother or by her aunt, as a matter of duty.

Mrs Leigh-Perrot was a determined socialiser of the head-hunting variety: at her home in Hare Hatch she boasted of dining with thirty families (six more than Mrs Bennet at Longbourn).[23] At Bath the state of her husband's health would not allow her to indulge in many public appearances, but she was forever inviting people to tea-and-card parties, which were in any case becoming more popular than public gatherings ('another stupid party', Jane once complained).[24] Mrs Leigh-Perrot almost certainly kept a look-out in the *Bath Chronicle* for names of new arrivals with whom she could claim acquaintance, and she was probably not averse to nosying for addresses in the Pump Room book during her husband's visits to drink the waters. Whilst the Austens were staying with her in the early winter months of 1797 she can hardly have helped knowing of the arrival of the young Michael Hicks-Beach, beginning his education as a gentleman of the Enlightenment and a man of the world by touring the country under the guidance of his tutor, the Revd Sydney Smith. Mrs Austen may well have heard of the young man's arrival herself from Mrs Bramston of Oakley Hall, for Michael's father was Wither Bramston's cousin, and Mrs Bramston and her husband, having no children of their own, took a great interest in the family which would one day inherit their property. Any of its members visiting Oakley Hall are bound to have been introduced to the neighbourhood at large: Mrs Austen in one of her poems mentioned 'Squire Hicks and his fair spouse' attending a Basingstoke assembly, and Jane herself knew the family well enough to write in reply to sad news in a letter from Cassandra in 1796: 'I am sorry for the Beaches loss of their little girl, especially as it is the one so much like me.'[25]

A clergyman tutor was exactly the sort of person a Master of Cere-monies would have introduced to a clergyman's daughter at a ball. There is no direct evidence to prove that Jane Austen met Sydney Smith, yet everything that a new acquaintance would have noticed about him bears a striking resemblance to her description of Henry Tilney. Smith was twenty-six years old, tall and pleasant-looking. His conver-sation, for which he was later to be celebrated, was already extraordinarily amusing, but of a kind also to puzzle a listener unac-customed to his vein of humour. It might even have been thought that he 'indulged himself a little too much with the foibles of others', as Catherine suspected of Henry Tilney.[26] A friend protested on his behalf that he meant no harm:

> He talked because he could not help it; because his spirits were excited and his mind full.[27]

He was, in fact, kind and capable of great sensitivity, as Henry proved to be. In spite of his sometimes absurd talk, he was intelligent, rational, wise and understanding: like Henry Tilney, he would have been capable on one occasion of baffling a young friend with his 'odd ways' and on another of giving sound advice in a manner both gentle and compelling. Like many young men at the time, Sydney Smith had entered the church without any conscious vocation, yet he proved to be a diligent clergyman and later a much valued parish priest. Henry Tilney, destined from birth by his father to take up the family living at Woodston, was as conscientious in his duties as the times required, and sufficiently assured in his religious faith to speak of it without embarrassment to Catherine as an essential feature of the age.[28]

Other characters in *Northanger Abbey* (Mrs Allen with her 'inactive good temper'; John Thorpe, who 'seemed fearful of being too handsome unless he wore the dress of a groom') are equally well drawn,[29] and the plot is as realistic as any reader could require. A young lady from a country parsonage is taken to Bath for entertainment and experience in the process of growing up. She has virtually to fend for herself, since her chaperon is too mindless and too involved in her own trivial concerns to give her proper advice or attention. In her loneliness she is glad to receive friendly advances from Isabella Thorpe, and in her innocence she does not recognise them as entirely self-seeking. Her brother James, equally unversed in the snares of the marriage market, is taken in by Isabella to the extent of becoming engaged to her, but fortunately discovers his mistake before it is too late.

At Bath, Catherine is introduced by the Master of Ceremonies, Mr King, to a young clergyman, Henry Tilney, whom she greatly admires. Invited to stay with him and his sister at their parental home, she is gratified and excited but also nervous: their house is much grander than any she has previously entered, and this is the first time she has been away from home entirely on her own. She is also puzzled and somewhat frightened by the autocratic behaviour of Henry's father, General Tilney. Her fears are exaggerated, but she is not entirely wrong in her suspicion that the General is not all that he should be. It eventually emerges that he has encouraged her attachment to his son in the belief that she is a great heiress – a misunderstanding that could easily occur at Bath, where visitors' backgrounds were not always known. On discovering his mistake he turns her unceremoniously from his house, obliging her to travel home alone by hired coach. Thanks to her own good sense she accomplishes the journey without alarm, and arrives home to weep for the loss of her young man – but not for long. Henry, discovering what has happened, has the moral courage to defy his father and stand by his unspoken commitment to Catherine until such time as the General grudgingly consents to their marriage. The novel ends with the prospect of happiness ever after in Henry's charming vicarage.

Jane Austen's decision to make this homely story into a vehicle for

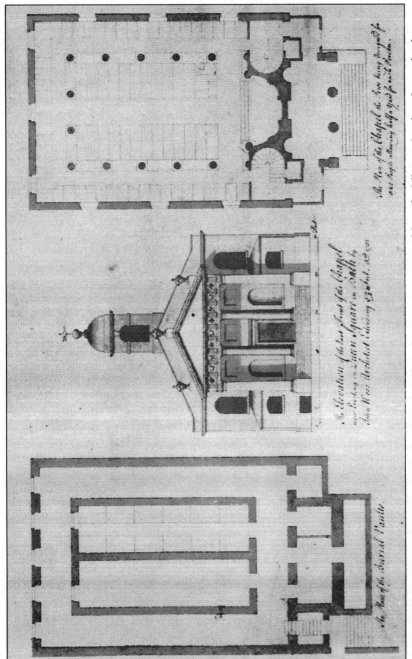

St Mary's Chapel, Queen Square, Bath, where it is thought Jane Austen worshipped whilst staying in a house in the square in 1799. (*Bath City Library*)

comment upon the novel-reading habits of her day has seemed to many people a step backwards in her progress as an author. At the time, however, there was much to be said for it. In the 1790s Bath had as many as nine circulating libraries, from which books could be borrowed on payment of a small subscription for the season. Visitors from the country, with few facilities at home for borrowing books, seized the opportunity to get abreast with the latest publications, especially novels, which were a commodity to be borrowed if possible, rather than bought: the 'horrid' novels listed in Isabella Thorpe's pocket book (which included some very recent titles) were presumably going to be obtained from a library and read whilst on holiday in Bath.[30] Among the literate classes, the reading of novels was in any case such an important part of their entertainment that many people lived with the characters and situations they had read about, and enjoyed allusions to them, much as people later were to live with characters and situations seen on television.

The craze for 'gothic' or macabre tales of wickedness and suspense set in terrifying surroundings had reached unprecedented levels with the publication of Mrs Radcliffe's *Romance of the Forest* (1792) and *The Mysteries of Udolpho* (1794). The paraphernalia of such novels – the gloomy castle, the old family retainer, the funereal bedchamber, the mysterious chests and cabinets, the dying embers of the fire, the guttering candle, the strange footsteps and distant moans – became so familiar that no explanations were needed when reference was made to them. Eliza de Feuillide, after a visit to a doctor's surgery in 1796, described how she had detected in the dim light of the waiting room two cabinets which she was convinced must be full of skeletons – until she surreptitiously opened the doors and found only surgical instruments inside.[31] Mrs Austen could describe the state bedchamber at Stoneleigh Abbey, with its 'high dark crimson Velvet Bed', as 'an *alarming* apartment just fit for a Heroine', and Jane Austen in her letters to Cassandra could lapse without warning into the style of Mrs Radcliffe: 'the shades of Evening are descending, and I resume my interesting Narrative'.[32] In these circumstances, burlesques flourished along with sequels, imitations and adaptations of all kinds.

It has often been assumed that *Northanger Abbey* was another to add to the list, but Jane Austen probably had an altogether different purpose in mind. There had grown up in recent years an increasingly vigorous campaign by moralisers and educational pundits to discourage parents and teachers from allowing children as they grew older to read novels. Many young people, starved of imaginative literature in childhood by a heavy diet of moral tales, devoured novels in their early 'teens. Girls, especially, took eagerly to a form of literature which for the first time gave a prominent position to a young female heroine. The idea that excessive reading of fiction could lead weak-minded persons into irrational behaviour was as old as Don Quixote: what now happened was that novels were perceived to have immoral as well as deranging effects, and the weak-minded were thought to include the entire body of adolescents, especially those of the female sex.

The term 'adolescence', though used by Laurence Sterne in Volume 5 of *Tristram Shandy* (1761), was not well-known in England; but theorists were beginning to recognise that there was a period between childhood and maturity when susceptibility to new influences was strong, expectation from life high, responsibilities few and experience slender. Samuel Johnson was in no doubt that Richardson, Fielding and other novelists of his day aimed to appeal specifically to such readers ('the Young, the Ignorant, and the Idle'); in his opinion, they ought therefore to be more careful about what they wrote.[33] Other moralists, including the influential Mrs Chapone, thought that there was more to be gained by restricting access to novels, especially on the part of young women. Maria Edgeworth and her father shared this view, claiming to know 'from common experience' that immoderate reading of novels by young ladies prematurely cultivated their hearts, lowered the tone of their minds, and rendered them indifferent to the common pleasures and occupations of daily life.[34]

Many women novelists, flattered rather than annoyed by the influence attributed to them, believed that young readers would be attracted to novels all the more if they were told that they were a risqué commodity. Hence they often included in their novels some young female character who was warned against reading such trash, or who herself professed to be disgusted with it. Jane deplored such tactics as likely to bring novels further into contempt among the adult public. In *Northanger Abbey*, as Catherine and Isabella 'shut themselves up to read novels together', she insists defiantly:

> Yes, novels; – for I will not adopt that ungenerous and impolitic custom so common with novel writers, of degrading by their contemptuous censure the very performances, to the number of which they are themselves adding – joining with their greatest enemies in bestowing the harshest epithets on such works, and scarcely ever permitting them to be read by their own heroine ... Alas! if the heroine of one novel be not patronized by the heroine of another, from whom can she expect

protection and regard? I cannot approve of it. Let us leave it to the
Reviewers to abuse such effusions of fancy at their leisure, and over
every new novel to talk in threadbare strains of the trash with which
the press now groans. Let us not desert one another; we are an injured
body.[35]

In view of such a declaration, it seems unlikely that she intended her
novel to be another version of *The Female Quixote* (Charlotte Lennox's
minor classic of 1752), although it is sometimes seen as such.

Charlotte Lennox's novel (which Jane enjoyed so much that she read
it three times) was itself an updated version of Cervantes's *Don Quixote*,
with a young female as the central figure.[36] The rich Lady Arabella,
growing up in a remote castle, reads nothing but translations of French
seventeenth-century romances. Realising that she is very beautiful, she
becomes convinced that she is destined to be a heroine. On entering
the world, she assumes that the circumstances described in the romances
are operative in eighteenth-century London and Bath, and proceeds
to behave as a fictional heroine would have done. In doing so, she not
only makes herself ridiculous but wreaks havoc upon the people she
encounters. She is rescued only after years of attention on the part of
her devoted lover, who eventually marries her.

Jane Austen cannot possibly have believed that novels were likely to
have such an effect on any girl brought up in ordinary surroundings.
She herself had read novels avidly from childhood onward. Admittedly
she was lucky in that all the members of her family were 'great Novel-
readers & not ashamed of being so'. Her mother willingly gave her the
money to subscribe to a new circulating library which opened in Basingstoke in 1798, and it seems to have been George Austen who
introduced her to Francis Lathom's fantastic tale, *The Midnight Bell*,
which he borrowed on an overnight stop at Dartford on his way home
from Godmersham to read before going to bed.[37] A leading critic
assumed that this latest addition to the accounts of haunted castles
would be read only by 'the misses';[38] for many educated adults, particularly males, either despised or pretended to despise novels and hence
left younger readers without guidance on them. Nevertheless, in *Northanger Abbey* Jane Austen set out to show that even without adult help a
young girl brought up to exercise common sense could conceivably
read novels without very much harm resulting. Most of the gothic
novels, though worthless as literature, were after all harmless enough.
The heroines are moral and much given to prayer and meditation, and
strange happenings are eventually attributed to earthly rather than

supernatural causes. Mrs Radcliffe's works were actually admired by notable critics such as Hazlitt and Walter Scott for their stunning (if inaccurate) descriptions of mountain scenery. The only novel which caused Jane any doubts was Matthew Lewis's *The Monk*, a disturbing tale which she had probably not read but had seen condemned by Coleridge in the *Monthly Mirror* as tasteless, poisonous, libidinous and brutalising. This she decided would appeal only to such coarse characters as John Thorpe.[39]

Catherine Morland, the readers of *Northanger Abbey* are informed, is not a heroine of romance, nor (unlike the Lady Arabella) does she imagine herself destined to be one. She is not exceptionally beautiful, her mother has not died in childbed, her father is neither poor nor wicked and she does not commune with nature or write sonnets in contemplative hours. Her expectations on visiting Bath are not outlandish: she is satisfied for one evening when she hears two gentlemen describing her as a pretty girl, and thinks herself in 'high luck' when, on another evening, the Master of Ceremonies introduces her to a lively young clergyman who, 'if not quite handsome was very near it'. Catherine as a girl has been seen to prefer novels to works of information, but in her country parsonage new ones have seldom come her way; the only novel she mentions by name as having read is the unexceptionable *Sir Charles Grandison*, which she thinks 'very entertaining' and which her mother has read too. It is left to Isabella Thorpe, her new-found friend at Bath, to intoduce her to *The Mysteries of Udolpho* and to forecast the thrills she will experience from 'horrid' novels in general. Isabella's entire conversation is couched in the exaggerated terms common to the novels. Mrs Chapone had warned that too much reading of novels inevitably made a young woman 'ridiculous in conversation', but in Isabella's case it is an affectation which she has deliberately adopted because she thinks it adds to her modishness and will help to attract the men.[40] Many of her effusive remarks puzzle Catherine rather than impress her, especially when they bear little relation to the speaker's behaviour. The bond between the two girls is a mutual enthusiasm for Mrs Radcliffe's *Mysteries of Udolpho*, which has long since lost its power to freeze the blood but which countless readers at the end of the eighteenth century found compelling. Henry Tilney, failing to realise just how much Catherine has been carried away by the novel, inadvertently heightens its effect by pretending to her that she is going to experience some of its frightening aspects at his home, Northanger Abbey. The latter is of course not a mouldering edifice redolent of secret fears and mysterious deaths but a building much more common in eighteenth-century England: an abbey taken over at the Reformation by a lay proprietor, who has refurbished such parts as could be made comfortable, pulled down the rest, and built on a startlingly new wing. Stoneleigh Abbey in Warwickshire may well have been a model for it (assuming that James Austen had visited his patroness there and described the architecture to Jane). Catherine Morland has already begun to be disenchanted by it when a series of coincidences reminds her of Henry's predictions. One stormy night, she indulges in a little vicarious terror, and frightens herself more than she expected. Daylight, however, soon banishes her fantasies, and she determines never to be so foolish again.

This laudable resolution falters as Catherine tries to find an explanation for General Tilney's disturbing behaviour. Again, however, common sense reasserts itself and she is already ashamed of her folly by the time Henry Tilney takes her to task. In her new-found maturity she resists any temptation she might have had to rush to the other extreme and despise gothic novels altogether. Like Henry, who admits to having read *The Mysteries of Udolpho* with his hair standing on end the whole of the time, she determines to see them from then on as works of fiction whose particular forms of good and evil are unlikely to be found in an English environment. She has nevertheless been alerted by them to the continuing existence of good and evil. General Tilney is not guilty of locking up innocent females in a gloomy castle, but he tyrannises over his son and daughter to further his own ambitions. Catherine Morland, throughout the novel, shows that an understanding of right and wrong is not confined to highly educated persons but is available, as Locke maintained, to anybody with good will. No special training has been required to show her how to behave courteously in a ballroom or how to judge Isabella Thorpe's flirtations with Captain Tilney whilst engaged to someone else. From start to finish, *Northanger Abbey* illustrates the combination of reason and morality which Jane had been brought up to employ.

Whilst she was writing *Northanger Abbey*, two people she knew personally were successful in publishing novels, both of which she must have known to be inferior to her own. Samuel Egerton Brydges' *Arthur Fitz-Albini* was despised even by his relatives at Ashe parsonage, for which reason Jane thought it hardly fair that her family should read it. Her father nevertheless decided to buy a copy, thinking that Mrs Lefroy may have been over-critical. Not so, for George Austen as an experienced novel-reader was disappointed before he had finished the first volume, and Jane reported disparagingly to Cassandra that it contained no story and very little characterisation.[41] The following year, the family received a copy of *Battleridge*, by Mrs Austen's cousin Cassandra Cooke. Its many pro-Stuart asides (to the 'usurpation' by Cromwell, to 'the sacred hand' of Charles the Martyr, and so on), no doubt met with approval at Steventon, but the contrived plot and pedestrian writing cannot have created a favourable impression.[42] Jane nevertheless either continued to lack confidence in her own work or could not see her way to approaching a publisher. Not until 1802–3 was she persuaded, possibly by her brother Henry, to make a fair copy of 'Susan', as the novel was still called, and to allow William Seymour, his legal adviser, to offer it to Richard Crosby and Son of Stationers Hall Court, London, for purchase of copyright. This method may have been chosen because Mrs Cooke had experienced annoying delays in getting her book published by the alternative method of commission.[43] The choice of Crosby and Son was strange, in that the firm was small, not particularly well thought of, and better known for publishing reliable sellers such as reference books and extracts from literature. It can only be assumed that Seymour had contacts there.

The £10 which Crosby paid for the copyright was not generous, but Jane was probably pleased to think that she had at last got her foot on the first step of the publishing ladder without any threat of further expense to herself – especially as she believed that Seymour had been given a guarantee of early publication. In 1803 the novel was advertised in one of Crosby's own journals, *Flowers of Literature*, as being 'in the Press', but time passed and *Susan* did not appear. Eventually years passed. In 1809, in answer to an enquiry from Jane under an assumed name, the firm replied to the effect that there had never been an obligation to publish, early or otherwise; they gave no promise to publish at any time in the future, and threatened to stop her from taking the work elsewhere unless she repaid them their £10 for the copyright.[44] A possible explanation for their behaviour is that, having published one or two gothic novels, they had got cold feet at the thought of offending future authors and purchasers of such works. It seems more likely, however, that the advertisement in *Flowers of Literature* had failed to produce the desired response from persons in the trade (such as suppliers of books to circulating libraries), and Crosby had decided to write off the £10 already paid rather than risk throwing good money after bad.[45] Not until 1816, when four of her novels had appeared in print, did Jane ask Henry to retrieve the manuscript from Crosby, who had already pocketed his £10 when Henry gleefully informed him that the novel he had rejected was by the author of *Pride and Prejudice*.[46]

Jane had by now learnt that the title 'Susan' had already been used by another author, and that she must go through the laborious process of altering the heroine's name to Catherine throughout the manuscript. Having done this, she again put the novel aside, probably because she dared not risk the financial outlay needed to launch it. Not until after her death did Henry once more rescue it from oblivion. He devised a new title for it, but otherwise published it as she had left it; with a sad little preface she had written in 1816, appealing to readers to remember that thirteen years had elapsed since the novel was finished and that 'places, manners, books and opinions' had undergone considerable changes since that time.[47]

Chapter 14

Dread and Terrible Times

Whilst Mrs Austen and her two daughters were visiting Bath, in November 1797, the newspapers available at the Pump Room reported contentious developments in the nation's fortunes. On 10 November the Prime Minister, William Pitt, faced the House of Commons with the news that his attempts to make peace with Revolutionary France had broken down. During the summer months, in spite of opposition from the King, he had felt it his duty 'as an English minister and a Christian' to make every effort to end a war he could see no chance of winning. His country's only remaining ally, Austria, was about to make peace with the enemy; Ireland was on the verge of revolution; the navy was simmering with discontent after recent mutinies; and there seemed little hope of repelling the Dutch army waiting at the Texel for favourable weather to sail for the invasion of Britain. At first, Pitt's peace overtures had seemed likely to succeed, for the French people too were reported to be tired of war. Yet the French government, purged by Bonaparte's troops of those members who were thought to be in favour of peace, had rejected Britain's generous terms. Pitt ended his speech with a rousing call to arms against a power so clearly determined to destroy the nation's liberty. The House rose spontaneously to sing 'Britons Strike Home', but the response from the country as a whole was less unanimous. Whilst Canning tried to stir up hostility to France with a new journal, the *Anti-Jacobin*, Pitt received numerous petitions from county assemblies demanding the dismissal of Ministers for failing to bring an end to the war. Even Hampshire produced a petition from an unruly gathering of 4000 people at Winchester.[1]

The patriotic Austens are more likely to have signed the counter-petition collected shortly afterwards in support of the government. The peace terms, which had envisaged the sacrifice of much that Britain had fought for overseas during the past twenty years, cannot have been popular with a family with colonial and seafaring interests. Jane took to wearing 'a black military feather' in her cap that winter; and Eliza de Feuillide, preparing for marriage with the man she was proud to introduce as *Captain* Henry Austen, added Dibdin's patriotic songs to her cosmopolitan collection – songs which were all the more popular with Jane because so many of them dealt with the sea.[2]

Britain was now the only target left for France's ambitious general. In January 1798, Bonaparte was appointed Commander-in-Chief of the Army of England, and in February British spies reported that he was preparing to transport a huge army across the Channel. His agents spread rumours of great rafts, each capable of carrying two whole divisions complete with artillery and horses and propelled by giant windmills. Eliza was not taken in by such hoaxes, but she knew that the threat of invasion was serious. The government hastily increased the militia from 45,000 to 100,000 men: in March Henry was transferred to Henley-on-Thames to help in the training of the new recruits, over 350 of whom were added to his regiment.[3]

George Austen was now too old to join the multitude of clergy rushing to enlist in their local Volunteer troop, even had he wished to do so. It is a sign of the increasing importance attached to a clergyman's role among his flock that, in April 1798, the archbishops urged members of the clergy to refrain from taking up arms except in dire circumstances. Their task, they were told, was to keep the nation strong in faith, though 'if the danger should be realised and the enemy set foot on our shores, our hand with that of every man must in every way be set against those who come for purposes of rapine and desolation, the vowed champions of anarchy and irreligion, defying the living God'. This was not the image that Bonaparte wished France's troops to possess; but, whilst the massacre of priests in the prisons of Paris in September 1792 was still fresh in people's minds, it was easy for Englishmen to portray their country as a righteous power crusading against the forces of evil. Edmund Burke, in his *Reflections on the Revolution in France*, had argued strongly that church and state stood or fell together. Discussing with the Bishop of Lincoln the sermon to be preached in thanksgiving for the victory over the Dutch fleet at Camperdown, Pitt approved of a text from the Acts of the Apostles, 'Except these abide in the ship, ye cannot be saved', which could be expanded to show that faith in God and devotion to duty were twin weapons in the fight against apparently overwhelming forces. The idea of the clergy – especially the unpretentious country clergy – as the backbone of the nation began from this point to gain ground. It was to be expounded by Edmund Bertram and become an important theme in Jane Austen's *Mansfield Park*.[4]

Bonaparte's anger at hearing of Nelson's victory at Aboukir Bay. A cartoon by
James Gillray, December 1798.

Meanwhile George Austen served his country in a more prosaic way also. The Defence of the Realm Act, rushed through Parliament in April 1798, required parish clergy to submit to the Lord Lieutenant of their county details of the number of able-bodied men in their parish; what service each was prepared to offer and what weapons he could provide; the amount of livestock, grain, mills, carts, boats and barges that were available; the number of aliens that would need to be watched; and the number of elderly and infirm that would have to be evacuated in case of invasion. To the surprise of politicians, who had assumed that the most enthusiastic response would come from rural areas where people had property to defend, many country parsons either proved dilatory or failed to send in returns at all. Not so George Austen, who in his careful handwriting soon assured the Lord Lieutenant that thirty-five able-bodied men from Steventon, out of a total population of 153, would be willing to serve the country in time of danger. This was a higher proportion than any achieved elsewhere in rural Hampshire.[5]

In May 1798 rebellion broke out in Ireland. With few troops available to reinforce the small number on the spot, the government at Westminster invited English militia regiments to volunteer. The majority did so, the Oxfordshires among them;[6] but the Irish rebels, vainly awaiting help from France, were defeated before the regiments could be despatched. During the summer, it was learnt that Bonaparte's troops, instead of sailing for Ireland, had withdrawn from the Channel coast and embarked from Mediterranean ports for Egypt, with Nelson in pursuit. No longer threatened with imminent invasion of England's southern counties, George Austen took a holiday from his unaccustomed work on wartime statistics and in August 1798 accompanied his wife and daughters to Godmersham. They were probably joined there by Henry, on leave of absence from his regiment for the first time in two years.[7] On 2 October, newpapers carried the joyful tidings that on 1–2 August 1798 (a whole two months earlier, such was the difficulty of communications) Nelson had destroyed the French fleet at anchor in Aboukir Bay. Bonaparte and his army were still at large in the Middle East, but for the forseeable future they could not threaten England's shores.

When details of Bonaparte's campaign in Egypt became known in England, radical poets and politicians praised him for initiating an era of science and culture in an area too long exploited by the tyrannical Mameluke Beys, the Egyptian aristocracy which ruled the country in the name of the Turkish Sultan. The patriotic British public, however, looked upon Mamelukes and Turks alike as gallant allies. Things

Egyptian became all the rage. Charles Fowle, trying to think of a suitable gift for his friend James Austen's wife at Deane, bought Mary a Mameluke cap – a fez-like creation – which Jane was allowed to borrow for a Kempshott Ball. 'It is all the fashion now,' she assured Cassandra, 'worn at the Opera, & by Lady Mildmays at Hackwood Balls.'[8]

The whole of the time that these exciting events were taking place in the Mediterranean, Frank Austen was serving as Lieutenant in HMS *London*, on blockade duties outside the port of Cadiz. The tediousness of such a life was too much for the good behaviour of many of the crews, and Frank had stories of fearsome disciplinary measures to relate to the family in later years.[9] On 30 April 1798, the log of the *London* had recorded the arrival of Nelson, returning to duty after a long convalescence from wounds received at Tenerife. Nelson was not looking forward to what promised to be a summer of inactivity off Cadiz, and was delighted when Earl St Vincent, as commander of the fleet, sent him instead to the Mediterranean in search of Bonaparte. Three battleships – not, however, including HMS *London* – went with him. On 27 September the news of his victory at Aboukir Bay was read on the deck of the *London* to the assembled crew, and a month later the men saw Nelson's prizes limping by.[10] It is not known whether Frank grumbled in his letters home, or whether his father realised himself that Frank would never get either promotion or prize money unless he saw more action, but a few weeks later George Austen was found once again trying to pull strings on behalf of his son. Learning from past experience, he applied this time not to Warren Hastings, although the family was still in touch with him and had rejoiced at his acquittal by the House of Lords, but to a more remote acquaintance who had the advantage of access to the First Lord of the Admiralty. James Austen's first wife's father had a niece who was married to Admiral Gambier, a man of deep religious principles and a friend of the First Lord, who might be both willing and able to put in a good word for so dutiful and devout a young man as Frank.[11]

Jane Austen was not on principle averse to seeking patronage, even from so remote a connection. It was the only system she knew and, providing it could be made to work in favour of her deserving brother, it was well and good. In *Mansfield Park*, Fanny Price, who is not only the heroine but the moral exemplar of the novel, is delighted when her brother William is promoted Lieutenant as the result of an equally extended chain of personal approaches; her only regret is that it was her unwelcome admirer, Henry Crawford, who set the process in motion and would almost certainly expect her in return to favour his suit.[12]

Jane was embarrassed, however, when she learnt that her father, within days of writing to Admiral Gambier about Frank, was planning to write again on behalf of his other sailor son, Charles. The Admiral might reasonably regard this as too much, she thought, for Charles was only nineteen and had seen nothing like Frank's length of service. Charles, however, was impatient and perhaps a little spoilt. In 1796 he had set sail under the captaincy of his cousin by marriage, Thomas Williams, for duties in the Channel. In June, the newspapers had carried thrilling accounts of an action in which his 32-gun frigate, *Unicorn*, without loss of life or injury to anyone on board, had kept up a running fight for ten hours with the 44-gun French ship *La Tribune*, finally dismasting her and towing her into port as a prize. Prints had been sold showing the enemy ship enveloped in smoke from the *Unicorn's* broadsides; Thomas Williams had received a knighthood (which prompted Jane to refer to him thereafter as 'His Royal Highness'), and Charles had believed that he was set fair for a career in the limelight. Not so, for as Frank could have told him the navy, even in wartime, was more often engaged in routine duties than in chases and battles. At the end of two years as Lieutenant in the little 16-gun *Scorpion*, Charles was determined to get something bigger.[13]

Jane was sorry that he had begun to feel 'the Dignity of ill-usage'. If he *must* make a fuss, she would have preferred him to write to his former captain, Sir Thomas Williams. The latter had always been on good terms with the family and had recently been brought even closer to them in mutual sorrow over the death of his wife Jane – the cousin Jane who had accompanied the Austen sisters to school.[14] Charles, however, would have none of this. Echoes of his impatience are to be heard in *Mansfield Park*, when Sir Thomas Bertram advises William Price to visit the wealthy Mr Rushworth whom he would find 'sincerely disposed to regard all the connections of our family as his own'.

> 'I would rather find him private secretary to the First Lord than anything else,' was William's only answer, in an under-voice.[15]

In the end, Charles threatened to write in person to the First Lord, and his father, in the hope of forestalling such an unheard of proceedings, sent off another letter to Admiral Gambier. Before a reply could arrive, Charles carried out his threat and wrote to Earl Spencer at the Admiralty – a piece of audacity which Jane fancied would send 'His Serene Highness' into such a passion that he would order some of their heads to be cut off. No such dire result followed, however, and, two days later, news from the Admiral enabled her to write jubilantly to Cassandra:

> Frank is made. He was yesterday raised to the Rank of Commander, & appointed to the *Petterel* [*sic*] sloop, now at Gibraltar ... As soon as you have cried a little for Joy, you may go on and Learn ... that Lieut Charles John Austen is removed to the *Tamar* Frigate.[16]

Charles, as Jane feared, was not quite satisfied with his share of the success, for the *Tamar* was currently being refitted and was not known to be scheduled to leave for any theatre of action. However, on arriving somewhat reluctantly at the Downs to join the ship, he met Sir Thomas Williams, who readily agreed to take him as Second Lieutenant on board his own vessel, the *Endymion*, bound for more rewarding times in the western Mediterranean. For the next eighteen months, Charles had the excitement of attacking enemy gunboats off the coast of Spain and of taking several prizes in hazardous conditions. For one of the latter he received £40 as his share of the prize money and promptly spent some of it on a present for his sisters. Topaz crosses on gold chains were an elaborate choice of ornament for two unpretentious ladies ('We shall be unbearably fine', Jane said); but she cherished her gift as much as Fanny Price cherished the amber cross she received from her sailor brother William, and made sure she thanked Charles for it as well as scolding him.[17]

Frank, meanwhile, in charge of the *Peterel*, had the distinction of being sent with despatches to Admiral Nelson, who began from that time to have an increasingly good opinion of Captain Austen. In June 1799 he took part in an action which resulted in the capture of the French Rear-Admiral Perrée and his squadron whilst attempting to reach Bonaparte's troops marooned in the Middle East; in May 1800 he was appointed Post Captain for driving two French ships onto the rocks off Marseilles and capturing a third, the brig *La Ligurienne*, without damage to the *Peterel* and without the loss of a single member of her crew. In August 1800, whilst serving with Sir Sydney Smith's squadron blockading Alexandria, he set fire to a Turkish ship which had run aground and was in danger of being taken by the French – an exploit which Jane read about in the newspaper kindly handed on by Mr Holder from Ashe Park. The period of time in which Frank described himself to Jane as 'guiltless of prizes' must have been short, for in eighteen months in the *Peterel* he picked off forty small vessels as they crept along the coast between Marseilles and Genoa.[18]

Henry Austen's activities in the militia, which feature in *Pride and*

Prejudice in their early, carefree stage, play no further part in Jane's fiction – perhaps because they fell outside the area in which she trusted herself to write with accuracy. In March 1799 the Oxfordshire Regiment, with two others, sailed for Ireland, where there was still a threat of rebellion and hence a remaining possibility, though slight now, of invasion by the French. The crossing was stormy, but the duties during the nine months that the regiment stayed in the country were of a policing nature and unpleasant rather than dangerous. This would have been the time for Henry to fulfil his earlier ambition to join the Regulars, for Pitt was anxious to start an offensive against the French, and militiamen were given the option of transferring to the army without loss of rank and without purchase money. Thousands accepted the offer, but Henry was now a married man and had no wish to go campaigning in Holland or Egypt. With the militia winding down, it was imperative for him to think of an alternative career. As regimental paymaster he had made a good many contacts in the banking world, and he had always made the best of his socialising opportunities. Eliza, who had something in common with Mrs Elton when it came to name dropping, referred to Lord Charles Spencer, the Colonel of the Oxfordshires, as Henry's 'very good friend'; and mentioned also the pleasing relationship her husband had established with Lord Cornwallis, the Viceroy of Ireland. Capitalising on such contacts, Henry decided to become an army agent and banker. At the end of the year 1800 he paid a short visit to Steventon, where he charmed everybody as usual. On New Year's Day, 1801, he set off for London where he established business premises at St James's and set up house with Eliza in Upper Berkeley Street. He was to flourish as a banker in London throughout the Napoleonic Wars. Jane was both fascinated by him and proud of him. Finance, like trade, was not necessarily a dirty business in her eyes: money, like any other resource, should be made to work. In *Sanditon*, her last (unfinished) novel, she is clearly on the side of Mr Parker, who invests the money from his estate in a speculative enterprise, rather than on that of his brother, Arthur, who lives idly on the interest. By then, however, she was only too well aware that risks were involved and that businesses could fail: Henry became bankrupt in the uncertain times after the war. There is an air of unreality about Mr Parker's enterprise at Sanditon; in spite of Jane's obvious affection for this ebullient character a crash seems certain.[19]

Jane had no doubt heard of Henry's doings in Ireland from Eliza, who had moved from Ipswich to Dorking, near Box Hill in Surrey. She may or may not have written to him herself, for Cassandra was the chief letter writer of the family. Letters were too expensive to allow of more than one person sending the same news if it could possibly be avoided, so Jane took over mainly when Cassandra was away from home, reporting to her as she did so: 'I shall not forget to write to Frank', or 'I will write to Charles soon'. It was as Cassandra's deputy that Jane wrote the family's formal letter of condolence to their cousin Philadelphia Walter when her father died. It was Jane who wrote round to numerous members of the family concerning the birth of a nephew or niece at Godmersham, where Cassandra was in attendance. The task could sometimes be tedious. On 25 November 1798, having written to her mother's girlhood friend Mrs Birch, to her mother's cousin Miss Elizabeth Leigh and to the family's friend Mrs Elizabeth Heathcote, she confessed to Cassandra: 'I am tolerably tired of letter writing, and, unless I have anything new to tell you of my mother or Mary, I shall not write again for many days.' [20]

It was a threat she did not carry out, for she never really tired of writing to her sister. Sometimes her eyes troubled her – they were prone to irritation with dust from a ballroom and to inflamation when she had a cold – but she usually persevered when her correspondent was Cassandra.[21] She had grown closer to her sister after the death of Tom Fowle, almost as though she had found her again after an absence from home. When writing to Cassandra, she could feel that her reactions to people and events mattered: that when she sat against the wall waiting to be asked to dance her observations were important because Cassandra would want to know about them. She could put herself in charge of the situation by analysing ruthlessly the people she saw, as she did at the Hurstbourne Ball in November 1800:

There were very few Beauties, & such as there were, were not very handsome. Miss Iremonger did not look well, & Mrs Blount was the only one much admired. She appeared exactly as she did in September, with the same broad face, diamond bandeau, white shoes, pink husband, & fat neck. The two Misses Coxes were there; I traced in one the remains of the vulgar, broad featured girl who danced at Enham eight years ago ... I looked at Sir Thomas Champneys & thought of poor Rosalie; I looked at his daughter & thought her a queer animal with a white neck. Mrs Warren, I was constrained to think a fine woman, which I much regret.[22]

With Cassandra one could have fun and be a little wicked, knowing that she would not take the remarks too seriously.

Letters were beginning to be regarded as an art form, and as one

especially suited (like novels) to female pens. Jane, like Catherine
Morland, doubted whether women were in fact better than men at the
task, particularly as they were also believed to be worse at grammar
and spelling and to have very little to say, but she liked to pretend that
she was practising the art with a view to future publication. 'I am very
much flattered by your commendation of my last Letter, since I write
only for Fame, and without any view to pecuniary Emolument', she
informed Cassandra in January 1796. Sometimes she made fun of banal
advice on the subject. More often she practised literary conceits –
half-hidden parodies of famous writers such as Mrs Thrale with her
'dear Dr Johnson', or comic inversions as in her announcement of one
of Frank's postings: 'Frank has rec:d his appointment on Board the
Captn John Gore commanded by the Triton'. She indulged in a good
deal of foolery, as when she learnt that John George Children, an
acquaintance at Tonbridge, was about to marry: 'Mr Children's two
Sons are both going to be married, John & George. They are to have
one wife between them.' Cassandra's letters to Jane have not survived,
but it seems she replied in equally light-hearted vein, for Jane frequently
said how much she had laughed at a letter, and on one occasion
described her sister as 'the finest comic writer of the present age'.[23]

Whenever the sisters were apart, they wrote to each other every few
days, often starting another letter as soon as one had been posted off.
Jane sometimes felt she was making too many demands on Cassandra,
but she could not contain her eagerness for a reply. Cassandra seldom
failed her.[24] During Jane's visit to Bath in the summer of 1799 her
Uncle Leigh-Perrot was surprised at the number of letters the sisters
exchanged with each other, possibly because of the expense. Paper was
dear: only a wealthy person such as Mr Darcy could afford to enclose
a letter in an envelope.[25] The general practice was to fold the sheet
(or sheets) in two, leaving a panel on the outside clear for the address,
and to affix a wafer. The cost of postage, which was charged to the
recipient, was calculated in accordance with the number of sheets sent
and the mileage covered: Jane calculated that Martha Lloyd would have
to pay three pence for two leaves quarto sent over the short distance
from Steventon to Hurstbourne Tarrant. With only £20 a year for
personal expenditure, Jane was naturally aggrieved when she was once
charged eight pence for a letter from Godmersham which by her own
calculation should only have cost sixpence; she even felt obliged to
write to the postmaster at Overton about it.[26] Sprawling handwriting
or failure to fill a sheet were causes for apology, since they meant that
the recipient was being charged for short measure. Jane often felt

herself at fault in the matter of untidy handwriting and wished hers was as neat as Cassandra's, but she usually made good use of her space: if she found herself needing a few more lines to finish her news, she employed the common device of writing them upside down between the previous lines. She seldom 'crossed' her letters by writing both horizontally and vertically on the same page, for Cassandra, unlike Miss Bates, could hardly be considered so impecunious as to warrant being burdened with 'all that checker work'.[27]

Letters for Steventon were sometimes delivered to the Wheatsheaf Inn on Popham Lane and had to be fetched from there. More often they were sent via Overton and had to be delivered (or chaperoned, as Jane called it) to the rectory by the post boy. For this there was an extra charge: it was a mark of real thoughtfulness on Sir John Middleton's part to offer to convey the Dashwoods' mail along with his own when driving to and from the post office. Members of Parliament were allowed to send letters free of charge – a privilege which was sometimes the sole reason why Members with business interests entered Parliament. They could extend the favour to their friends by providing them with franks, and Jane, in spite of her dislike of politicians, was known to hide her feelings for the sake of obtaining a 'ditto' (the slang term she sometimes used for a frank): she once told Cassandra that it was worth 'laying out a few kisses' for the purpose. They were both of them grateful when in 1798 their father, who regarded communication between members of the family as very important, offered to reimburse Cassandra for the postal charges she had incurred in receiving letters from Steventon during her lengthy stay in Kent.[28]

Jane's own financial worries may have accounted to some extent for the importance attached to money in her novels, though literary convention was also a factor. A sudden reversal of fortune, actual or threatened, was a standard device in the novels of the time for placing the future of the heroine in jeopardy. Hence when a banking firm in Basingstoke ran into difficulties in the late 1790s Jane wrote facetiously to Cassandra: 'The partnership between Jeffereys Toomer & Legge is dissolved – the two latter are melted away into nothing, & it is to be hoped that Jeffereys will soon break for the sake of a few heroines whose money he may have.'[29] In the three novels Jane wrote at Steventon, she pays lipservice to this convention. The Dashwood sisters in *Sense and Sensibility* are reduced to poverty and driven from their home by the sudden disclosure of the terms of their grandfather's will; the Bennet girls in *Pride and Prejudice* are doomed to future poverty by the entail on their father's estate; and Catherine Morland in *Northanger*

Abbey, although she does not undergo any actual change of fortune, crashes from riches to poverty in General Tilney's imagination. In no case, however, does the financial position of the various heroines ultimately matter: their happiness is not dependent on money. Unfortunately, Jane was unable for a long time to apply this hardest of all Christian messages to her own situation. She worried about money more than her mother or Cassandra did, although all three of them must have known that whenever George Austen died they would be turned out of the parsonage with only their meagre savings to live on, for the Church of England made no provision for clergy widows. Like many people at the time, Jane hoped vaguely for a legacy: infertility rates and early deaths led to many a distant inheritance. In her family's case she felt there were real possibilities. James Austen was generally supposed to be first in line for money from Uncle Leigh-Perrot; and other members of the family, especially Mrs Austen, might reasonably look forward to a small bequest. There was also the Honourable Mary Leigh of Stoneleigh Abbey, elderly and unmarried, who could be considered: her estate was destined to devolve upon the Adlestrop Leighs in the person of the Revd Thomas Leigh, Mrs Austen's cousin, who was himself elderly and childless and had been known to show little acts of generosity to the family at Steventon parsonage. All these hopes were to prove vain, but they occupied the recesses of Jane's mind for a long time. Not until the last few weeks of her life, when she was immeasurably grateful for the loving care she received from the members of her family, did she accept the lesson she had been taught regularly since childhood: 'Take no thought for your life, what ye shall eat, or what ye shall drink; nor yet for your body, what ye shall put on ...'

As the century drew to a close, anxiety about rising costs became, not without reason, a national concern. Pitt had been determined for some time to finance the war as far as possible from annual income rather than from loans, so as not to mortgage the revenue of future governments. To this end, duties on tea, sugar and spirits were increased at an early stage, and others were newly imposed on tallow, wax, indigo and raw cotton. Taxes on horses used for pleasure were joined by others on animals kept for husbandry, which meant that wily gentlemen such as Mr Bennet would no longer be able to escape charges by employing their carriage horses occasionally on the farm. In 1797 the so-called 'assessed' taxes on large houses, windows, carriages, servants, sporting dogs, clocks and watches and a variety of luxury items were tripled and in some cases quadrupled, causing Fanny Burney to block up several windows in her newly-built Camilla Cottage and Eliza de Feuillide (just before her marriage to Henry) to decide that she would have to give up living in London. In lighter vein, the increased cost of hair powder helped to finish off the declining fashion among men for wigs and powdered locks. Amongst Jane Austen's brothers, Edward clung for a while to the old style, which had been associated with Tory respectability, but the younger Charles, eager to be 'up to the knocker', as the phrase went, appeared before admiring friends at Kintbury with his hair 'cropped' and unpowdered.[30]

By March 1798 Parson Woodforde was complaining that 'Pitt's taxes' fell 'very heavy indeed on the Clergy': he hoped fervently that no new ones would be invented. Yet the government needed more money. In December 1798, Pitt offered huge subsidies to Russia, Austria and Prussia in return for a Second Coalition of European Powers against France, and proposed to meet the added burden with an innovative tax on all forms of income. In spite of his intentions the tax, which was self-assessed, fell heaviest on landowners, whose assets were visible. As landowners, the clergy suffered along with the gentry: by 1800 Parson Woodforde's payments had risen to three or four times their pre-war level.[31]

An added burden upon landowners was the increasing level of Poor Rate. The problem was not new. Enclosure had proceeded rapidly in some counties, including rural Hampshire, depriving cottagers of their rights on common land. Competition from factories had almost killed off the spinning of flax and wool by labourers' wives in the home: Jane Austen's nephew could just remember the practice existing at Steventon during his childhood at the end of the century. Families were dependent almost entirely on agricultural wages, which admittedly rose during the war but not as rapidly as prices. Six years of bad harvests increased the price of food beyond the capacity of more and more families to survive unaided. As purchasing power decreased, firms went bankrupt; Jane Austen knew of a few such in Basingstoke. Parish officials, struggling to find jobs for an increasing number of 'able-bodied' as distinct from the usual 'impotent' poor, were glad to see large numbers of them joining the militia, but found that their wives, if left at home, soon became a burden on the Poor Rate. Bounties were offered by the government to men who volunteered for the regular forces, but the money was soon swallowed up and the men's families too were thrown on the rate.[32]

With a government that seemed to have no settled financial policy, and with writers like Malthus suggesting that the problem of the poor was virtually insoluble, gentlemen of ordinary means became wary of unnecessary expenditure. Carriages and horses were given up, and balls and public entertainments became increasingly short of patrons. In December 1798 Jane complained to Cassandra, 'People get so horridly poor & economical in this part of the World, that I have no patience with them. Kent is the only place for happiness. Everybody is rich there'. Two years later she was reporting a rumour that the Assembly Rooms at Canterbury were to close for lack of support.[33]

George Austen was not a man to overreact in such circumstances. Towards the end of 1798 he gave up the carriage he had bought a year or so earlier, but otherwise he made no difference to his lifestyle. Jane regretted the loss of the carriage, which was a status symbol among small-minded persons in country neighbourhoods, as we learn from Mrs Bennet; but she consoled herself for its loss with the thought that the Basingstoke assemblies had declined so much in popularity as to be hardly worth attending. Their demise was due more to changing fashion than to economic hardship, as Jane in her more thoughtful mood may well have acknowledged. Noble families and wealthy persons generally were ceasing to take seriously their duty to attend such neighbourhood gatherings. Mrs Austen signalled the problem shrewdly in a rhyming report she wrote on the Basingstoke assembly as early as 1796:

> It would have been a better dance
> But for the following circumstance;
> The Dorchesters, so high in station,
> Dined out that day, by invitation,
> At Heckfield Heath, with Squire Le Fevre;
> Methinks it is not quite so clever
> For one subscriber to invite
> Another, on assembly night.

As the aristocracy fell off, so did others.[34]

Having given up the carriage, George Austen continued to spend money on items which, though more expensive than they had been before the war, were not a liability in the form of annual taxation. Books, for instance, had been steadily increasing in price throughout the eighteenth century, but he had budgeted for an annual sum of money to go to a Winchester bookseller and he continued to spend it. His choice of reading matter had played an important part in Jane's education and was to continue to have its influence to the end of his ministry. In November 1798 he purchased, in addition to his neighbour's novel *Fitz-Albini*, two of James Boswell's lengthy evocations of the personality and opinions of Samuel Johnson: his *Journal of a Tour to the Hebrides* (published in 1785); and *The Life of Samuel Johnson LL.D*, of which a second edition appeared in 1793. These, rather than any of Johnson's own works, provided the reading public, and probably Jane also, with a knowledge of Johnson's thoughts, prejudices, conversational talents and deeply religious soul-searchings. As there was still some money left with the bookseller, Jane thought that her father would probably spend it on 'Cowper's works'. He apparently did so, for in December he was reading the poems aloud in the evenings, with Jane 'listening when she could'.[35]

Reading aloud to the family became more common as candles became too expensive to allow of everyone having enough light to read by. It resulted in a community of knowledge which Jane reveals again and again in her certainty that other members of her family and of her circle of friends are acquainted with the same books as herself: 'I could not do without a Syringa, for the sake of Cowper's line', she told Cassandra some years later. The poet's skill with words had obviously caught her imagination more than the sight or scent of flowers had ever done: remembering his lines about 'Laburnum, rich in streaming gold; syringa, iv'ry pure' made her think that she would like to have specimens of both shrubs in her garden. Cowper's long poem *The Task*, from which the lines were taken, confirmed in its gentle, meandering way views that many readers in Christian homes already held: that the countryside, unlike the towns, was God's handiwork; that the sights and sounds of England's countryside, more than any other, revealed their creator's beneficent purposes; and that landscape should therefore be treated with respect, not altered ruthlessly for the sake of mere fashion. In this vein, Emma Woodhouse was to gaze appreciatively at what she saw as a typically English scene at Donwell; and Fanny Price, on hearing of plans to employ Repton to cut down the avenue of oaks at Sotherton Court, was to murmur in Cowper's own words, 'Ye fallen avenues! once more I mourn your fate unmerited'.[36]

A surprising move for so unpretentious a man as George Austen was that, in the first year of the new century, he was prevailed upon to buy several pieces of new furniture for the parsonage. Jane Austen's nephew, writing in 1870, imagined that the furniture in his grandfather's house must have been like that in other small houses of the time – both uncomfortable and 'lamentably scanty'.

There would often be but one sofa in the house, and that a stiff, angular, uncomfortable article. There were no deep easy-chairs, nor other appliances for lounging. But perhaps we should be most struck with the absence of those elegant little articles which now embellish and encumber our drawing room tables. We should miss the sliding bookcases and picture stands, the letter-weighing machines and envelope cases, the periodicals and illustrated newspapers.[37]

The inventory of George Austen's furniture made when he left Steventon bears out the conjecture about the lack of sofas and easy chairs, but in other respects there were signs of modernisation. Jane had probably already noticed, in the large houses that she visited, the profusion of small tables and desks that the Musgrove girls were to introduce into their parents' old home in *Persuasion*. The few small pieces of furniture George Austen ordered from Basingstoke were subject to irritating delays, but in November 1800 Jane was finally able to write in great excitement to Cassandra:

> The Tables are come, & give general contentment. I had not expected that they would so perfectly suit the fancy of us all three, or that we should so well agree in the disposition of them; but nothing except their own surface can have been smoother; The two ends put together form our constant Table for everything, & the centre peice stands exceedingly well under the glass; holds a great deal most commodiously, without looking awkwardly. They are both covered with green baize & send their best Love. The Pembroke has got its destination by the sideboard, & my mother has great delight in keeping her Money and papers locked up ... we are now only in want of the chiffoniere, which is neither finished nor come.[38]

None of this expenditure was allowed to interfere with the charitable work incumbent on a clergyman's family. Old Testament writers had regarded charity as a means of softening the discrepancy between rich and poor in a society where the gap was wide. This association with the Bible had linked the act of giving to the poor inseparably with piety, and the Christian church had continued to commend it. In parishes throughout England, the parsonage house traditionally stood open to the poor of the village: according to Mrs Norris, it was unknown how much was consumed in her kitchen 'by odd comers and goers'. Parsons' wives were noted for handing out home-made herbal remedies: Mrs Norris's ministrations to the coachman at Mansfield Park were probably reminiscent of the cures for nose bleeds, stomach upsets, bruises and sprains ('Thieves Vinegar') and general weakness ('Strengthening Jelly') Mrs Austen kept on her shelves. The old partnership

between clergy and landowners, which had once ensured that the peasants did not starve, had broken down in urbanised areas during the
eighteenth century; but it survived in rural counties such as Hampshire,
where landowners and clergy continued to exercise their right of entry
to the cottages of the peasants in order to minister to the sick and
needy and to distribute gifts of food, medicine, clothing and sometimes
money to the poor at Christmas and at times of bad harvest and bad
weather. Needless to say, Lady Catherine de Bourgh and Mr Collins
abuse the right in order to dominate the lives of the villagers.[39]

At Steventon, George Austen acted not only on behalf of the church
but as representative of the absentee landlord – his son Edward. Whilst
he himself wrote letters of recommendation for young people of the
parish seeking jobs, and exhorted parishioners to give generously to
the church's charitable funds, the task of visiting the sick and lonely
and of distributing relief was left, as in most gentry and clergy families,
to the womenfolk. Cassandra was in charge, with Jane taking over and
reporting to her when she was away from home. The two sisters knitted
and sewed during the year, and purchased such items as they could
afford to add to the largesse received from Edward. On Christmas Eve
1798 Jane returned in the morning from a visit to Manydown, and in
the evening wrote to Cassandra:

> Of my charities to the poor since I came home, you shall have a faithful
> account. I have given a p^r of Worsted Stock^{gs} to Mary Hutchins, Dame
> Kew, Mary Steevens & Dame Staples; a shift to Hannah Staples, & a
> shawl to Betty Dawkins; amounting in all to about half a guinea. But I
> have no reason to suppose that the Battys *would* accept of anything,
> because I have not made them the offer.

Earlier in the year Dame Tilbury's daughter had lain in and Jane had
written to Cassandra to ask if she should give her some of their stock
of baby clothes. Worsted stockings were apparently the main standby
for older women: in October 1800 Jane took the precaution of buying
ten pairs when she passed by the shop at Oakley. She also bought a
shift for Betty Dawkins, having discovered that she preferred it to the
rug she had been offered.[40]

Apart from a passage in *Emma* describing a charitable visit to a
labourer's cottage, Jane Austen notoriously says little or nothing about
the poor in her novels. It seems that she shared Emma Woodhouse's
attitude to her duties: she was competent, conscientious and sensitive
to individual wants and deserts, but also unromantic and almost professional in her refusal to become emotionally involved. 'I hope it may

be allowed', says Emma to Harriet, 'that if compassion has produced exertion and relief to the sufferers, it has done all that is truly important. If we feel for the wretched, enough to do all we can for them, the rest is empty sympathy, only distressing to ourselves.'[41]

Jane was not always satisfied with her own efforts, especially at visiting. On one occasion she confessed to Cassandra:

> I called yesterday on Betty Londe, who enquired particularly after you, and said she seemed to miss you very much, because you used to call upon her very often. This was an oblique reproach at me, which I am sorry to have merited, and from which I will profit.

She sometimes found it difficult, too, to keep up with another kind of social duty: that of paying calls upon those families which set the tone of the neighbourhood and conducted its political and religious life. She knew only too well that neighbours could be tedious, nosy, interfering and downright mischievous; she could sympathise with Marianne Dashwood's attitude to the Middletons. She sometimes regarded her mother's insistence on visiting as one of her more annoying habits: 'We have been exceedingly busy since you went away', she told Cassandra one autumn.

> In the first place we have had to rejoice two or three times every day at your having such delightful weather for the whole of your Journey – & in the second place we have been obliged to take advantage of the delightful weather ourselves by going to see almost all our Neighbours. On Thursday we walked to Deane, Yesterday to Oakley Hall & Oakley, & to day to Deane again.

Yet she recognised, like Elinor Dashwood, that it was 'civility' that made life bearable in small communities. She once deferred setting off on a visit to Ibthorpe because the neighbourhood expected to see her at a local gathering.[42]

It has sometimes been wondered why Jane, after completing 'Susan' in the summer of 1799, attempted no more novels for a number of years. It may have been because, for a part of this time, her brother Henry, on whose opinion she very much relied, was either away in Ireland or engaged in winding up his affairs in the militia; the family at Steventon saw little of him. Or it could simply have been because she was very busy. In addition to charitable and neighbourly duties, her sewing continued to be in demand for members of her family: her brother Charles, back in port after two years at sea, demanded that she send him shirts by the half dozen, as soon as they were finished.[43]

Meanwhile, her mother had begun to value her services as nurse and housekeeper during Cassandra's lengthy absences in Kent. During Mrs Austen's many illnesses, real and imagined, she was glad to have Jane on hand to dole out the medicine and consult the doctor about possible remedies she had heard of, such as dandelion tea. She even came to think better of Jane's housekeeping abilities than had once been the case:

> I had the dignity of dropping out my mother's Laudanum last night, I carry about the keys of the Wine & Closet; & twice since I began this letter, have had orders to give in the Kitchen ...

Jane reported during one of her mother's 'visitations'. Before long she was priding herself on having ordered a meal which she had no reason to be ashamed of when the doctor unexpectedly stayed to dinner. To Cassandra she decribed her housekeeping abilities jokingly as her 'chief excellence'.[44] She was already more or less permanently in charge of the household's wine and beverage supplies. The beverage drunk at the parsonage was mainly tea, with some coffee being kept for visitors and for Edward when he stayed a night or so. Maintaining supplies of tea required attention and forethought, since tea came from China and was expensive – sixteen to eighteen shillings a pound for the better brands, which could only be obtained in London. Cheaper tea such as Bohea, which was produced by mixing in sloe, liquorice, ash or elder leaves, or even used tea leaves, might be sold for half a crown, but even this was kept in locked tea caddies and used sparingly.[45]

George Austen did not have the problem which faced Parson Woodforde when Pitt's taxes, combined with the hazards of war in the Channel, caused the local smuggler to put up his prices, for the Austen family did not drink spirits and the household produced its own wine. Fruit was harvested from the garden and glebe and processed in the outhouses. The state of the fruit trees thus became one of Jane's major concerns. Gardening had long been recommended by educational pundits and conduct writers as 'a truly feminine amusement', bringing rewards both practical and spiritual, but Jane refused to be interested in growing flowers; it is in one of Henry Tilney's teasingly didactic moods that she has him recommend a love of flowers to Catherine Morland. At the parsonage it was taken for granted that flowers were Cassandra's concern; Jane willingly collected plants for her from the neighbours, but her own interest was in fruit. On arriving home from Godmersham, in October 1798, she at once enquired from the servants as to whether there was any late fruit in the garden. She also genuinely loved trees, which had begun to be valued by many people for their beauty rather than merely for their economic value since Gilpin published his book on *Forest Scenery* in 1791. She therefore took a great interest in her father's plans in 1800 for new developments in the garden.

Many clergy towards the end of the eighteenth century were busy trying to copy on a small scale in their parsonage gardens the Natural Style fashionable on large estates. A favourite scheme, adopted by Parson Woodforde at Weston Longeville and Henry Tilney at Woodston, was to take a part of the glebe and transform it from pasture into shrubbery and wilderness. With his sons away, and no pupils to feed, George Austen embarked on a similar design. The bank along the Elm Walk was to be sloped down and planted on one side with shrubs and on the other with forest trees such as larch, beech and mountain ash. A month later, however, he had been persuaded, probably by his wife, to consider planting fruit rather than forest trees. Nothing had been done when a great storm swept the locality in November 1800 and distressed Jane by wreaking havoc among the already existing trees, sweeping one huge elm into the drive and another into the screen of firs and chestnuts at the front of the house, where it beheaded a spruce fir and brought down a host of branches from the chestnuts. Even so, work began on the planting of fruit trees rather than larch or birch, fruit trees being the more immediately profitable.[46]

Whatever else was happening, time and money were regularly found for Mrs Austen and one or both of her daughters to visit relatives at a distance. In the summer of 1799, Jane and her mother had no sooner arrived home from Bath than there was a round of visits to clergy relatives in their parsonage houses: to Thomas Leigh and his sister Elizabeth at Adlestrop; Samuel Cooke and his wife in their spacious yellow brick vicarage at Great Bookham; and Edward Cooper and his growing family at Harpsden. Jane did not necessarily like these people. She was fond of Elizabeth Leigh, who was Cassandra's godmother, but she had mixed feelings about the Revd Thomas Leigh, whose determination to cut a figure in the world by employing Humphry Repton to landscape his garden was probably the origin of her scathing remarks about the latter in *Mansfield Park*. As for Samuel Cooke and his wife, she had hoped against hope that something would happen to prevent the visit – although it is difficult to know what she found wrong with them, except that the one was a fusspot and the other hypochondriac. It was Edward Cooper who was her prime bugbear, however. Edward had been good fun in his younger days, but as curate of Harpsden he had become, in Jane's view, pompous and insensitive. He was noted already for preaching Evangelical sermons of a kind he was to publish in large quantity in subsequent years. Jane could neither like nor approve of Evangelicals, by whom she meant not Methodists, with whom she seems to have been unacquainted, but the Evangelizing wing of the Church of England founded by Wilberforce. She disliked their emotional preaching, which was designed, like Wesley's, to appeal to the unconverted (a term they applied to the larger number of lukewarm Christians who attended church regularly). Jane could not see the need for anybody to be 'regenerated' or 'born again': in her view, they merely needed to correct their faults.[47]

In spite of these reservations, she was prepared to carry out her family duties. She once said that she 'liked first cousins to *be* first cousins, & interested about each other', so she probably felt she had to visit them.[48] Fortunately, she loved travelling. Even a tragic incident, such as the death of her cousin Jane Cooper in a carriage accident on the Isle of Wight, left no fears: the more hazardous she could say a journey had been, the more she revelled in it. She always admired the countryside through which she drove on her ten and a half hour journey from London to Godmersham, and nothing would have delighted her more than to go on a 'Picturesque Tour', visiting Derbyshire or the Lake District and calling at stately homes to ask the housekeeper to show her round. She had never seen the celebrated Picturesque areas of the country, and sometimes laughed at her own prejudices regarding them: in *Northanger Abbey*, Catherine Morland, even when she has been enlightened as to the unreality of gothic novels, is inclined to think that they might have some application to the 'northern and western extremities' of the country.[49] She would have loved to visit Scotland to see the 'Lakes & Mountains', although she had no doubt imbibed Johnson's hostile views of the Scots.[50]

Unfortunately, she had neither the money nor the male companionship needed for such a journey. She could indulge her love of the countryside only by taking long walks whenever opportunity offered. Cassandra was seldom equal to such strenuous exercise, and Jane was therefore doubly looking forward, in November 1800, to visiting Martha Lloyd at Ibthorpe, in the hillier northern part of Hampshire. In the event, the weather kept the two friends indoors for most of the time, but Jane could still write excitedly to Cassandra:

> Martha has promised to return with me & our plan is to [have] a nice black frost for walking to Whitchurch, & there throw ourselves into a

postchaise, one upon the other, our heads hanging out at one door & our feet at the opposite.

It was when they arrived at the parsonage that Jane received the shock of her life. The story as handed down by the family is that, as soon as Mrs Austen heard the carriage arrive at the gate, she rushed into the hall and greeted the two young ladies with: 'Well, girls, it is all settled, we have decided to leave Steventon ... and go to Bath'; whereupon Jane fainted away.[51]

Chapter 15

Leaving Steventon

No one has ever been able to explain for a certainty why George Austen decided to leave Steventon and move to Bath. He was approaching seventy, but there was no rule of the Church of England which would then have obliged him to retire from his duties, let alone vacate his house. Unless condemned by an ecclesiastical court for improper conduct, a parson could retain his benefice to the end of his life. With the permission of his bishop (not difficult to obtain), he could at any time resign his duties to a curate: many did so from the beginning of their incumbency whilst others, like Dr Shirley in *Persuasion*, remained at the helm into a frail old age. Having appointed a curate, he could either give up the parsonage house to the latter or continue to live in it himself and leave the curate to find alternative accommodation anywhere within reach of the church. George Austen's decision was to retain his benefice, transfer his duties at Steventon wholly to James as his curate, give up his house to the latter and appoint a new curate to take up residence at Deane.

According to Frank Austen, his father retired because he felt 'too incapacitated from age and increasing infirmities to discharge his parochial Duties in a manner satisfactory to himself'.[1] Frank was writing long after the event, however, and may simply have been imagining, from the standpoint of a different age, why his father acted as he did. There is no evidence that George Austen was in anything but fine fettle. With James in charge at Deane, his religious obligations, in a parish which contained a mere 153 souls, were not heavy. Admittedly, the secular burdens laid on a parish priest had increased significantly with the war, but George Austen had carried out his share with exemplary efficiency and (unlike Parson Woodforde) without any sign that they weighed on his mind. As the invasion threat subsided, food shortage took its place as the country's major concern. No sooner had George Austen handed in statistics of the men and materials that would be available in case of attack than he was required to report on the amount of land under cultivation in his parish should famine strike elsewhere. He complied as readily with this new demand as he had done with the others: for the year 1801 he noted that farmers in Steventon were cultivating 267 acres of wheat, 250 acres of barley, 250 acres of oats, sixty acres of turnips or rape, twelve acres of peas and one and a half acres of potatoes. The Austens themselves were amongst the few people to cultivate potatoes, which were considered a luxury by the villagers.[2]

Much has been made of financial anxieties as a reason for George Austen's retirement. Incomes from agriculture fluctuated wildly during the 1790s, with good and bad harvests and with the movement of militia regiments causing increased demand in areas where they were stationed. Yet apart from a single reference by Jane, in November 1800, to her father's disappointment at the profits from his farm, there is no evidence that economic factors played a part in his decision. Like many other farmers, he had probably nursed inflated hopes for that year. Even if his income from farming had been a consideration, it would have had to be weighed against other factors. On leaving Steventon he would need to employ two curates instead of one. He would have to pay for accommodation in Bath for himself, his wife and his two daughters instead of enjoying a rent-free parsonage house. Moreover, his income would still be dependent on agricultural yields and prices. There were no pensions for retired clergy: his only regular source of income would be the tithe, which as rector he would continue to receive. In the days when he was running a school and a farm, he had taken few pains over collecting tithes; now that he was retiring he needed to make a push to ensure that he would receive his proper dues for land newly taken into cultivation or changed from one type of cultivation to another. This was a tedious and time-consuming task, and one which might also have been unpleasant.[3]

In spite of frequent contacts with members of the Austen family, James Leigh-Perrot and his wife were so surprised by their brother-in-law's decision to leave Steventon that they imagined it must have been occasioned by some recent development of a confidential nature, such as the desire to extricate Jane from an undesirable love affair. Speculation failed to reveal a likely suspect, but the decision must indeed have been sudden, for George Austen had not only recently bought new furniture for his house but had started on major works in the garden.

Other members of the family could have told the Leigh-Perrots that George Austen was one of those placid people who could easily allow things to go on as usual for long enough and then suddenly decide to make a change. His wife may have been urging him for some time to leave his parish and move to Bath. Between bouts of vigorous activity, Mrs Austen enjoyed a good deal of ill-health.

> My Mother continues hearty, her appetite & nights are very good, but her Bowels are still not entirely settled, & she sometimes complains of an Asthma, a Dropsy, Water in her Chest & a Liver Disorder ...

Jane wrote in December 1798. At such times Mrs Austen no doubt thought how much better off she would be in Bath, with its many doctors, than at Steventon, where Mr Lyford had to be fetched from Basingstoke.[4] In other respects, too, life in a tiny village had its problems. Servants of a tolerable standard were hard to get, yet they were required to work on a variety of tasks from churning butter and brewing beer to serving at table. Nanny Hilliard was the prop and stay of the establishment at Steventon. When she was ill, two charwomen had to be employed to do her work, 'which is not very comfortable', Jane confessed. When Dame Bushell left her job as washerwoman, Dame Steevens, who took her place, hardly inspired confidence: 'She does not look as if anything she touched would ever be clean', Jane said. Debility and general ill-health were rampant in the villages: James Austen at Deane doubted whether a girl his wife had taken on as her 'scrub' would be strong enough for the task, whilst another whom she hired shortly afterwards 'jilted' her to go elsewhere. At Bath, with its many shops, the Austen household would not have to grow or otherwise produce every item of food and drink consumed, and the few servants needed for domestic chores would be easier to obtain in a city with crowded working-class areas.[5]

Mrs Austen, like many women at the time, regarded herself upon marriage as having sacrificed all her friends and home comforts to follow her husband into a far country. It was something Darcy had to consider before asking Elizabeth Bennet to marry him: would she be prepared to leave Hertfordshire for Derbyshire? '*You* cannot have a right to such very strong local attachment. *You* cannot have been always at Longbourn', he suggests hopefully. Mrs Austen had been happy enough at Steventon whilst her children were growing up, but now that most of them had left home she hankered after her roots. She had not spent many of her early years at Bath, but she had married from there, and her brother James and his wife lived there for half the year. She believed (not unreasonably, though as it turned out, wrongly) that her own wealthy relations, properly cultivated, might prove a help to her if she became a widow. A few days before Jane left for her visit to Ibthorpe, her mother heard that a distant relative, Lady Saye and Sele, was about to move to Bath. This could easily have set her going once more on her recurrent theme.[6]

Cassandra, Frank, Charles and Henry were all away from home when George Austen made his crucial decision. Besides his wife, the only persons near enough at hand to have influenced him were his eldest son and daughter-in-law at Deane. It is noticeable that Mary was careful to be present when the news was broken to Jane. James had been designated in Thomas Knight's will as the next incumbent at Steventon, but the couple had much to gain without waiting for George Austen to die. In addition to his stipend as curate, James would be able to take over the glebe. His father could have continued to farm it through an agent, or rented it out for his own profit, but it seems he was content to hand it over to James, who would be able to use it to graze his horses. Perhaps even more important to Mary was the opportunity to move from Deane into the roomier and more prestigious parsonage house at Steventon. Space had been a problem at Deane ever since her baby was born. When Martha and Jane stayed there for a night in 1799, in order to be able to get a lift from James to the Kempshott Ball, they had to sleep together in a 'shut-up bed' whilst nurse and baby slept on the floor beside them. Jane thought it great fun, but other guests might not. Mary had become socially ambitious since her marriage, describing the only spare bedroom at Deane as 'the Nursery', employing a nursemaid to wheel out the baby in his pram, copying baby clothes worn by her well-off nieces and nephews at Godmersham, subscribing to a circulating library (although according to Jane she never read a book in her life), driving about in her own carriage and giving dinner parties for the local gentry. Mrs Austen had never thought it necessary to show off her aristocratic connections to her neighbours, although she was proud of them in her way. Mary, with less confidence than her mother-in-law, believed she had to keep up appearances.[7]

Although Jane had never been so delighted with Bath as to wish to live there, she had not yet conceived the dislike of it she was to feel later. She had but recently finished writing a novel which, whilst indicating the city's drawbacks, did full justice to its amenities. In that same novel, however, the heroine, like many another young woman, had been taken to Bath to find a husband. Was this one of the reasons why Jane's parents had decided to go there – so that she could find a husband? If so, it was the first indication they had given that she had disappointed them. She had for some time been aware that she was not immediately attractive to young men: they hardly flocked to her side at balls as they did to Eliza's. After an evening at Kempshott Park in January 1799, she wrote ruefully to Cassandra:

> I do not think I was very much in request. People were rather apt not to ask me [to dance] till they could not help it. There was one Gentleman, an officer of the Cheshire, a very good looking young Man, who I was told wanted very much to be introduced to me: but as he did not want it quite enough to take much trouble effecting it, We never could bring it about.[8]

She was now approaching twenty-five. Her parents were perhaps hoping that in Bath she would meet some older clergyman who had just acquired a parish and needed a wife.

Whatever they thought about their parents' decision to move to Bath, Jane and Cassandra had no alternative but to go too. Cassandra, with her more placid disposition, probably found it easier to acquiesce than Jane, but the latter soon began to make the best of it, as was her duty. If there had been any letters in which she expressed her resentment, Cassandra destroyed them: a few appear to be missing for the month of December 1800. Those which followed, in January and February 1801, reveal her efforts at composure whilst trying to help her father to cope with the problems created by the move.[9] By January she was searching for arguments in favour of leaving Steventon. 'I get more and more reconciled to our removal', she assured Cassandra. 'We have lived long enough in this Neighbourhood, the Basingstoke Balls are certainly on the decline, there is something interesting in the bustle of going away, & the prospect of spending future summers by the Sea or in Wales is very delightful.' She was aware that her parents would not be able to do more than rent accommodation in Bath, possibly on short-term leases only. This too she tried to see positively: 'For a time we shall now possess many of the advantages which I have often thought of with Envy in the wives of Sailors or Soldiers', she wrote.[10]

Seaside holidays were becoming fashionable, yet the Austens had never taken one. Her parents could perhaps now be prevailed upon to accept the pressing invitation they had had from Mr Austen's former pupil Richard Buller, son of the Bishop of Exeter, to visit him in his Tudor parsonage house at Colyton. From there, they could perhaps travel on to Dawlish, which they had for some time talked of visiting. Sidmouth had been heard of as a good centre: Jane asked Cassandra to find out about it from one of Edward's in-laws, who apparently knew it well. These were dreams which came true: during the five years Jane lived in Bath she became acquainted with much of the Dorset and Devon coastline. She became fond of sea-bathing, in spite of its rigours: at Lyme in 1804 she stayed so long in the water during the morning that she was tired out by the middle of the day. With her usual perception, she realised that seaside resorts were not so much natural beauty spots as speculative ventures on the part of businessmen, who promoted their health-giving facilities and social amenities in brochures whose language she parodied to perfection in her last, unfinished, novel.[11]

As soon as Mrs Austen knew she was moving to Bath, she became lively and well. Her mind began to run excitedly on the subject of servants, with Jane reporting her ideas in an accurately garbled form to Cassandra:

> We plan having a steady Cook, & a young giddy Housemaid, with a sedate, middle-aged Man, who is to undertake the double office of Husband to the former and sweetheart to the latter. No Children of course to be allowed on either side.[12]

Mr Austen, who had weightier matters to occupy his mind, was wisely not informed of these ambitions. A clergyman leaving a parish had a great deal to settle. George Austen's immediate concern was to extricate himself from the lease on his farm at Cheesedown, which had not yet run out, and to provide if possible for his steward John Bond, who had served him faithfully and well for many years. He did not welcome the prospect of applying to the owner of the land, William Portal, to terminate the lease prematurely, especially since it would mean that the farm could then pass to a tenant such as Mr Harwood, who already had a steward. John Bond boasted that he would have no difficulty in finding another place, and indeed it was not long before Harry Digweed offered to take him on as manager of his estates at Steventon – a prospect which delighted Jane, who knew that Harry would be a generous employer. Unfortunately, it would have meant John Bond leaving his cottage on the farm at Cheesedown, and Bond, who was in his early sixties, had no wish to move. The problem was solved for the time being when Mr Holder of Ashe Park agreed to take on the farm until the lease ran out and to employ Bond on the same terms as before. Jane was not entirely happy with this makeshift solution, but John Bond seemed satisfied and there was no more that could be done.[13]

Meanwhile, her father had the task of making satisfactory arrangements for the parish of Deane. His first concern was to put in hand any repairs that were necessary to the parsonage house, so that when he died his executors would not have to deal with claims for 'dilapidations' from his successor. Fortunately, these were assessed at little more than £100, James having taken good care of the place. It was to be offered to the new curate, so that he would have no excuse for non-residence, and the next task, therefore, was to find a suitable appointee ready to move in. In spite of the glut of clergy seeking posts, the curacy at Deane proved surprisingly difficult to fill – the reason being that a country parson did not immediately advertise: he considered his acquaintance. George Austen first of all approached Peter Debary, the son of his old friend, the vicar of Hurstbourne Tarrant; but Peter had lived long enough in a village and now hankered after a more exciting life. To Jane's disgust he turned down her father's offer on the grounds that Deane was not near enough to London. George Austen then felt obliged to offer the post to James Digweed, currently living with his parents at Steventon Manor. Since his ordination in 1797, James had been helping out at the church at Steventon. The curacy at Deane would give him a house – an important factor if, as rumour had it, he was planning to marry. However, he too seems to have turned it down, perhaps because he agreed with Jane that it would be better for him to look for a curacy which offered £75 a year (as happened in some wealthier areas) rather than the statutory £50, which was all her father could afford.

The next candidate in line was the Revd Henry Rice, who had recently become engaged to Madam Lefroy's daughter Lucy and was hoping to marry in the summer. Lucy's father had engaged him as his curate at Ashe, and he was currently living in lodgings in Andover: the curacy at Deane would double his income and give him a house in which to install his bride. The appointment of Rice sounds so obvious a step that one wonders why George Austen had placed him only third on his list. Perhaps he already suspected that the charming Henry's gambling debts were not altogether the fault of a tight-fisted mother but were signs of a deeply engrained habit. Jane was inclined to be critical of the widowed Mrs Rice, who was rumoured to be threatening to cut off her son's allowance unless he returned to live near her at Canterbury, but she may have had her reasons: by 1812 her son was so deeply in debt that he had to flee the country to escape his creditors. Whatever threats his mother made in 1801, Henry Rice took the curacy at Deane and escaped her domineering ways at the cost of placing himself at the mercy of two equally domineering women: Mary Austen at Steventon and Mrs Lefroy at Ashe. Jane foresaw what would happen: 'It will be an amusement to Mary to superintend their Household management, & abuse them for expense, especially as Mrs L. means to advise them to put their washing out', she wrote wickedly.[14]

Jane was hopeful that the installation of the Rices at Deane would at least solve another of their problems – that of finding a place for the maidservant, Nanny Hilliard. Mrs Hilliard's husband and child lived nearby: at Steventon parsonage she had been luckier than many women domestics in that she could look forward to having the child with her on occasions (admittedly rare) when the whole family went away. She had some thoughts of giving up service now that the Austens were leaving, but her husband did not think it wise for her to do so 'in times such as these'. She hinted that she would be prepared to go with the Austens to Bath, but they were hoping to employ more of a maid-of-all-work. It suddenly occurred to Jane that 'Mrs H. Rice's place would be very likely to do for her. It is not many, as she is herself aware, that she is qualified for'.[15] The idea came to nothing, however, and Mrs Hilliard had to go to London to find work.

There was much discussion between Jane and her parents, and with Cassandra by correspondence, as to where to live in Bath. They were united in wishing to avoid Axford Buildings (a continuation of the Paragon), which they knew would be Mrs Leigh-Perrot's choice for them. Mrs Austen was persuaded by a neighbour that Westgate Buildings was a pleasant prospect, but Cassandra was against it and her view prevailed with her father. Mrs Austen then fell back on her earlier choice of Queen's Square, for which she solicited support from her brother, James Leigh-Perrot. Mr Austen, who at first had seemed indifferent as to where they lived, gradually got more interested and began to require 'a comfortable & creditable looking house'. Like Jane and Cassandra (and perhaps in support of their views) he fancied the environs of Laura Place. 'It would be very pleasant to be near Sydney Gardens!' Jane wrote. 'We might go into the Labyrinth every day.' [16]

They had been invited to stay with the Leigh-Perrots at the Paragon until they found somewhere suitable, but meanwhile their discussions served to turn their minds into positive channels. The sad business of leave-taking had begun all too early: from January, hardly a day passed without visitors coming to say goodbye. The ladies of the neighbour-hood were only too eager to take over Mrs Austen's stock of poultry – a carriage load of ladies from Manydown and Deane arrived solely for the purpose. James and Mary could hardly wait to get their parents off the premises: they took away at once one of the two horses they had been promised, '& everything else I suppose will be seized by degrees in the same manner', wrote Jane bitterly.[17]

Cassandra, who was at Godmersham when the news of the pending move was broken to Jane, remained there for another nine or ten weeks, leaving her sister to safeguard her concerns at Steventon. Jane reported in January that most of the pictures in the house, including the large painting of the battle of 1565 between the Swedes and the Poles which hung over the chimney-piece in the rectory dining room, the portraits of former pupils given to George Austen by grateful parents, '& all the old heterogeneous, miscellany, manuscript, Scriptural pieces' were to be left for James. She had ensured, however, that Cassandra would be able to keep her own drawings and a few other items of special interest to her, such as a couple of paintings on tin. Cassandra, for her part, joined Mrs Austen in advising Jane on what to do with her own possessions: she should give a particular piece of furniture to Anna; a particular book to Fanny, and so on. Jane was slightly annoyed, and refused to have generosity dictated to her; but she ended by giving the items away after all.[18]

In her determination to make the best of a situation she could not avoid, Jane remembered that heroines were supposed to be desolated when torn from home. 'It must not be generally known ... that I am not sacrificing a great deal in quitting the Country – or I can expect to inspire no tenderness, no interest in those we leave behind', she wrote in mock seriousness.[19] In fact she sacrificed a great deal: her piano, her most cherished items of furniture and her books. She was to be without a piano for five or six years. Her parents thought at first of taking some of their furniture with them – beds, especially, and perhaps a sideboard and a table or two – but they soon decided that it would be better to sell the lot, along with the farm stock and the equipment from the outhouses and stables, and buy whatever they wanted when they got to Bath. James Bayle, cabinet maker and furniture dealer from Winchester, arrived on 16 January 1801 to begin making an assessment, but found that there was too much to get through in the short winter days and left the job until the spring. The business was thereupon taken out of his hands and entrusted to Benjamin Stroud of Newbury, who advertised the sale for 5–7 May 1801. Jane was disappointed to learn that the new tables fetched only eleven guineas. She was satisfied with the eight guineas given for the piano, although it was probably worth more.[20] It is not clear how much money was obtained, either for her father's books or for her own: Jane had wanted James to take all their father's books at half a guinea a volume, but he does not appear to have done so. One way or another, all the books went. Jane was never again to have so large a collection at her disposal: in later years she was to be almost entirely dependent on circulating libraries and book societies.

Among the many decisions that she had to make was the perennial one regarding clothes. Her pink gown, she said, would last out her time at Steventon but no longer. She would need two new gowns for the summer, one of which would be needed on arrival at Bath and should be 'of plain brown cambric muslin, for morning wear'. Would Cassandra please buy the material on her way through London from Godmersham? Her mother wanted a similar gown, so would Cassandra buy *two* lengths of material, one seven yards long for her mother and the other seven and a half yards for the slightly taller Jane, both dark brown but slightly different in shade so as to allow for discussion as to which was the prettier? At one stage, Mrs Austen had thought of having a mourning gown made up also, and had asked Cassandra (via Jane) to match a length of material she already had in the drawer, but she changed her mind and the material was put away again.[21]

There was doubt to the end as to when and in what order the family would leave Steventon. Cassandra returned from Godmersham sometime in February but left again not long afterwards for Ibthorpe and Kintbury. George Austen went to London to settle a number of bills and took the opportunity to spend a fortnight in Kent. It seems, therefore, that it was left to Jane, with her mother, to close the doors of the parsonage for the last time on 3 May 1801 and leave for Bath. The fine weather, in which she usually rejoiced, could do nothing on this occasion to dispel her sadness.

Jane Austen spent the next five years of her life in Bath. The suspicion that her failure to marry had worried her parents and contributed to their decision to move from Steventon may account for her strange behaviour the following year. During the evening of 2 December 1802, when she was visiting her friend Catherine Bigg for the first time since moving to Bath, she received a proposal of marriage from Catherine's brother Harris and accepted it. He was not in love with her, but it was his duty to marry, and as a shy young man he turned confidently to Jane, who was six years his senior and whom he had known since childhood. His unmarried sisters may have encouraged him, for Jane had long been their friend and could be relied upon not to turn them out of the house when Harris inherited his father's estate at Manydown. His manners and appearance were not prepossessing, and Jane had never been on terms of more than ordinary friendliness with him, but she knew him to be respectable and reliable. As her niece afterwards remarked, 'a great many would have taken him *without* love'. On the one evening when he made his proposal, Jane perhaps believed that she would grow to like him enough to make marriage with him tolerable. The night brought different counsel, however, and she withdrew her promise in the morning. Whatever welcome Harris's sisters had given to the match, Jane would probably have been regarded by the neighbourhood as marrying above her station and as trapping a man much younger than herself into marriage in order to avoid being left on the shelf.[22]

Accompanied by Cassandra, she left Manydown at once and fled to Steventon, where the startled James was prevailed upon to escort her home at once to Bath. The affair continued for a while to cause her some distress, but she was relieved by her decision and thereafter she stuck to her principles. Many years later, Cassandra divulged to her niece that a young man whom they had met on holiday in Devonshire had been attracted to Jane and she to him, but he had died suddenly before the relationship could develop.[23] The encounter was too brief to leave deep scars. Unresentful and without cause for self-reproach, Jane like Cassandra remained unmarried.

For the first three years, George Austen's determination to have a 'comfortable and creditable house' resulted in his taking out a short-term lease on No. 4, Sydney Place. The house was not quite in 'the Environs of Laura Place', which he had previously fancied; but it was even nearer to Sydney Gardens, whose trees and lawns could be seen from all the principal windows. There were holidays each year at the seaside, including Lyme, whose scenery Jane was to describe in glowing terms in *Persuasion*.[24] Unfortunately, the lease ran for only three and a half years. In the autumn of 1804 the family moved to Green Park Buildings, a situation they had previously rejected on the grounds that the houses were probably damp. There, on the morning of Monday, 21 January 1805, George Austen died.

Jane wrote off at once to Frank – a fine, controlled letter such as might be thought suitable for a deeply religious man to receive on such an occasion:

> Our dear Father has closed his virtuous & happy life, in a death almost as free from suffering as his Children could have wished ... Heavy as is the blow, we can already feel that a thousand comforts remain to us to soften it. Next to that of the consciousness of his worth & constant

preparation for another World, is the remembrance of his having suffered, comparatively speaking, nothing.[25]

Next day, she discovered in a letter newly arrived from Frank that his ship was not at Dungeness, as she had supposed, but was on its way to Portsmouth; so she wrote again. By this time her distress was apparent:

> Everything I trust & beleive was done for him that was possible! It has been very sudden! – within twenty four hours of his death he was walking with only the help of a stick, was even reading! We had however some hours of preparation, & when we understood his recovery to be hopeless, most fervently did we pray for the speedy release which ensued. To have seen him languishing long, struggling for Hours, would have been dreadful! – & thank God! we were all spared from it. Except the restlessness & confusion of high Fever, he did not suffer & he was mercifully spared from knowing that he was about to quit the Objects so beloved, so fondly cherished as his wife and Children ever were. His tenderness as a Father, who can do justice to?[26]

James and Henry attended the funeral at Walcot church a few days later (ladies did not attend funerals, Edward remained at Godmersham, Charles was far away in Nova Scotia and Frank unable to leave his ship). During the next few weeks the brothers consulted each other about the future of their 'dear trio' of womenfolk. Henry agreed to act as banker. Mrs Austen's small investments, along with the interest from the £1000 Tom Fowle had left Cassandra, were expected to yield about £200–250 a year. James offered another £50, which Henry agreed to match. Frank wanted to give £100 a year, but Mrs Austen would take only £50. Edward, it seems, was expected to give at least £100 a year. Henry, optimistic as ever, but in terms uncomfortably reminiscent of John Dashwood discussing his step-mother's prospects in the second chapter of *Sense and Sensibility*, pointed out to to the others that the ladies would have £450 a year regardless of anything extra that Edward might contribute.

> As a smaller establishment will be as agreeable to them, as it cannot but be feasible, I really think that My Mother & Sisters will be full as rich as ever. They will not only suffer no personal deprivation, but will be able to pay occasional visits of health and pleasure to their friends.

This assessment ignored the fact that the three women would from now on be dependent on young men, all of whom had their own commitments and priorities.[27] Fears were justified when, in 1816, Henry's bank failed and the brothers lost heavily: Henry and Frank had to withdraw

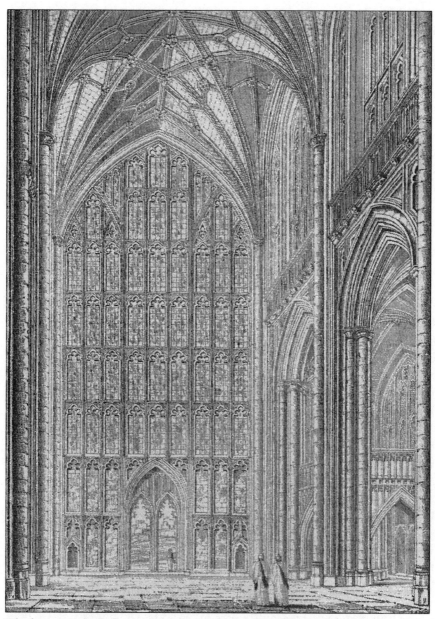

Winchester Cathedral, where Jane Austen is buried: the west end of the nave.
From John Britton, *Chronological History of English Architecture* (1821).

their contributions, and James and Edward were uncertain as to how long they could continue theirs. The £500 which Jane had stated to be a very modest income for the Dashwood ladies was further than ever from being met.

Jane was likely to have been more conscious of their dependent situation than her mother and Cassandra, since she was the only one who could contribute nothing to the family funds. Friends in Bath were not slow to recognise their lowered status: they were beset with invitations kindly meant. 'What request we are in!', wrote Jane, after being invited to drink tea with friends on two successive evenings.

> Our Tea & sugar will last a great while. I think we are just the kind of people & party to be treated about among our relations; we cannot be supposed to be very rich.[28]

Whilst living at Sydney Place she had begun to write another novel, now known as 'The Watsons'; but after the death of her father she had no heart to continue and it was never finished. The impoverished daughters of an ailing clergyman did not make a cheering subject. Circumstances, too, were no longer propitious for writing. James Austen had been quick to realise that his mother and sisters would not be able to buy or even rent a house in Bath for any length of time: they would have to stay with relatives during the summer months and move for the winter into furnished lodgings vacated at the end of the season.[29] He dutifully offered them a home at Steventon Parsonage, but it would not have been the same to them as before, and they declined the invitation. For the next two years they lived without settled abode, visiting Godmersham, Steventon, Worthing, Adlestrop, Stoneleigh Abbey and Hamstall-Ridware and moving house in Bath first to Gay Street and then to the previously rejected Trim Street. Society in Bath had many gradations, and so, in society's estimation, had the city's terraces: the Austens appeared to be sliding rapidly down the scale. With diminishing hopes, they were searching for yet more lodgings they could afford to take when Frank came to their rescue by suggesting that they should share a house with him and his bride in Southampton.

Frank married Mary Gibson, a young lady he had met whilst organising the Sea Fencibles at Ramsgate, in July 1806. After a spell in lodgings in Southampton, the two families moved in March 1807 into a large house confronting the castle. They took with them Jane's friend Martha Lloyd – another clergyman's daughter recently made homeless (Mrs Lloyd had died at Ibthorpe in April 1805). Jane soon detected snubs where they may or may not have been meant. When the Sheriff

of Southampton and his wife left cards (having been informed of the
Austens' arrival in the town by the Sheriff's brother, a clergyman they
had met at Hurstbourne Tarrant), Jane wrote after returning their call:

> They will not come often, I daresay. They live in a handsome style and
> are rich, and she seemed to like to be rich, and we gave her to understand
> that we were far from being so; she will soon feel therefore that we are
> not worth their acquaintance.[30]

Southampton nevertheless provided a reasonably happy interlude.
The house in Castle Square had a garden where Jane could plant her
syringa 'for the sake of Cowper's line'; a friend of Aunt Leigh-Perrot's
had unexpectedly left the sisters £50 each, which emboldened Jane to
hire a piano; and there were plays to attend and dances at the Long
Rooms and the Dolphin Inn. Jane enjoyed watching Frank, during his
periods of leave, busy like Captain Harville at his hobbies; Frank's wife,
Mary, was loved by all and Martha Lloyd was a pleasant and comforting
companion. Yet it could not last. Mary had her first child in April 1807
and she and Frank soon found that they would like to have a home of
their own. Mrs Austen was already considering the possibility of moving
to Alton, where Henry had set up a branch of his bank, when Edward
finally intervened. Perhaps the death of his wife in October 1808 had
made him more dependent on affection from his family. For whatever
reason, he now gave his mother and sisters a choice of two houses: one
near Godmersham, the other near to his older manor house at Chawton,
about a mile to the south east of Alton. They unhesitatingly chose the
latter and moved into the house in July 1809.

Jane settled with relief into the 'cottage', as members of the family
called it, and lived there uncomplainingly until her death in 1817. It
was an old-fashioned building, said at one time to have been an inn.
More recently it had been occupied by Thomas Knight's steward. James
Edward Austen-Leigh described it as having small rooms and low
ceilings like the majority of parsonage houses at the time, which perhaps
helped to endear it to Jane. The dining-room window was so close to
the road that travellers in passing coaches could observe Mrs Austen
and her daughters at breakfast,[31] and accommodation was so restricted
that Jane's cherished writing-desk had to be set up in the parlour,
frequented by all comers. Still, the house was rent free. It had a garden
with flower beds for Cassandra, fruit trees for Jane and enough space
for Mrs Austen to grow potatoes. It was in a village, surrounded by the
Hampshire countryside which Jane loved. She had continued her
churchgoing and her charitable giving through all her vicissitudes: at

Southampton, pew rents and charities had accounted for a quarter of her annual expenditure.[32] The churches, however, had been fashionable neoclassical structures and the charities impersonal.[33] Now, she could walk a short way up a lane every Sunday to a small country church of a kind familiar to her and help to distribute 'Edward's charity' to people in the parish whose needs she knew. Moreover, the village provided her with a salutary reminder of the depths to which she might have fallen. Mary Benn, the unmarried sister of a nearby clergyman, was condemned to live in a draughty cottage rented from a tight-fisted farmer, and to be handed around for meals by neighbours anxious to do their duty by her. Jane was to write feelingly in *Emma* of the fate of Mrs and Miss Bates, widow and daughter of the former vicar of Highbury, living in a 'very moderate sized apartment' up a dark narrow staircase in someone else's house whilst the whole of the neighbourhood conspired to enable them to keep up appearances.[34]

Mrs Knight liked to think that the thirty-three-year-old Jane would marry the bachelor rector of Chawton, the Revd John Rawstorne Papillon, who had built himself a new rectory on acquiring the benefice and was now living in it with his spinster sister as hostess. Jane laughed when she heard of the idea, and told Cassandra, who was at Godmersham, to thank Mrs Knight for her kind wishes and assure her 'that I *will* marry Mr Papillon, whatever may be his reluctance or my own'.[35] Papillon was forty-five, but clergymen were often known to wait until middle age to marry. Catherine Bigg, at the age of thirty-three, had recently married the Revd Herbert Hill, twenty-five years her senior ('Tomorrow we must think of poor Catherine', Jane wrote, as the wedding day approached.)[36] After rejecting Edward Bridges' proposal in 1805, Jane was firm in her decision to remain unmarried.

Relatives and friends continued to find in her a lively and warm-hearted companion, but they noticed that she had become reserved in company.[37] In fact, she seems to have been leading a secret life, for she had decided, on leaving Southampton, to make real efforts to become a published author; and, to Jane, anonymity meant anonymity. Nobody outside the immediate family circle must know. After publishing *Sense and Sensibility* and *Pride and Prejudice*, she recovered the inventive powers she had known at Steventon and, in the few years between 1812 and her death in 1817, wrote three novels and began a fourth, all entirely new. The three that she completed – *Mansfield Park*, *Emma* and *Persuasion* – are regarded by many critics as the height of her achievement. Her brother Henry, alas, could never keep a secret: it was largely due to his proud revelations that his sister's authorship of *Sense and Sensibility* and *Pride and Prejudice* became known in London. Nephews and nieces were then told also and, from 1813, knowledge of the author's identity gradually spread around the Chawton neighbourhood. 'I am trying to harden myself', Jane told her brother Frank. 'After all, what a trifle it is in all its Bearings, to the really important points of one's existence even in this World!' [38] Fortunately, she derived genuine entertainment from the frank comments of not very intelligent acquaintances: Mrs Bramston, for instance, who preferred *Mansfield Park* to the earlier novels 'but imagined *that* might be her want of Taste'; her sister-in-law Augusta Bramston, who 'having finished the 1st vol. flattered herself she had got through the worst'; and Mrs Digweed, who declared on reading *Emma* that 'if she had not known the Author [she] could hardly have got through it'.[39]

Once the publication of her first two novels had convinced her of her own capabilities and restored her self-respect, Jane could accept more contentedly her marginal position among the gentry. It was an admirable position from which to observe the conventions governing social acceptance in the exclusive neighbourhoods of rural England – conventions difficult to analyse but apparently understood by everybody concerned at the time. In *Emma* they are described with tolerant amusement. Jane Austen's comments on class have long been questioned because of their lack of a clear economic basis: at Highbury, for instance, Mr Woodhouse's gentle manners, hereditary fortune (which is of distant and long-forgotten origin) and long residence in the place make him as much sought after as Mr Knightley, although the latter owns large estates and Mr Woodhouse has hardly any land at all. With the waning popularity of economic determinism, however, her awareness of the subtle criteria governing the acceptance of a businessman like Mr Cole, along with the equally subtle differences in attitude towards the various professional men and their womenfolk, may result in her descriptions of society receiving more serious consideration.

Jane and Cassandra sometimes went their separate ways, on visits to relatives and friends. Jane enjoyed visits to London; Cassandra continued to keep in touch with Tom Fowle's family at Kintbury. Jane had always admired the fortitude with which Cassandra bore Tom's tragic death: like Elizabeth Bennet when her sister was in trouble, she had tried hard 'to contribute to the recovery of her spirits by all that affection could do'.[40] Cassandra in her turn supported Jane with unstinting devotion in the last and greatest trial of her life. After a painful and distressing illness, later thought to be Addison's disease, Jane Austen died on 18 July 1817, her head pillowed in her sister's lap.

Among her last words, she appealed to God to grant her patience and begged her sister to pray for her. She had been taken to Winchester in the vain hope of receiving beneficial treatment and was buried there, in the cathedral: 'a Building', wrote Cassandra, 'she admired so much'.[41]

For some years after her death, early Victorian readers preferred a type of novel which was more openly didactic and covered a broader canvas than the 'little bit (two inches wide) of ivory' on which Jane Austen had written 'with so fine a Brush'; but, by 1870, appreciation had revived to a point at which her nephew James Edward believed there was a demand for information about her life and environment.[42] His *Memoir* opened the floodgates of biography and literary criticism which have established her position as the outstanding novelist of her age, and perhaps of all time.

It would be presumptuous to ascribe the rise of so bright a genius to any earthly cause, but Jane would no doubt have been the first to recognise the debt she owed to her early training. Her relationship with her father did not end with his death. She remembered him with affection and respect and remained true to his teaching. In one of the prayers which she wrote for use in family worship at Chawton, she implored God 'above all other blessings ... to quicken our sense of the value of that holy religion in which we have been brought up, that we may not, by our own neglect, throw away the salvation thou hast given us'.[43] It is true that in her novels she seldom writes of religion directly. According to a friend, Mrs Barrett, whom she met at Chawton, she was put off from doing so by her dislike of strident religious enthusiasts;[44] but, even without this deterrent, she would not have considered novels a suitable vehicle for preaching. Religion was to her a private matter: to discuss it in a novel would have been a breach of good taste. Moreover, readers expected novels to be entertaining and were not ready, in her day, to find entertainment in religious soul-searchings. Although Jane believed that the English had become, during the wars against France, 'a Nation improving in Religion', she nevertheless feared that she had made *Mansfield Park* too serious for the majority of readers: comparing it with *Pride and Prejudice*, she thought it was 'not half so entertaining'.[45] The mere idea of introducing sermons into novels struck her as funny: in a letter to her nephew James-Edward, who was experimenting with writing fiction. Her brother Henry, his wife Eliza having died in 1813 and his banking business failed, had at last, in December 1816, taken Holy Orders without any prospect of a benefice and had entered on what turned out to be a life of comparative poverty by serving as curate to Mr Papillon at Chawton. He was by all accounts a stunning preacher but it was merely as a joke that Jane wrote:

> Uncle Henry writes very superior Sermons. You & I must try to get hold of one or two, & put them into our Novels; it would be a fine help to a volume; & we could make our Heroine read it out aloud of a Sunday Evening.[46]

Religion, as her father had taught it, is nevertheless inherent in Jane Austen's novels. In *Mansfield Park*, Edmund Bertram expresses what may be assumed to have been George Austen's view of the role of a parish priest in rural England: namely, to set an example of godly living. A clergyman, Edmund explains to the sceptical Mary Crawford,

> has the charge of all that is of the first importance to mankind, individually or collectively considered, temporally and eternally – the guardianship of religion and morals and consequently of the manners which result from their influence.

A good sermon, he continues, will always be admired;

> but it is not in fine preaching only that a good clergyman will be useful in his parish and his neighbourhood, where the parish and neighbourhood are of a size capable of knowing his private character, and observing his general conduct ... And with regard to [the clergy] influencing public manners ... the *manners* I speak of, might rather be called *conduct*, perhaps, the result of good principles; the effect, in short, of those doctrines which it is their duty to teach and recommend.

Similarly, Jane told her friend Mrs Barrett, a novelist must rely on example. In her novels, she sought, through the words and actions of her characters, to give examples of good and evil in daily life.[47]

The Cathechism, on whose teaching Jane had been brought up, represented moral behaviour as the visible part of a human being's duty to God. On this understanding, ordinary domestic activities such as visiting the Middletons in *Sense and Sensibility*, rehearsing amateur theatricals in *Mansfield Park* or playing word games in *Emma* are of eternal significance. Hence Jane wrote in one of her evening prayers:

> May we now, and on each return of night, consider how the past day has been spent by us, what have been our prevailing thoughts, words and actions during it, and how far we can acquit ourselves of evil. Have we ... disobeyed thy commandments, have we neglected any known duty, or willingly given pain to any human being? Incline our hearts to

ask these questions oh! God, and save us from deceiving ourselves by pride or vanity.[48]

The individuals who grow in moral stature in Jane Austen's novels – Marianne Dashwood, Elizabeth Bennet, Darcy, Emma Woodhouse, Captain Wentworth – are the ones who ask themselves these questions, whilst also learning to set aside the personal delusions Jane Austen saw as an inevitable part of the human condition. By doing so, they achieve happiness: Jane had learnt in childhood that virtue must have its reward.

It is not surprising, therefore, that Richard Whateley (later Archbishop of Dublin), who was one of the earliest scholars to review Jane Austen's novels, perceived them at once to be 'evidently' the work of 'a Christian writer'. Whilst regarding this as a great asset, their value was enhanced in his eyes by their usefulness – their 'practical good sense', derived from the author's observation of real life.[49] On both counts, Jane Austen as her father's pupil could have received no higher praise.

Notes

Jane Austen's novels, letters and minor works are cited without her name first. The editions used are:

The Novels of Jane Austen: The Text Based on Collation of the Early Editions, ed. R. W. Chapman (3rd edn, 5 vols, Oxford, 1923).

The Works of Jane Austen, vi, *Minor Works*, ed. R. W. Chapman (Oxford, 1954).

Jane Austen's Letters: New Edition, ed. Deirdre Le Faye (Oxford, 1995).

Introduction

1. J. E. Austen-Leigh, *A Memoir of Jane Austen* (3rd edn, London, 1872), pp. 9–10.
2. *Emma*, pp. 28–29, 361–62; J. E. Austen-Leigh, *Memoir*, p. 10.
3. Nikolaus Pevsner, 'The Architectural Setting of Jane Austen's Novels', *Journal of the Warburg and Courtauld Institutes*, 31 (1968), p. 410.
4. Irene Collins, *Jane Austen and the Clergy* (London and Rio Grande, OH, 1993), pp. 35–44.
5. *Northanger Abbey*, pp. 249–50.
6. J. Walsh, S. Taylor, and C. Hayden, *The Church of England, c. 1689 – c. 1883*, (Cambridge, 1993), p. 14.
7. Collins, *Jane Austen and the Clergy*, pp. 48–60.
8. Michael Lewis, *A Social History of the Navy, 1793–1815* (London, 1960), pp. 36–38.
9. J. E. Austen-Leigh, *Memoir*, p. 47.

Chapter 1: A Goodly Heritage

1. R. Austen-Leigh, *Austen Papers, 1704–1856* (University Microfilms International, Ann Arbor, MI, 1980), pp. 28, 31; Laurence Sterne, *The Life and Opinions of Tristram Shandy, Gentleman*, ed. Graham Petrie (Harmondsworth, 1967), pp. 33–35.

2.   R. Austen-Leigh, *Austen Papers*, pp. 32–33.
3.   William Buchan, *Domestic Medicine* (2nd edn, London, 1772), pp. 12–16.
4.   Irene Collins, *Jane Austen and the Clergy* (London and Rio Grande, OH, 1993), pp. 61–62; Deirdre Le Faye, *Jane Austen: A Family Record* (London, 1989), pp. 6, 99.
5.   Ibid., pp. 1–4.
6.   *Sense and Sensibility*, p. 295; Collins, *Jane Austen and the Clergy*, pp. 27–28.
7.   Ibid., pp. 28–29.
8.   Le Faye, *Family Record*, pp. 6–7; *Persuasion*, p. 74.
9.   Collins, *Jane Austen and the Clergy*, pp. 45–46, 135–36.
10. Maggie Lane, 'The Very Reverend Thomas Powys', Jane Austen Society, *Report for 1993*, pp. 8–11.
11. *Letters*, no. 25, p. 56; Le Faye, *Family Record*, pp. 12, 14.
12. Ibid., pp. 8, 15; R. Austen-Leigh, *Austen Papers*, pp. 153–54.
13. Jane Austen Society, 'Anna Lefroy's Description of Steventon Parsonage in the Rev. George Austen's Time', *Collected Reports, 1966–75*, p. 246; *Northanger Abbey*, p. 213.
14. J. E. Austen-Leigh, *A Memoir of Jane Austen* (3rd edn, London, 1872), pp. 19–20, 35–36; *Northanger Abbey*, pp. 184, 212; Collins, *Jane Austen and the Clergy*, p. 65.
15. *Mansfield Park*, pp. 55, 241–44; *Persuasion*, p. 36; Hesketh Pearson, *The Smith of Smiths* (London, 1984), p. 146.
16. J. E. Austen-Leigh, *Memoir*, p. 19; R. Austen-Leigh, *Austen Papers*, p. 24.
17. Ibid., p. 25.
18. Ibid., p. 32.
19. *Letters*, no. 13; p. 25, no. 18, p. 38; Robin Vick, 'The Sale at Steventon Parsonage', Jane Austen Society, *Report for 1993*, pp. 13–16.
20. *Persuasion*, p. 102.
21. Paul Langford, 'British Politeness and the Progress of Western Manners', *Transactions of the Royal Historical Society*, 6th series, 7 (1997), pp. 53–72.
22. R. Austen-Leigh, *Austen Papers*, p. 27; Brian Southam, 'A Source for Names?', Jane Austen Society, *News Letter* (April 1996), p. 1.
23. J. E. Austen-Leigh, *Memoir*, pp. 8–10.
24. W. Page, ed., *The Victoria History of the Counties of England: Hampshire*, v (London, 1973), p. 355.
25. R. Austen-Leigh, *Austen Papers*. pp. 29, 30–31.

Chapter 2: Upbringing

1.   D. Selwyn, ed., *Jane Austen: Collected Poems and Verse of the Austen Family* (Manchester, 1996), pp. 25–28; Lloyd de Mause, ed., *The History of Childhood* (London, 1974), p. 36.
2.   *Spectator*, no. 246 (12 December 1711); William Buchan, *Domestic Medicine* (2nd edn, London, 1772), pp. xxix, 3–5; J. Steven Watson, *The Reign of George III, 1760–1815* (Oxford, 1960), pp. 11–12; Jean-Jacques Rousseau, *Emile* (Everyman Library, London, 1974), p. 13.

3. William Cadogan, *An Essay upon Nursing* (London, 1748), pp. 14–19; R. Austen-Leigh, *Austen Papers, 1704–1856* (University Microfilms International, Ann Arbor, MI, 1980), p. 29; J. E. Austen-Leigh, *A Memoir of Jane Austen* (3rd edn, London, 1872), p. 41.

4. Claire Tomalin, *Jane Austen: A Life* (London, 1997), pp. 5–7; J. E. Austen-Leigh, *Memoir*, p. 41; R. Austen-Leigh, *Austen Papers*, p. 29.

5. Rousseau, *Emile*, p. 13; Deirdre Le Faye, 'The Austens and the Littleworths', *Jane Austen Society, Report for 1987*, pp. 15–21.

6. R. Austen-Leigh, *Austen Papers*, pp. 28, 31; Jane Austen's christening gown is illustrated in Jane Austen Society, *Collected Reports, 1966–75*, p. 37.

7. R. Austen-Leigh, *Austen Papers*, p. 24.

8. Ibid., pp. 29–31.

9. Phillis Cunnington and Anne Buck, *Children's Costume in England: From the Thirteenth to the Nineteenth Century* (London, 1965), pp. 106–15; Penelope Byrde, *A Frivolous Distinction: Fashion and Needlework in the Works of Jane Austen* (Bath, 1979), p. 24.

10. *Northanger Abbey*, pp. 1–3; J. E. Austen Leigh, *Memoir*, p. 20; Jane Austen Society, 'Anna Lefroy's Description of Steventon Parsonage in the Rev. George Austen's Time', *Collected Reports, 1966–75*, p. 246; *Letters*, no. 69(D), p. 176.

11. Deirdre Le Faye, *Jane Austen: A Family Record* (London, 1989), pp. 38, 52; R. Austen-Leigh, *Austen Papers*, pp. 148, 265.

12. Ibid., pp. 27, 130; William Buchan, *Domestic Medicine*, p. 551; George Armstrong, *An Account of the Diseases Most Incident to Children* (London, 1777), pp. 51–60; Le Faye, *Family Record*, pp. 42; Caroline Austen, *Reminiscences of Jane Austen* (Jane Austen Society, 1986), pp. 49, 58; George Tucker, *A Goodly Heritage: A History of Jane Austen's Family* (Manchester, 1983), p. 117.

13. R. Austen-Leigh, *Austen Papers*, pp. 65–66.

14. Ibid., p. 23.

15. Le Faye, *Family Record*, pp. 39–40, 42; Selwyn, *Collected Poems and Verse*, pp. 25–28; *Mansfield Park*, p. 32.

16. *Northanger Abbey*, pp. 14–15, 109–10; Jan Fergus, *Jane Austen: A Literary Life* (Basingstoke, 1991), p. 37; S. Roscoe, *Newbery – Carnan – Power: A Provisional Checklist of Books for Children and Young People, Issued under the Imprint of John Newbery and his Family, 1742–1802* (Harrow, 1966), p. 15; *Minor Works*, pp. 139–50; Jane Austen, *The History of England: A Facsimile* (London, 1993); J. David Grey, ed., *Jane Austen's Beginnings* (Ann Arbor, MI, 1989), pp. 61–62.

17. Caroline Austen, *Reminiscences*, pp. 12–13; Isaac Watts, *Divine Songs: Attempted in Easy Language for the Use of Children* (London, 1715), p. 33; Geoffrey Summerfield, *Fantasy and Reason: Children's Literature in the Eighteenth Century* (London, 1984), pp. 73–81.

18. Paul Sangster, *Pity My Simplicity: The Evangelical Revival and the Religious Education of Children* (London, 1963), pp. 43, 50–51, 62, 82.

19. David Gilson, *A Bibliography of Jane Austen* (Oxford, 1982), p. 422; Percy Muir, *English Children's Books* (London, 1954) pp. 64, 68; F. J. Harvey Darton, *Children's Books in England* (Cambridge, 1966), pp. 130–35, 137; [John Newbery], 'ed.', *The History of Little Goody Two-Shoes* (London, 1765), pp. 3, 24–31, 65–75, 132.

20. John Gay, *Fables* (reprint of 1727 and 1738 eds, California, LA, 1967), pp. 170–73; *Northanger Abbey*, p. 14; *Emma*, pp. 319–20; *Letters*, no. 39, p. 94.
21. Thomas Percival, *A Father's Instructions to his Children* (2 vols in one, London, 1776), pp. 21–32, 42; *Letters*, no. 57, p. 145; *Northanger Abbey*, p. 14.
22. Summerfield, *Fantasy and Reason*, p. 294.
23. *Northanger Abbey*, p. 14; Henry Austen, *Biographical Notice of the Author* (R. W. Chapman, ed., *The Novels of Jane Austen*, 3rd edn, 5 vols, Oxford, 1954), v, p. 3.
24. Tucker, *Goodly Heritage*, pp. 66–67.
25. Le Faye, *Family Record*, p. 43.
26. Ibid., pp. 40–41.
27. *Emma*, p. 96.

Chapter 3: School

1. Elizabeth Jenkins, 'Some Banking Accounts of the Austen Family', Jane Austen Society, *Collected Reports, 1949–65*, p. 61.
2. Deirdre Le Faye, 'Anna Lefroy's Original Memories of Jane Austen', *Review of English Studies*, new series, 39 (1988), p. 421.
3. Idem, *Jane Austen: A Family Record* (Oxford, 1989), pp. 8, 9, 42; R. Austen-Leigh, *Austen Papers* (University Microfilms International, Ann Arbor, MI, 1980), pp. 23, 29; Deirdre Le Faye, 'Three Austen Family Letters', *Notes and Queries*, 32 (1985), pp. 329–30.
4. T. A. B. Corley, 'Jane Austen's Schooldays', Jane Austen Society, *Report for 1996*, p. 10.
5. *Emma*, p. 22; John Gore, 'Sophia Sentiment: Jane Austen?', Jane Austen Society, *Collected Reports, 1966–75*, pp. 9–10.
6. Corley, 'Jane Austen's Schooldays', p. 10–11; *Letters*, no. 24, p. 54.
7. *Pride and Prejudice*, p. 202.
8. Irene Collins, *Jane Austen and the Clergy* (London and Rio Grande, OH, 1993), pp. 124–25; *Mansfield Park*, p. 289.
9. *Pride and Prejudice*, pp. 105–6.
10. Ibid., p. 44;
11. Le Faye, *Family Record*, p. 47; Henry Austen, Biographical Notice of the Author' (*The Novels of Jane Austen*, ed. R. W. Chapman, 5 vols. Oxford, 1923), v, p. 5; Lady Balfour, 'The Servants in Jane Austen', *Cornhill Magazine*, new series, 67 (1929), p. 695; *Letters*, no. 13, p. 24; *Sense and Sensibility*, p. 375.
12. Michael Lewis, *A Social History of the Navy, 1793–1815* (London, 1960), pp. 60–68.
13. R. Austen-Leigh, *Austen Papers*, pp. 105, 110.
14. F. B. Sullivan, 'The Royal Naval Academy at Portsmouth', *Mariner's Mirror*, 63 (1977), pp. 311–15, 321.
15. David Gilson, *A Bibliography of Jane Austen* (Oxford, 1982), p. 440.
16. Le Faye, *Family Record*, p. 53.
17. Jane Austen Society, 'Jane Austen 's French Primer', *Collected Reports, 1966–75*, p. 257.

18. F. J. Harvey Darton, ed., *The Life and Times of Mrs Sherwood* (London, 1910), p. 36; Rosamund Bayne-Powell, *The English Child in the Eighteenth Century* (London, 1939), pp. 50–52; Le Faye, *Family Record*, p. 55, 209.
19. Ibid., pp. 46–47.
20. Deirdre Le Faye, 'Anna Lefroy's Original Memories', p. 420. For Dr Valpy and the Abbey School, see Darton, *Mrs Sherwood*, pp. 84, 85, 121–34, 142–51; and Corley, 'Jane Austen's Schooldays', pp. 10–20.
21. *Emma*, pp. 21–22.
22. Ibid., pp. 61–62.
23. Dorothy Gardiner, *English Girlhood at School* (Oxford, 1929), pp. 437–38; *Sense and Sensibility*, p. 160; *Pride and Prejudice*, pp. 164–65.
24. Gardiner, *English Girlhood*, pp. 336–38.
25. Ibid., pp. 435–37; *Mansfield Park*, p. 425; Ann Murry, *Mentoria: or The Young Ladies' Instructor* (3rd edn, London, 1782), pp. 21–34.
26. Gardiner, *English Girlhood*, p. 334; Maria and Richard Lovell Edgeworth, *Practical Education* (3 vols, London, 1798), ii, p. 529.
27. Gardiner, *English Girlhood*, pp. 428–31; Hester Chapone, *Letters on the Improvement of the Mind: Addressed to a Young Lady* (3rd edn, London, 1774), p. 150; *Northanger Abbey*, p. 108.
28. Gilson, Bibliography, p. 432; Darton, *Mrs Sherwood*, p. 132.
29. Gardiner, *English Girlhood*, p. 339.
30. *Northanger Abbey*, p. 19.
31. Gardiner, *English Girlhood*, pp. 400–8.
32. Ibid., p. 337.
33. *Emma*, p. 27.
34. *Letters*, no. 4, p. 5.
35. Jenkins, 'Some Banking Accounts', p. 61; Corley, 'Jane Austen's Schooldays', pp. 16–17; Sullivan, 'The Royal Naval Academy', pp. 314–15.
36. Darton, *Mrs Sherwood*, p. 151.

Chapter 4 : Reason and Godliness

1. George Austen, 'Memorandum for the Use [of] Mr F. W. Austen on his Going to the East Indies Midshipman on Board his Majesty's Ship Perseverance Cap: Smith Decr 1788' (unpublished MS).
2. W. B. Norris, *Jane Austen and Steventon* (Basingstoke, 1975), pp. 18–20.
3. Jocelyn Creigh Cass, 'In Defence of George Austen', *Persuasions*, 16 (1994), pp. 58–61; *Letters*, no. 15, p. 31.
4. Irene Collins, *Jane Austen and the Clergy* (London and Rio Grande, OH, 1993), pp. 37–40.
5. Idem, 'Displeasing Pictures of Clergymen', *Persuasions*, 18 (1996), pp. 109–19.
6. *Sense and Sensibility*, p. 102; *Emma*, p. 484.
7. Peter Virgin, *The Church in an Age of Negligence, 1700–1840* (Cambridge, 1989), pp. 134–37.
8. Ford K. Brown, *Fathers of the Victorians* (Cambridge, 1961), pp. 18, 38–40.
9. B. W. Young, 'Knock-Kneed Giants: Victorian Representations of Eighteenth-

Century Thought', in Jane Garnett and Colin Matthew, eds, *Revival and Religion since 1700: Essays for John Walsh* (London and Rio Grande, OH, 1993), pp. 81–83.

10. George Austen, 'Memorandum'.

11. In a poem by Mrs Austen, two of the pupils at the school promise George Austen they will pray faithfully if he grants them a favour: David Selwyn, ed., *Jane Austen: Collected Poems and Verse of the Austen Family* (Manchester, 1996), p. 28.

12. George Austen, 'Memorandum'.

13. Deirdre Le Faye, *Jane Austen: A Family Record,* London, 1989), p. 25.

14. George Austen, 'Memorandum'; Paul Sangster, *Pity My Simplicity: The Evangelical Revival and the Religious Education of Children* (London, 1963), p. 40.

15. *Emma*, p. 320.

16. Vicesimus Knox, *Liberal Education: or A Practical Treatise on the Methods of Acquiring Useful and Polite Learning* (London, 1781).

17. Idem, *Elegant Extracts: or Useful and Entertaining Passages in Prose, Selected for the Improvement of Scholars at Classical and Other Schools in the Art of Speaking, in Reading, Thinking, Composing and in the Conduct of Life* (2nd edn, London, 1785), pp. 1–180.

18. George Austen, 'Memorandum'.

19. Knox, *Elegant Extracts in Prose*, pp. 18–19, 21–22, 51.

20. *Sense and Sensibility*, p. 331.

21. *Mansfield Park*, p. 92.

22. Ibid., pp. 339–40; *Minor Works*, pp. 453–57; Bruce Stovel, '"A Nation Improving in Religion": Jane Austen's Prayers and their Place in her Life and Art', *Persuasions*, 16 (1994), p. 189.

23. Charles Smyth, *The Art of Preaching in the Church of England, 1747–1939* (London, 1940), pp. 157–58.

24. Gordon Rupp, *Religion in England, 1688–1791* (Oxford, 1968), p. 515; George Eliot, *Scenes of Clerical Life* (Everyman Library, London, 1910), p. 71 ('Mr Gilfil's Love Story', chapter 1).

25. *Pride and Prejudice*, p, 68.

26. Emma Austen Leigh, *Jane Austen and Steventon* (2nd edn, London, 1937), pp. 2–3.

27. *Northanger Abbey*, p. 175.

28. W. Page, ed., *The Victoria History of the Counties of England: Hampshire*, v (London, 1973), p. 442.

29. *Letters*, no. 6, p. 9.

30. Elizabeth Jenkins, 'The Marriage Registers at Steventon', Jane Austen Society, *Collected Reports, 1949–65*, pp. 294–95.

31. *Northanger Abbey*, p. 15; Isabel Rivers, 'Shaftesburian Enthusiasm and the Evangelical Revival', in Jane Garnett and Colin Matthew, eds., *Revival and Religion since 1700: Essays for John Walsh* (London and Rio Grande, OH, 1993), pp. 24–25; James Thomson, *The Seasons*, ed. James Sambrook (Cambridge, 1981), introduction, pp. xvii–xix.

32. H. Pratt, *Eclectic Notes* (London, 1856), p. 272.

33. Book of Proverbs, 3: 1–4.

34. George Austen, 'Memorandum'; Le Faye, *Family Record*, pp. 61–62.

35. George Austen, 'Memorandum'.
36. *Persuasion*, p. 19.
37. William Vickers, *A Companion to the Altar* (appended to Book of Common Prayer, Edinburgh, 1776).

Chapter 5: Reading and Learning

1. Deirdre Le Faye, *Jane Austen: A Family Record* (London, 1989), p. 54; *Letters*, no. 30, p. 72, no. 31, p. 74; David Gilson, *A Bibliography of Jane Austen* (Oxford, 1982), p. 431.
2. Vicesimus Knox, *Elegant Extracts: or Useful and Entertaining Pieces of Poetry Selected for the Improvement of Young Persons* (new edn, London, 1801), preface, p. iv.
3. J. David Grey, ed., *Jane Austen's Beginnings* (Ann Arbor, MI, 1989), p. 9.
4. Henry Austen, 'Biographical Notice of the Author', *The Novels of Jane Austen* (ed. R. W. Chapman, 3rd edn, 5 vols, Oxford, 1923), v, p. 7; Gilson, *Bibliography*, p. 443.
5. *Mansfield Park*, p. 20; *Pride and Prejudice*, p. 70.
6. Laurence Sterne, *The Life and Opinions of Tristram Shandy, Gentleman*, ed. Graham Petrie (Harmondsworth, 1967), pp. 106–7.
7. *Letters*, no. 27, p. 62.
8. Ibid., no. 92, p. 237; no. 96, p. 253.
9. *Sense and Sensibility*, p. 232; *Emma*, p. 219.
10. *Letters*, no. 53, p. 129; no. 54, p. 134; no. 89, p. 226; no. 91, p. 233.
11. Henry Austen, 'Biographical Notice', p. 7; Le Faye, *Family Record*, p. 54.
12. *Northanger Abbey*, p. 111.
13. *Sense and Sensibility*, p. 97.
14. William Gilpin, *Observations on Several Parts of England, Particularly the Mountains and Lakes of Cumberland and Westmoreland, Relative to Picturesque Beauty: Made in the Year 1772* (3rd edn, 2 vols, London, 1808), ii, pp. 210–12.
15. *Minor Works*, pp. 187–89.
16. *Sense and Sensibility*, p. 98.
17. Brian Southam, '*Sir Charles Grandison* and Jane Austen's Men', *Persuasions*, 18 (1996), pp. 74–87; *Minor Works*, pp. 25–26.
18. *Pride and Prejudice*, p. 165.
19. Ibid., p. 203.
20. *Mansfield Park*, p. 22; J. E. Austen-Leigh, *A Memoir of Jane Austen* (3rd edn, London, 1872), p. 12.
21. *Mansfield Park*, p. 22.
22. *Letters*, no. 86, pp. 214–15.
23. *Mansfield Park*, p. 113.
24. *Letters*, no. 42, p. 98; Robin Vick, 'The Sale at Steventon Parsonage', Jane Austen Society, *Report for 1993*, pp. 14–15.
25. Gilson, *Bibliography*, p. 441.
26. *Minor Works*, pp. 139–50.
27. Ibid., pp. 139, 144.

28. Ibid., p. 144.
29. Brian Southam, 'Jane Austen and Politics' (manuscript to be published in *Women's Writing*).
30. G. H. Tucker, *Jane Austen the Woman* (London, 1994), pp. 111–15.
31. R. G. Thorne, ed., *History of Parliament: The House of Commons, 1790–1820* (5 vols, London, 1986), i, pp. 4–5, 9, 11, 121, iii, pp. 433–34; Stephen Terry, *The Diaries of Dummer: Reminiscences of an Old Sportsman, Stephen Terry of Dummer* (London, 1934), p. 153; Robin Vick, 'The Basingstoke Assemblies', Jane Austen Society, *Report for 1993*, p. 25; *Letters*, no. 23, p. 50.
32. *Minor Works*, pp. 145–46.
33. *Letters*, no. 82, p. 208.
34. Gilson, *Bibliography of Jane Austen*, p. 433.
35. *Mansfield Park*, pp. 18–19.
36. *Northanger Abbey*, p. 241.
37. James Fordyce, *Sermons to Young Women* (7th edn, 2 vols, London 1771), i, pp. 148–49.
38. *Minor Works*, pp. 243–313; *Letters*, no. 3, p. 5.
39. E. E. Duncan Jones, 'Lydia Languish, Lydia Bennet and Dr Fordyce's Sermons', Jane Austen Society, *Collected Reports, 1949–1965*, pp. 241–43.
40. Irene Collins, *Jane Austen and the Clergy* (London and Rio Grande, OH, 1993), pp. 143–50; *Pride and Prejudice*, p. 126; *Emma*, p. 5.
41. Deirdre Le Faye, 'Anna Lefroy's Original Memories of Jane Austen', *Review of English Studies*, new series, 30, p. 420.
42. R. Austen-Leigh, *Austen Papers, 1704–1856* (University Microfilms International, Ann Arbor, MI, 1980), pp. 130–31.
43. Gilson, *Bibliography*, p. 445.

Chapter 6: Dramatic Times

1. R. Austen-Leigh, *Austen Papers, 1704–1856* (University Microfilms International, Ann Arbor, MI, 1980), pp. 34–37, 44, 52–53, 56–57, 60, 66–68, 71–72, 76, 78–80.
2. Ibid., pp. 83–84, 89–90.
3. Ibid., p. 92; Deirdre Le Faye, *Jane Austen: A Family Record* (London, 1989), p. 34.
4. R. Austen-Leigh, *Austen Papers*, pp. 97–98.
5. Ibid., pp. 99–100, 125.
6. Ibid., pp. 106, 110–11; Deirdre Le Faye, 'Three Austen Family Letters', *Notes and Queries*, 32 (1985), p. 331; idem, 'Jane Austen and her Hancock Relatives', *Review of English Studies*, new series, 30, no. 117 (February 1979), pp. 25–26.
7. Deirdre Le Faye, *Family Record*, p. 51; R. Austen-Leigh, *Austen Papers*, p. 116.
8. Ibid., p. 106.
9. Ibid., pp. 115–16, 117–18.
10. Le Faye, 'Three Austen Family Letters', pp. 333–34.
11. R. Austen-Leigh, *Austen Papers*, pp. 124.
12. Le Faye, 'Three Austen Family Letters', pp. 333–34.

13. Idem, 'Jane Austen and her Hancock Relatives', pp. 25–26.
14. David Gilson, *A Bibliography of Jane Austen* (London, 1982), pp. 438–39; Le Faye, 'Three Austen Family Letters', p. 333; F. J. Harvey Darton, *Children's Books in England* (2nd edn, Cambridge, 1958), p. 150. The copy of Berquin's tales given to Jane Austen was the original French version, published in London.
15. *Letters*, no. 71, p. 185.
16. Robert R. Wallace, 'Jane Austen's Neglected Song Book', Jane Austen Society, *Collected Reports, 1976–85*, pp. 121–25.
17. *Mansfield Park*, p. 18.
18. The sampler is illustrated in Jane Austen Society, *Collected Reports, 1976–85*, pp. 4–5.
19. Evelyn M. Howe, 'Amateur Theatricals', Jane Austen Society, *Collected Reports, 1966–75*, pp. 126–27; *Mansfield Park*, pp. 12–27.
20. R. Austen-Leigh, *Austen Papers*, p. 126; Betty Askwith, 'Jane Austen and the Theatre', Jane Austen Society, *Collected Reports, 1976–85*, p. 277.
21. Howe, 'Amateur Theatricals', p. 121; Robin Vick, 'The Sale at Steventon Parsonage', Jane Austen Society, *Report for 1993*, pp. 13–16.
22. F. J. Harvey Darton, ed., *The Life and Times of Mrs Sherwood, 1775–1851* (London, 1910), p. 133.
23. Anne Vincent-Buffault, *The History of Tears* (London, 1991), pp. 54–56; Roger Sales, *Jane Austen and Representations of Regency England* (London, 1994), pp. 125–26; *Mansfield Park*, p. 124.
24. J.-J. Rousseau, *Lettre à d'Alembert sur les spectacles*, ed. M. Fuchs (Geneva, 1948).
25. Askwith, 'Jane Austen and Theatre', p. 278; *Mansfield Park*, pp. 130–31.
26. R. Austen-Leigh, *Austen Papers*, pp. 124, 126–28.
27. *Mansfield Park*, p. 123, 141; Askwith, 'Jane Austen and the Theatre', p. 271.
28. Le Faye, *Family Record*, pp. 59–60; *Minor Works*, pp. 55–57.
29. R. Austen-Leigh, *Austen Papers*, p. 130.
30. Peter Virgin, *The Church in an Age of Negligence, 1700–1840* (Cambridge, 1989), pp. 141, 220.
31. R. Austen-Leigh, *Austen Papers*, p. 131.
32. *Letters*, no. 51, p. 122.
33. R. Austen-Leigh, *Austen Papers*, p. 131.
34. Ibid., pp. 131–32.
35. F. B. Sullivan, 'The Royal Naval Academy at Portsmouth, *Mariner's Mirror*, 63 (1977), pp. 316–17, 322–23, 324; Richard Vesey Hamilton, ed., *Letters and Papers of Admiral of the Fleet Sir Thomas Byam Martyn*, i (London, 1903), p. 23.
36. J. H. and E. C. Hubback, *Jane Austen's Sailor Brothers* (London, 1906), pp. 16–17.
37. Sullivan, 'The Royal Naval Academy', p. 315; Michael Lewis, *A Social History of the Navy, 1793–1815* (London, 1960), pp. 228–29, 267.
38. Hubback, *Jane Austen's Sailor Brothers*, p. 19.
39. C. N. Parkinson, *Trade in the Eastern Seas, 1793–1813* (New York, 1969), pp. 101–3.

Chapter 7: Stories

1. *Pride and Prejudice*, p. 68. James Austen read out Scott's newly published *Marmion* whilst staying at Godmersham in 1808: *Letters*, no. 53, p. 131.
2. *Minor Works*, pp. 47–49.
3. Percy Muir, *English Children's Books, 1600–1900* (London, 1954), p. 71.
4. *Minor Works*, pp. 44–47.
5. Patrick Piggott, *The Innocent Diversion: A Study of Music in the Life and Writings of Jane Austen* (London, 1979), p. 159.
6. *Minor Works*, pp. 40–42, 43–44.
7. Henry Austen, 'Biographical Notice of the Author', *The Novels of Jane Austen* (ed. R. W. Chapman, 5 vols, Oxford, 1923), v, p. 7.
8. J. David Grey, *Jane Austen's Beginnings* (Ann Arbor, MI, 1989), p. 153.
9. R. Austen-Leigh, *Austen Papers, 1704–1856* (University Microfilms International, Ann Arbor, MI, 1980), p. 133. For *The Loiterer*, see A. Walton Litz, 'The Loiterer, A Reflection on Jane Austen's Early Environment', *Review of English Studies*, new series, 11 (1961), pp. 251–61.
10. *Minor Works*, pp. 29–33.
11. Ibid., pp. 5–12.
12. James Austen, *The Loiterer* (Oxford, 1789–90), no. 9.
13. Deirdre Le Faye, *Jane Austen: A Family Record*, London, 1989), p. 55; Idem, 'Jane Austen and William Hayley', *Notes and Queries*, 232, no. 1 (March 1987), pp. 25–26.
14. *Minor Works*, pp. 76–109.
15. Ibid., p. 102.
16. Ibid., pp. 6, 43–44; *Northanger Abbey*, p. 68.
17. *Minor Works*, p 31; R. D. Richards, 'The Lottery in the History of English Government Finance', *Economic History* (1934), p. 74; Le Faye, *Family Record*, p. 68.
18. J. E. Austen-Leigh, *A Memoir of Jane Austen* (3rd edn, London, 1872), p. 45.
19. *Minor Works*, pp. 1–2.
20. David Gilson, 'Jane Austen and Sir Egerton Brydges', Jane Austen Society, *Collected Reports, 1976–85*, pp. 9–11; *Minor Works*, pp. 40–41.
21. Caroline Austen, *Reminiscences of Caroline Austen* (Jane Austen Society, 1986), pp. 12–15; *Letters*, no. 26, p. 58, no. 28, p. 64; Deirdre Le Faye, 'To Dwell Together in Unity', Jane Austen Society, *Report for 1989*, p. 30; *Northanger Abbey*, p. 15.
22. Caroline Austen, *Reminiscences*, p. 11.
23. Ibid., p. 7; J. E. Austen-Leigh, *Memoir*, p. 54.
24. *Minor Works*, pp. 76, 109.
25. R. Austen-Leigh, *Austen Papers*, pp. 130, 134, 137–38.
26. Ibid., pp. 116, 134, 138–40.
27. *Letters*, no. 63, pp. 160–61.
28. Deirdre Le Faye, 'Jane Austen and her Hancock Relations', *Review of English Studies*, new series, 30 (1979), pp. 12–14; R. Austen-Leigh, *Austen Papers*, pp. 140–144.
29. Ibid., p. 143.

30. Ibid., pp. 147–48.
31. *Mansfield Park*, p. 28.
32. R. Austen-Leigh, *Austen Papers*, pp. 148–49; Le Faye, *Family Record*, pp. 71–72.
33. R. Austen-Leigh, *Austen Papers*, p. 144.
34. *The Loiterer*, no. 21; William Wilberforce, *The Correspondence of William Wilberforce: Edited by his Sons* (2 vols, London, 1840), ii, p. 273; *Persuasion*, p. 217.
35. *Letters*, no. 27, p. 61; Le Faye, 'To Dwell Together', pp. 26–27.
36. Robin Vick, 'Court House at Overton', Jane Austen Society, *News Letter*, no. 8 (1997), p. 5.
37. *Sense and Sensibility*, pp. 276–77; Irene Collins, *Jane Austen and the Clergy* (London and Rio Grande, OH, 1993), p. 33.
38. *Minor Works*, p. 57.
39. J. David Grey, ed., *Jane Austen's Beginnings* (Ann Arbor, MI, 1989), p. 116.
40. *Minor Works*, p. 194.
41. Ibid., pp. 57–71.
42. Ibid., pp. 12–29.
43. Ibid., pp. 192–240.
44. Ibid., p. 198.
45. Ibid., pp. 113–15.
46. *Pride and Prejudice*, p. 369.
47. *The Loiterer*, no. 21.
48. R. Austen-Leigh, *Austen Papers*, pp. 142, 145, 149.

Chapter 8: Dancing

1. *Pride and Prejudice*, pp. 92–94.
2. Jacqueline Reid-Walsh, '"Entering the World" of Regency Society: The Ballroom Scenes in *Northanger Abbey*, "The Watsons" and *Mansfield Park*', *Persuasions*, 16 (1964), pp. 116–18.
3. *Pride and Prejudice*, p. 91.
4. Ibid., p. 165; *Mansfield Park*, p. 49.
5. *Minor Works*, pp. 150–52.
6. *Letters*, no. 10, p. 16.
7. R. Austen-Leigh, *Austen Papers* (University Microfilms International, Ann Arbor, MI, 1980), pp. 148, 150.
8. *Letters*, no. 27, p. 61.
9. A. G. L'Estrange, ed., *A Life of Mary Russell Mitford: Related in a Selection from her Letters to her Friends* (London, 1870), p. 235.
10. R. Austen-Leigh, *Austen Papers*, p. 144. Contemporary and near-contemporary references to Jane Austen's appearance can be found in Henry Austen, 'Biographical Notice of the Author', *The Novels of Jane Austen*, ed R. W. Chapman, 3rd edn, 5 vols (Oxford, 1923), v, p. 5; J. E. Austen-Leigh, *A Memoir of Jane Austen* (3rd edn, London, 1872), p. 82; Caroline Austen, *My Aunt Jane Austen* (Jane Austen Society, 1991), p. 5; and Egerton Brydges, *The*

Autobiography, Times, Opinions and Contemporaries of Sir Egerton Brydges (2 vols, London, 1834), ii, p. 41.

11. *Northanger Abbey*, p. 74; Penelope Byrde, *A Frivolous Distinction: Fashion and Needlework in the Works of Jane Austen* (Bath, 1979), pp. 2, 3, 12.

12. Patrick Piggott, *The Innocent Diversion; A Study of Music in the Life and Writings of Jane Austen* (London, 1979), pp. 5–6, 131–37, 143–54, 162–64; H. Neville Davies, 'More Light on Mr Chard', Jane Austen Society, *Report for 1989*, pp. 12–14; Robin Vick, 'The Sale at Steventon Parsonage', Jane Austen Society, *Report for 1993*, pp. 13–16; *Pride and Prejudice*, p. 25.

13. *Northanger Abbey*, pp. 16–17.

14. *Letters*, no. 9, p. 15; no. 15, p. 31; no. 18, p. 38; no. 27, p. 62; no. 33, p. 78.

15. Ibid., no. 25, pp. 56–57; no. 33, p. 78.

16. Ibid., no. 1, pp. 1–2; no. 2, p. 4.

17. *Sense and Sensibility*, p. 33.

18. *Minor Works*, p. 401; *Pride and Prejudice*, pp. 66, 169; *Emma*, p. 213.

19. *Letters*, no. 5, p. 8; no. 15, p. 29; no. 17, p. 35; no. 18, p. 37; no. 25, pp. 55–56.

20. *Mansfield Park*, p. 82; *Letters*, no. 1, pp. 1–2; no. 15, p. 29; no. 18, p. 37; no. 27, p. 61.

21. R. G. Thorne, ed., *History of Parliament: The House of Commons, 1790–1820* (5 vols, London, 1986), i, pp. 4–5, 9, 11, 12; iii, pp. 433–34; *Letters*, no. 2, p. 4; no. 23, p. 50; no. 24, p. 53; no. 29, p. 66; no. 30, pp. 70, 71.

22. Ibid., no. 18, p. 38; no. 24, p. 53.

23. *Mansfield Park*, p. 152; *Letters*, no. 17, p. 35; no. 23, pp. 49–50; no. 27, p. 62; William Jarvis, '"Those Will Last Us Some Time"', Jane Austen Society, *Report for 1988*, pp. 19–23.

24. *Letters*, no. 24, pp. 52–53; no. 28, p. 65; David Selwyn, ed., *Jane Austen: Collected Poems and Verse of the Austen Family* (Manchester, 1996), pp. 29–30; Robin Vick, 'The Basingstoke Assemblies', Jane Austen Society, *Report for 1993*, pp. 22–25; *Pride and Prejudice*, pp. 11, 13.

25. *Letters*, no. 27, p. 61; no. 24, p. 53.

26. Ibid., no. 15, p. 30; no. 16, p. 32; no. 17, pp. 33–35; no. 27, pp. 60–61.

Chapter 9: War

1. William Pitt, *The War Speeches of William Pitt the Younger*, ed. R. Coupland (Oxford, 1940), p. 76.

2. For information on Britain's war effort, see Clive Emsley, *British Society and the French Wars, 1793–1815* (London, 1979), pp. 11–12, 33–39, 40, 43–54, 73–74. On the Irish Militia, Thomas Bartlett, '"A Weapon of War Untried": Irish Catholics and the Armed Forces of the Crown, 1760–1830', in T. G. Fraser and Keith Jeffery, eds, *Men, Women and War* (Dublin, 1993), p. 76.

3. *Letters*, no. 132(D), p. 306.

4. Ibid., no 80, p. 203.

5. *Emma*, p. 200; *Letters*, no. 67, p. 173; Edmund Burke, *The Works of the Rt*

Hon. Edmund Burke (2 vols, London, 1834), i, p. 455; Alfred Cobban, *Edmund Burke and the Revolt against the Eighteenth Century* (London, 1929), pp. 97–99; William Stafford, 'Religion and the Doctrine of Nationalism in England at the Time of the French Revolutionary and Napoleonic Wars', in S. Mews, *Religion and National Identity* (Oxford, 1982), pp. 381, 385–86.

6. Irene Collins, *Jane Austen and the Clergy* (London and Rio Grande, 1993), pp. 172–75; *Emma*, pp. 149, 358, 360.

7. *Letters*, e.g. no. 13, p. 23; no. 14, p. 28; no. 15, p. 29; no. 27, p. 63.

8. *Mansfield Park*, pp. 233, 236.

9. See Lord Chesterfield's advice to his son, quoted in Margaret Lane, 'The Insufferable Bad Manners of Mr Darcy', Jane Austen Society, *Collected Reports, 1976–85*, p. 327.

10. *Letters*, no. 17, pp. 33, 35; no. 27, p. 60.

11. *Mansfield Park*, p. 249.

12. *Persuasion*, pp. 26–30; *Letters*, no. 153, p. 333; J. H. and E. C. Hubback, *Jane Austen's Sailor Brothers* (London, 1906), pp. 205–7.

13. *Persuasion*, pp. 26, 65.

14. *Mansfield Park*, p. 60; *Persuasion*, pp. 65–66, 67, 170.

15. Ibid., p. 389.

16. G. J. Marcus, *Hearts of Oak: A Survey of British Sea Power in the Georgian Era* (Oxford, 1975), pp. 209, 211; C. W. Chalklin, *The Provincial Towns of Georgian England* (London, 1974), pp. 122–28.

17. Deirdre Le Faye, 'James Austen: Army Chaplain', Jane Austen Society, *Report for 1984*, pp. 8–11.

18. *Sense and Sensibility*, p. 103; Patrick Piggott, *The Innocent Diversion: A Study of Music in the Life and Writings of Jane Austen* (London, 1979), p. 150–51; *Letters*, no. 63, p. 161; no. 78, p. 198.

19. *Pride and Prejudice*, p. 312–13, 314, 387.

20. *Sense and Sensibility*, p. 51.

21. *Persuasion*, p. 252.

22. On Henry Austen as a militia officer, see Clive Caplan, 'Jane Austen's Soldier Brother: The Military Career of Captain Henry Thomas Austen of the Oxfordshire Regiment of Militia, 1793–1801', *Persuasions*, 18 (1996), pp. 122–43.

23. R. Austen-Leigh, *Austen Papers, 1704–1856* (University Microfilms International, Ann Arbor, MI, 1980), p. 148.

24. *Mansfield Park*, p. 234; Hubback, *Jane Austen's Sailor Brothers*, pp. 154–56.

25. *Letters*, no. 5, p. 8; no. 6, p. 10.

26. R. Austen-Leigh, *Austen Papers*, pp. 139–40, 321–23; Piggott, *The Innocent Diversion*, pp. 152–53.

27. James Woodforde, *The Diary of a Country Parson*, ed. John Beresford (5 vols, Oxford, 1981), iv, p. 169.

Chapter 10: Love and Tragedy

1. Deirdre Le Faye, *Jane Austen: A Family Record* (London, 1989), p. 83.

2. J. M. S. Tomkins, *The Popular Novel in England, 1770–1800* (London, 1932), p. 120.
3. Joyce Hemlow, *The History of Fanny Burney* (Oxford, 1958), p. 99.
4. *Letters*, no. 30, p. 70.
5. Paul Langford, 'British Politeness and the Progress of Western Manners', *Transactions of the Royal Historical Society*, 6th series, 7 (1997), pp. 59–61, 71.
6. *Letters*. no. 77, p. 197.
7. T. J. Wise and J. A. Symington, eds, *The Brontës: Their Lives, Friendships and Correspondence* (4 vols, Oxford, 1932), ii, pp. 179–80.
8. John Wiltshire, *Jane Austen and the Body* (Cambridge, 1992), pp. 37, 117–18.
9. *Minor Works*, pp. 110–39.
10. *Sense and Sensibility*, p. 378.
11. For Jane's own account of her love affair with Tom Lefroy, see *Letters*, no. 1, pp. 1–2, and no. 2, pp. 3–4.
12. *Pride and Prejudice*, p. 9; *Sense and Sensibility*, p. 54.
13. G. H. Tucker, *Jane Austen the Woman* (London, 1994), p. 56; *Letters*, no. 1, p. 2; no. 2, pp. 3, 4.
14. J. A. P. Lefroy, 'Jane Austen's Irish Friend: Rt Hon. Thomas Langlois Lefroy, 1776–1869', *Proceedings of the Huguenot Society of Great Britain and Ireland* (London, 1979), pp. 148–55; Deirdre Le Faye, 'Tom Lefroy and Jane Austen', *Jane Austen Society, Collected Reports, 1976–85*, pp. 336–38; idem, *Family Record*, pp. 251–52.
15. *Pride and Prejudice*, pp. 21–22, 197; *Mansfield Park*, p. 471; *Northanger Abbey*, p. 243; *Minor Works*, p. 432.
16. *Letters*, no. 11, p. 19.
17. Le Faye, *Family Record*, pp. 82–83, 84–85; R. Austen-Leigh, *Austen Papers, 1704–1856* (University Microfilms International, Ann Arbor, MI, 1980), pp. 226–27.
18. Le Faye, *Family Record*, p. 85; Irene Collins, *Jane Austen and the Clergy* (London and Rio Grande, OH, 1993), pp. 25–26, 29, 31.
19. Clive Emsley, *British Society and the French Wars, 1793–1815* (London, 1979), pp. 51, 81; Arthur Bryant, *The Years of Endurance, 1793–1802* (London, 1942), p. 106.
20. Ruth Perry, 'Austen and Empire: A Thinking Woman's Guide to British Imperialism', *Persuasions*, 16 (1994), pp. 95–98.
21. *Letters*, no. 2, p. 4.

Chapter 11: Publishing

1. David Gilson, *A Bibliography of Jane Austen* (Oxford, 1982), pp. 439–40.
2. *Letters*, no. 4, p. 6; no. 5, p. 9; no. 6, p. 9.
3. Deirdre Le Faye, *Jane Austen: A Family Record* (London, 1989), pp. 68–69.
4. Idem, 'Anna Lefroy's Original Memories of Jane Austen, *Review of English Studies*, new series, 39 (1988), p. 418.
5. Jane Austen Society, *News Letter*, 8 (May 1997), p. 1.

6. Darryl Jones, 'Frekes, Monsters and the Ladies: Attitudes to Female Sexuality in the 1790s', *Literature and History*, 3rd series, 4 (1995), pp. 1–24.

7. *Letters*, no. 18, p. 37.

8. Le Faye, *Family Record*, p. 69.

9. *Letters*, no. 13, p. 24.

10. Isobel Grundy, 'The Early Women Writers: Lives and Times', *Female Spectator*, 1, no. 2 (1996), p. 9.

11. *Pride and Prejudice*, p. 87.

12. Clive Caplan, 'Jane Austen's Soldier Brother', *Persuasions*, 18 (1996), p. 125–26; Lewis Melville, *Brighton: Its History, its Follies, and its Fashions* (London, 1909), pp. 88–89.

13. *Letters*, no 79, p. 202; *Pride and Prejudice*, pp. 406–7.

14. William Page, ed., *The Victoria History of the Counties of England: Hampshire* (5 vols, London, 1973), v, p. 356.

15. Caplan, 'Jane Austen's Soldier Brother', pp. 123–29.

16. Ibid., p. 130.

17. Clive Emsley, *British Society and the French Wars, 1793–1815* (London, 1979), p. 39.

18. Melville, *Brighton*, pp. 39–41, 52–60, 76; *Pride and Prejudice*, p. 232.

19. Ibid., p. 97.

20. William Gilpin, *Observations on the Mountains and Lakes of Cumberland and Westmoreland* (2 vols, London, 1786), has a brief description of 'The Peak of Derbyshire', ii, pp. 219–23.

21. Nikolaus Pevsner, 'The Architectural Setting of Jane Austen's Novels', *Journal of the Warburg and Courtauld Institutes*, 31 (1968), pp. 405–6.

22. Brian Southam, ed., *Jane Austen: The Critical Heritage*, i, *1811*–70 (London, 1968), pp. 9–10.

23. Irene Collins, 'Displeasing Pictures of Clergymen', *Persuasions*, 18 (1996), pp. 114–16.

24. *Pride and Prejudice*, pp. 63, 96–97, 101, 162–63, 166–67, 169, 296–97.

25. Collins, 'Displeasing Pictures', pp. 116–17.

26. Le Faye, 'Anna Lefroy's Original Memories', p. 418.

27. *Letters*, no. 17, p. 35.

28. Ibid., no. 21, p. 44.

29. On methods of publishing, see Jan Fergus, *Jane Austen: A Literary Life* (Basingstoke, 1991), pp. 14–21.

30. MS 279, St John's College, Oxford.

31. Le Faye, *Family Record*, p. 148.

32. *Sense and Sensibility*, pp. 345–47; *Minor Works*, p. 454.

33. Henry Austen, 'Biographical Notice of the Author' (*The Novels of Jane Austen*, ed. R. W. Chapman, 3rd edn, 5 vols, Oxford, 1923), v, p. 6.

34. *Letters*, no. 86, p. 217.

35. Chris Viveash, 'Jane Austen's First Royal Admirer', Jane Austen Society, *Report for 1994*, p. 19; *Letters*, no. 71, pp. 182–83.

36. Le Faye, *Family Record*, p. 169; Frank W. Bradbrook, *Jane Austen and her Predecessors* (Cambridge, 1966), p. 97; Robert Bage, *Hermsprong: or Man As He Is Not* (Folio Society reprint, London, 1960), p. 102.

37. Fergus, *Jane Austen: A Literary Life*, p. 140.

38. A. G. L'Estrange, *A Life of Mary Russell Mitford* (2 vols, London, 1870), i, p. 300; *Letters*, no. 79, p. 201.

Chapter 12: Marriage and Money

1. *Sense and Sensibility*, p. 36; *Mansfield Park*, p. 42.
2. *Letters*, no. 11, p. 19; no. 86, p. 216; G. H. Tucker, *Jane Austen the Woman* (London, 1994), pp. 58–59.
3. *Letters*, no. 28, p. 64.
4. *Pride and Prejudice*, p. 350.
5. *Letters*, no 14, p. 27; William Jarvis, 'Who was John Lyford?', Jane Austen Society, *Collected Reports, 1949–65*, pp. 216–18.
6. *Minor Works*, p. 421.
7. *Letters*, no. 4, p. 6; no. 5, p. 8.
8. On Elizabeth Bridges, see Deirdre Le Faye, 'To Dwell Together in Unity', Jane Austen Society, *Report for 1989*, pp. 23–26.
9. *Letters*, no. 27, p. 33; no. 14, p. 27.
10. Ibid., no. 4, p. 7; no. 6, pp. 10–11; no. 7, p. 12.
11. Ibid., no. 4, p. 6.
12. R. Austen-Leigh, *Austen Papers, 1704–1856* (University Microfilms International, Ann Arbor, MI, 1980), pp. 229–31.
13. *Letters*, no 10, p. 17; no. 13, p. 25; no. 15, p. 31.
14. Ibid., no. 51, p. 122.
15. Ibid., no. 10, p. 17; no. 13, p. 25; no. 15, p. 31; no. 52, p. 125; no. 55, pp. 137–39; no. 92, p. 252.
16. Nikolaus Pevsner, 'The Architectural Setting of Jane Austen's Novels', *Journal of the Warburg and Courtauld Institutes*, 31 (1968), p. 406.
17. Nigel Nicolson, *Godmersham Park, Kent* (Jane Austen Society, 1996), pp. 17–26; *Letters*, no. 52, p. 125; no. 53, pp. 131–32; no. 55, p. 139; no. 89, p. 228; no. 95, p. 249.
18. *Cornhill Magazine*, 973 (1947–48), pp. 72–73; *Letters*, no. 14, p. 27; *Pride and Prejudice*, p. 342.
19. *Letters*, no. 90, p. 230; no. 96, p. 252.
20. Ibid., no. 90, p. 234; no. 92, p. 237; no. 94, p. 245.
21. Deirdre Le Faye, *Jane Austen: A Family Record* (London, 1989), pp. 198–99; *Pride and Prejudice*, p. 57; *Minor Works*, p. 456.
22. Deirdre Le Faye, 'Anna Lefroy's Original Memories of Jane Austen', *Review of English Studies*, new series, 39 (1988), p. 419.
23. *Letters*. no. 4, p. 6; no. 5, p. 8; G. H. Tucker, *Jane Austen the Woman*, p. 51; *Pride and Prejudice*, p. 354.
24. R. Austen-Leigh, *Austen Papers, 1704–1856* (University Microfilms International, Ann Arbor, MI, 1980), pp. 156–57, 159, 163–64, 167.
25. Ibid., p. 155; *Letters*, no. 7, p. 12.
26. Caplan, 'Jane Austen's Soldier Brother', *Persuasions*, 18 (1996), p. 135; R. Austen-Leigh, *Austen Papers*, pp. 121, 168, 168–71.

27. Irene Collins, *Jane Austen and the Clergy* (London and Rio Grande, OH, 1993), pp. 26–27, 57.
28. *Letters*, no. 5, p. 8.
29. R. Austen-Leigh, *Austen Papers*, pp. 157, 228.
30. *Letters*, no. 10, p. 16.
31. Le Faye, *Family Record*, pp. 92–93, 101–2.
32. Irvine Loudon, *Death in Childbirth, 1800–1950* (Oxford, 1992), pp. 159–60.
33. *Letters*, no. 10, p. 17; no. 11, p. 20; no. 13, p. 24; no. 153, p. 332.
34. Ibid., no. 34, p. 81.
35. *Sense and Sensibility*, pp. 233–34; *Letters*, no. 107, p. 275.
36. Ibid., no. 153, p. 332.
37. *Emma*, p. 165.
38. Jan Fergus, *Jane Austen: A Literary Life* (Basingstoke, 1991), pp. 13, 15–16.
39. *Pride and Prejudice*, pp. 122, 125, 135.
40. Ibid., p. 109.

Chapter 13: Classical Scenes and Gothic Novels

1. *Northanger Abbey*, pp. 16–17.
2. *Minor Works*, p. 191; *Persuasion*, p. 157.
3. For Bath at the time of Jane Austen, see Phyllis Hembry, *The English Spa, 1560–1815* (London, 1990), pp. 111–274; and Maggie Lane, *A Charming Place: Bath in the Life and Novels of Jane Austen* (Bath, 1993).
4. *Letters*, no. 35, p. 82.
5. *Persuasion*, p. 135; *Northanger Abbey*, p. 19.
6. *Letters*, no. 19, p. 41; *Northanger Abbey*, p. 19.
7. *Letters*, no. 19, p. 40.
8. J. E. Austen-Leigh, *A Memoir of Jane Austen* (3rd edn, London, 1872), p. 67; David Gilson, *A Bibliography of Jane Austen* (Oxford, 1982), pp. 436–45.
9. R. Austen-Leigh, *Austen Papers, 1704–1856* (University Microfilms International, Ann Arbor, MI, 1980), pp. 179–219; G. H. Tucker, *Jane Austen the Woman* (London, 1994), pp. 157–60.
10. Deirdre Le Faye, *Jane Austen: A Family Record* (London, 1989), p. 104.
11. *Letters*, no. 20, p. 42.
12. *Sense and Sensibility*, pp. 208–10; *Mansfield Park*, pp. 192–93.
13. *Northanger Abbey*, p. 25.
14. Ibid., pp. 26–27, 78; R. Austen-Leigh, *Austen Papers*, p. 142.
15. *Letters*, no. 19, p. 41.
16. Ibid., no. 20, p. 42; no. 21, p. 44; no. 22, pp. 46–48; Bridget Duckinfield, 'Was Edward Knight Electrified?', Jane Austen Society, *Report for 1993*, pp. 20–21.
17. Patrick Piggott, *The Innocent Diversion: A Study of Music in the Life and Writings of Jane Austen* (London, 1979), pp. 17–19.
18. *Letters*, no. 20, p. 42; no. 22, p. 47.
19. Ibid., no. 20, p. 43; no. 21, p. 45.
20. Ibid., no. 20, p. 42; no. 21, p. 44; *Northanger Abbey*, p. 39.

21. *Letters*, no. 22, p. 47; no. 38, p. 91; Hembry, *The English Spa*, p. 154; *Northanger Abbey*, p. 76.
22. Betty Askwith, 'Jane Austen and the Theatre', Jane Austen Society, *Collected Reports, 1976–85*, p. 274; *Letters*, no. 22, p. 47; Chris Viveash, 'Jane Austen and Kotzebue', Jane Austen Society, *Report for 1996*, pp. 29–31; *Northanger Abbey*, pp. 92–93.
23. R. Austen-Leigh, *Austen Papers*, p. 291; *Pride and Prejudice*, p. 43.
24. *Letters*, no. 36, p. 85.
25. Hesketh Pearson, *The Smith of Smiths* (London, 1984), pp. 30–32; David Selwyn, ed., *Jane Austen: Collected Poems and Verse of the Austen Family* (Manchester, 1996), p. 29, *Letters*, no. 1, p. 2.
26. *Northanger Abbey*, p. 29.
27. Norman Taylor and Alan Hankinson, eds, *Twelve Miles from a Lemon: Selected Writings and Sayings of Sydney Smith* (Cambridge, 1996), p. 16.
28. *Northanger Abbey*, pp. 113, 197.
29. Ibid., pp. 20, 45.
30. Hembry, *The English Spa*, pp. 149–50; *Northanger Abbey*, p. 40.
31. Park Honan, *Jane Austen: Her Life* (London, 1987), pp. 137–38.
32. R. Austen-Leigh, *Austen Papers*, p. 246; *Letters* no. 96, p. 253.
33. Laurence Sterne, *The Life and Opinions of Tristram Shandy, Gentleman*, ed. Graham Petrie (Harmondsworth, 1967), p. 366; *The Rambler*, no. 4, in Samuel Johnson, *Collected Writings*, ed. R. T. Davies (London, 1965), pp. 76–80.
34. Hester Chapone, *Letters on the Improvement of the Mind* (new edn, London, 1820), pp. 168–69; Maria and Richard Lovell Edgeworth, *Practical Education* (2nd edn, 3 vols, London, 1801), ii, p. 105.
35. *Northanger Abbey*, p. 37.
36. J. David Grey, ed., *Jane Austen's Beginnings* (Ann Arbor, MI, 1989), p. 239.
37. *Letters*, no. 14, p. 26; no. 9, p. 15.
38. Cited in Francis Lathom, *The Midnight Bell*, The Northanger Set of Jane Austen Horrid Novels (London, 1968), introduction, p. x.
39. Louis F. Peck, *A Life of Matthew G. Lewis* (Cambridge, MA, 1961), pp. 24–25; *Northanger Abbey*, p. 48.
40. Chapone, *Letters*, p. 168.
41. *Letters*, no. 12, p. 22.
42. Cassandra Cooke, *Battleridge: An Historical Tale Founded on Fact* (London, 1799), pp. 1, 10.
43. *Letters*, no. 10, p. 17.
44. Ibid., no. 68, pp. 174–75.
45. Jan Fergus, *Jane Austen: A Literary Life* (Basingstoke, 1991), p. 112.
46. J. E. Austen-Leigh, *Memoir*, p. 130.
47. *Letters*, no. 153, p. 333. The novel was 'finished' in 1803 by the insertion of Maria Edgeworth's *Belinda* in the list of books eulogised on page 38.

Chapter 14: Dread and Terrible Times

1. William Pitt, *The War Speeches of William Pitt the Younger*, ed. R. Coupland (London, 1940), pp. 228–29; Arthur Bryant, *The Years of Endurance, 1793–1802* (London, 1942), pp. 208–12, 217; W. Page, *The Victoria History of the Counties of England: Hampshire*, v (London, 1973), p. 355.
2. *Letters*, no. 14, p. 26; R. Austen-Leigh, *Austen Papers, 1704–1856* (University Microfilms International, Ann Arbor, MI, 1980), p. 168; Patrick Piggott, *The Innocent Diversion: A Study of Music in the Life and Writings of Jane Austen* (London, 1979), pp. 142, 151, 157.
3. R. Austen-Leigh, *Austen Papers*, p. 170; Clive Caplan, 'Jane Austen's Soldier Brother', *Persuasions*, 18 (1996), p. 136.
4. Bryant, *Years of Endurance*, pp. 215, 223–24; *Mansfield Park*, p. 93: 'It will, I believe, be everywhere found that, as the clergy are or are not what they ought to be, so are the rest of the nation.'
5. Linda Colley, *Britons: Forging the Nation, 1707–1836* (London, 1994), p. 296.
6. Clive Caplan, 'Jane Austen's Soldier Brother', p. 137.
7. Ibid., p. 136.
8. Simon Bainbridge, *Napoleon and English Romanticism* (Cambridge, 1995), pp. 20–21, 33; *Letters*, no. 17, p. 33.
9. J. H. and E. C. Hubback, *Jane Austen's Sailor Brothers* (London, 1906), pp. 29–31.
10. Ibid., p. 45.
11. R. Austen-Leigh, *Austen Papers*, pp. 153–54; *Letters*, no. 14, p. 26.
12. *Mansfield Park*, pp. 298–308.
13. Hubback, *Jane Austen's Sailor Brothers*, pp. 21–23; *Letters*, no 1, p. 2; no. 6, p. 10.
14. Ibid., no. 14, p. 26.
15. *Mansfield Park*, p. 246.
16. *Letters*, no. 14, p. 27; no. 15, p. 31; no. 16, p. 32.
17. Deirdre Le Faye, *Jane Austen: A Family Record* (London, 1989), p. 111; *Letters*, no. 38, p. 91; G. H. Tucker, 'Jane Austen's Topaz Cross', Jane Austen Society, *Collected Reports, 1976–85*, pp. 76–77. (The crosses are illustrated in Jane Austen Society, *Collected Reports, 1966–75*, pp. 1, 4.)
18. *Letters*, no. 25, p. 57; no. 24, p. 52; Le Faye, *Family Record*, p. 111.
19. Caplan, 'Jane Austen's Soldier Brother', pp. 138–42; *Minor Works*, p. 388.
20. *Letters*, no. 10, p. 18; no. 20, p. 43; no. 8, pp. 13–14; no. 12, pp. 22–23.
21. Ibid., no. 17, pp. 33–34; no. 18, p. 36.
22. Ibid., no. 27, p. 61.
23. *Northanger Abbey*, p. 27; *Letters*, no. 2, p. 3; no. 29, p. 68; no. 7, pp. 12–13; no. 6, p. 10; no. 4, p. 5; no. 17, p. 33; no. 18, p. 38; no. 30, p. 69; no. 50, p. 121.
24. Ibid., no. 31, p. 72; no. 14, p. 25; no. 24, p. 52.
25. Ibid., no. 20, p. 43; *Pride and Prejudice*, p. 196.
26. *Letters*, no. 26, p. 58; no. 31, p. 74.
27. Ibid., no. 10, p. 17; no. 17, p. 36; no. 10, p. 18; no. 21, p. 46; no. 25, p. 57; no. 27, p. 63; Elizabeth Jenkins, 'All that Checker-Work', Jane Austen Society, *Report for 1988*, p. 8; *Emma*, p. 157.

28. *Letters*, no. 10, p. 17; *Sense and Sensibility*, p. 30; no. 24, p. 52; no. 30, p. 69; no. 16, p. 32; Sir Lewis Namier, *The Structure of Politics at the Accession of George III* (London, 1957), pp. 57–58.

29. *Letters*, no. 17, p. 35.

30. P. K. O'Brien, 'Public Finance in the Wars with France, 1793–1815', in H. T. Dickinson, ed., *Britain and the French Revolution* (London, 1989), pp. 176–82; Joyce Hemlow, ed., *The Journals and Letters of Fanny Burney* (4 vols, Oxford, 1973), iv, p. 49; R. Austen-Leigh, *Austen Papers*, p. 167; *Letters*, no. 18, pp. 37–38.

31. James Woodforde, *The Diary of a Country Parson*, ed. John Beresford (5 vols, Oxford, 1981), iv, p. 149; v, p. 105, 186; O'Brien, 'Public Finance', p. 184.

32. J. E. Austen-Leigh, *A Memoir of Jane Austen* (3rd edn, London, 1872), p. 39; Clive Emsley, *British Society and the French Wars, 1793–1815* (London, 1979), pp. 39–40, 54–55.

33. *Letters*, no. 14, p. 28; no. 28, p. 65.

34. Ibid., no. 11, p. 20; David Selwyn, ed., *Jane Austen: Collected Poems and Verse of the Austen Family* (Manchester, 1996), pp. 30, 93 n. 7.

35. *Letters*, no. 12, p. 22; no. 14, p. 27.

36. Ibid., no. 50, p. 119 (Jane Austen was quoting from Cowper's *The Task*, 'The Winter Walk at Noon', vi, lines 149–50); *Emma*, p. 360; *Mansfield Park*, p. 56.

37. J. E. Austen-Leigh, *Memoir*, p. 30.

38. *Persuasion*, p. 40; *Letters*, no. 25, p. 55.

39. *Mansfield Park*, pp. 30, 189; Diana Shervington, 'Family Receipts', Jane Austen Society, *Collected Reports, 1976–85*, pp. 250–53; *Pride and Prejudice*, p. 169.

40. *Letters*, no. 13, p. 24; no. 15, p. 31; no. 23, p. 50.

41. *Emma*, pp. 86–87.

42. *Letters*, no. 11, p. 21; no. 23, p. 49; no. 27, p. 61.

43. Ibid., no. 24, p. 53.

44. Ibid., no. 11, pp. 16–17; no. 11, p. 20.

45. Ibid., no. 21, p. 45; C. N. Parkinson, *Trade in the Eastern Seas, 1793–1813* (New York, 1969), pp. 75, 94–95.

46. James Woodforde, *Diary*, iv, p. 156; Dorothy Gardiner, *English Girlhood at School* (Oxford, 1929), pp. 357–58; *Northanger Abbey*, p. 174; *Letters*, no. 23, p. 50; no. 25, pp. 57–58.

47. *Mansfield Park*, pp. 53–55; *Letters*, no. 17, p. 33; no. 44, p. 106; Irene Collins, *Jane Austen and the Clergy* (London and Rio Grande, OH, 1993), pp. 184–88.

48. *Letters*, no. 112, p. 283.

49. *Northanger Abbey*, p. 200.

50. *Letters*, no. 90, p. 230.

51. *Letters*, no. 28, p. 65: Le Faye, *Family Record*, p. 113. For an alternative reading of the evidence regarding Jane's fainting fit and her reaction to leaving Steventon, see David Nokes, *Jane Austen: A Life* (London, 1997), pp. 220–23.

Chapter 15: Leaving Steventon

1. Cited by Park Honan in *Jane Austen: Her Life* (London, 1987), p. 156.

2. James Woodforde, *The Diary of a Country Parson*, ed. John Beresford (5 vols, Oxford, 1981), v, p. 329; 'George Austen's Crop Reports', Jane Austen Society, *Report for 1994*, pp. 22–23; J. E. Austen-Leigh, *A Memoir of Jane Austen* (3rd edn, Oxford, 1872) p. 30.
3. *Letters*, no. 24, p. 54; no. 29, p. 69.
4. J. E. Austen Leigh, *Memoir*, p. 56–57; *Letters*, no. 14, p. 27.
5. Ibid., no. 13, p. 22; no. 10, p. 18; no. 24, p. 54.
6. *Pride and Prejudice*, p. 179; *Letters*, 27, p. 63.
7. Ibid., no. 17, p. 34; no. 14, p. 26; no. 25, p. 56; no. 30, pp. 70–71.
8. Ibid., no. 17, p. 35.
9. *Letters*, nos 29–34, pp. 66–81.
10. Ibid., no. 29, p. 68.
11. *Minor Works*, pp. 369, 373.
12. *Letters*, no. 29, p. 66.
13. Ibid., no. 29, p. 66; no. 30, p. 70; no. 31, p. 73.
14. Ibid., no. 31, p. 74.
15. Ibid., no. 33, p. 79.
16. Ibid., no. 32, p. 76.
17. Ibid., no. 30, pp. 71–72.
18. Ibid., no. 29, p. 67; no. 30, p. 71; no 32, p. 77.
19. Ibid., no 29, pp. 68–69.
20. Robin Vick, 'The Sale at Steventon Parsonage', Jane Austen Society, *Report for 1993*. pp. 13–16; *Letters*, no. 36, p. 84.
21. Ibid., no. 32, p. 77.
22. Deirdre Le Faye, *Jane Austen: A Family Record* (London, 1989), pp. 121–22.
23. Ibid., pp. 250–51.
24. *Persuasion*, pp. 95–96.
25. *Letters*, no. 40, pp. 95–96.
26. Ibid., no. 41, pp. 97–98.
27. R. Austen-Leigh, *Austen Papers, 1704–1856* (University Microfilms International, Ann Arbor, MI, 1980), pp. 234–36.
28. *Letters*, no. 43, p. 101.
29. R. Austen-Leigh, *Austen Papers*, pp. 235–36.
30. *Letters*, no. 49, p. 117.
31. J. E. Austen-Leigh, *Memoir*, p. 81; Le Faye, *Family Record*, p. 161.
32. Park Honan, *Jane Austen: Her Life*, pp. 244–45.
33. At Bath, Jane probably worshipped either at the Octagon Chapel or at St Mary's Chapel (now demolished) at the corner of Queen Square (mentioned in *Letters*, no. 29, p. 67); at Southampton she attended All Saints Church, rebuilt in Grecian Ionic style (1792–95) and destroyed by bombs in the Second World War: R. A. Austen-Leigh, *Jane Austen and Southampton* (London, 1949), p. 21.
34. *Letters*, no. 83, p. 208; *Emma*, p. 155.
35. *Letters*, no. 62, p. 156.
36. Ibid., no. 60, p. 150.
37. Le Faye, *Family Record*, p. 247.
38. *Letters*, no. 90, p. 231.
39. *Minor Works*, pp. 453–54.
40. *Pride and Prejudice*, p. 188.

41. Le Faye, *Family Record*, pp. 228–29.
42. *Letters*, no. 146, p. 323.
43. *Minor Works*, p. 454.
44. Le Faye, *Family Record*, p. 210.
45. *Letters*, no. 86, p. 217; no. 106, p. 274.
46. Ibid., no. 146, p. 323.
47. *Mansfield Park*, p. 93.
48. *Minor Works*, p. 453–54.
49. Brian Southam, *Jane Austen: The Critical Heritage*, i, *1811–70* (London, 1968), pp. 92–95.

Bibliography

Adair, J. M., *Essays on Fashionable Diseases* (London, 1790).

Ariès, Philippe, *Centuries of Childhood* (Harmondsworth, 1960).

Armens, Sven M., *John Gay: Social Critic* (New York, 1970).

Armstrong, George, *An Account of the Diseases Most Incident to Children* (London, 1777).

Askwith, Betty, 'Jane Austen and the Theatre', Jane Austen Society, *Collected Reports, 1976–1985*, pp. 268–84.

Austen, Caroline, *My Aunt, Jane Austen* (new edn, Jane Austen Society, 1991).

——, *Reminiscences of Jane Austen* (Jane Austen Society, 1986).

Austen, George, 'Memorandum for the Use [of] Mr F. W. Austen on his Going to the East Indies Midshipman on Board His Majesty's Ship Perseverance Cap: Smith Decr 1788' (unpublished MS).

Austen, Henry, 'Biographical Notice of the Author' (R. W. Chapman, ed. *The Novels of Jane Austen*, 3rd edn, Oxford, 1923), v, pp. 1–9.

Austen, James, *The Loiterer* (Oxford, 1789–90).

Austen, Jane, *Jane Austen's Letters*, new edn, collected and edited by Deirdre Le Faye (Oxford, 1995).

——, *The Novels of Jane Austen: The Text Based on Collation of the Early Editions*, ed. R. W. Chapman (3rd edn, 5 vols, Oxford, 1954).

——, *The Works of Jane Austen*, vi, *Minor Works*, ed. R. W. Chapman (Oxford, 1954).

Austen-Leigh, Emma, *Jane Austen and Steventon* (2nd edn, London, 1937).

Austen-Leigh, J. E., *A Memoir of Jane Austen* (3rd edn, London, 1872).

Austen-Leigh, M. A., *Personal Aspects of Jane Austen* (London, 1920).

Austen-Leigh, R., *Austen Papers, 1704–1856* (University Microfilms International, Ann Arbor, MI, 1980).

Bage, Robert, *Hermsprong: or Man As He Is Not* (London, 1960).

Bainbridge, Simon, *Napoleon and English Romanticism* (Cambridge, 1995).

Balfour, Lady, 'The Servants in Jane Austen', *Cornhill Magazine*, new series, 67 (1929), pp. 694–705.

Bartlett, Thomas, '"A Weapon of War Untried": Irish Catholics and the Armed Forces of the Crown, 1760–1830', in T. G. Fraser and Keith Jeffery, eds, *Men, Women and War* (Dublin, 1993), pp. 66–85.

Bayne-Powell, Rosamond, *The English Child in the Eighteenth Century* (London, 1939).

Bradbrook, F. W., *Jane Austen and her Predecessors* (Cambridge, 1966).

Brown, Ford K., *Fathers of the Victorians: The Age of Wilberforce* (Cambridge, 1961).

Bryant, Arthur, *The Years of Endurance, 1793–1802* (London, 1942).

Brydges, Egerton, *The Autobiography, Times, Opinions and Contemporaries of Sir Egerton Brydges* (2 vols, London, 1834).

Buchan, William, *Domestic Medicine* (2nd edn, London, 1772).

Buck, Anne, *Dress in Eighteenth-Century England* (London, 1979).

Burke, Edmund, *The Works of the Rt Hon. Edmund Burke* (2 vols, London, 1834).

Burney, Frances, *Camilla: or A Picture of Youth* (5 vols, London, 1796).

Byrde, Penelope, *A Frivolous Distinction: Fashion and Needlework in the Works of Jane Austen* (Bath, 1979).

Cadogan, William, *A Dissertation on the Gout* (London, 1771).

——, *An Essay upon Nursing* (London, 1748).

Caplan, Clive, 'Jane Austen's Soldier Brother: The Military Career of Captain Henry Thomas Austen of the Oxfordshire Regiment of Militia, 1793–1801', *Persuasions*, 18 (1996), pp. 122–43.

Cass, Jocelyn Creigh, 'In Defence of George Austen', *Persuasions*, 16 (1994), pp. 55–62.

Chalklin, C. W., *The Provincial Towns of Georgian England* (London, 1974).

Chapman, R. W., 'Jane Austen's Books', *Book Collector's Quarterly*, 9 (1933), pp. 92–95.

Chapone, Hester, *Letters on the Improvement of the Mind: Addressed to a Young Lady* (new edn, London, 1820).

Cobban, Alfred, *Edmund Burke* (London, 1929).

Colley, Linda, *Britons: Forging the Nation, 1707–1837* (London, 1994).

Collins, Irene, *Jane Austen and the Clergy* (London and Rio Grande, OH, 1993).

——, 'Displeasing Pictures of Clergymen', *Persuasions*, 18 (1996), pp. 109–19.

Cooke, Cassandra, *Battleridge: An Historical Tale Founded on Facts* (London, 1799).

Corley, T. A. B., 'Jane Austen's Schooldays', Jane Austen Society, *Report for 1996*, pp. 10–20.

——, 'The Revd George Austen's Bank Account', Jane Austen Society, *Report for 1996*, pp. 21–23.

Cunnington, Phillis, and Buck, Anne, *Children's Costume in England: From the Thirteenth to the End of the Nineteenth Century* (London, 1965).

Darton, F. J. Harvey, *Children's Books in England* (2nd edn, Cambridge, 1958).

——, *The Life and Times of Mrs Sherwood, 1775–1851* (London, 1910).

Davies, H. Neville, 'More Light on Mr Chard', Jane Austen Society, *Report for 1989*, pp. 12–14.

Downes, Kerry, *The Georgian Cities of Britain* (Oxford, 1948).

Duckinfield, Bridget, 'Was Edward Knight Electrified?', Jane Austen Society, *Report for 1993*, pp. 20–21.

Edgeworth, Maria and Richard Lovell, *Practical Education* (2nd edn, London, 1801).

Eliot, George, 'Mr Gilfil's Love Story', in *Scenes of Clerical Life* (Everyman Library, London, 1910).

Ellis, Keith, *The Post Office in the Eighteenth Century* (Oxford, 1958).

Emsley, C., *British Society and the French Wars, 1793–1815* (London, 1979).

Fergus, Jan, *Jane Austen: A Literary Life* (Basingstoke, 1991).

Fordyce, James, *Sermons to Young Women* (7th edn, 2 vols, London 1771).

Gardiner, Dorothy, *English Girlhood at School* (Oxford, 1929).

Gay, John, *Fables* (reprint of 1727 and 1738 edns, California, LA, 1967).

Gilpin, William, *Observations on Several Parts of England, Particularly the Mountains and Lakes of Cumberland and Westmoreland, Relative Chiefly to Picturesque Beauty: Made in the Year 1772* (3rd edn, 2 vols, London, 1808).

Gilson, David, *A Bibliography of Jane Austen* (Oxford, 1982).

——, 'Jane Austen and Sir Egerton Brydges', Jane Austen Society, *Collected Reports, 1976–1985*, pp. 9–11.

——, 'Jane Austen's Books', *Book Collector*, 23 (1974), pp. 27–39.

Gore, John, 'Sophia Sentiment: Jane Austen?', *Collected Reports of the Jane Austen Society, 1966–1975*, pp. 9–12.

Grey, J. David (ed.), *Jane Austen's Beginnings* (Ann Arbor, MI, 1989).

Grundy, Isobel, 'The Early Women Writers: Lives and Times', *Female Spectator*, 1, no. 2 (1996), pp. 8–9.

Harper, Charles G., *The Brighton Road* (London, 1906).

——, *The Old Portsmouth Road* (London, 1895).

Harris, Stanley, *The Coaching Age* (London, 1885).

——, *The Old Coaching Days* (London, 1882).

Hembry, Phyllis, *The English Spa, 1560–1815* (London, 1990).

Hemlow, Joyce, *The History of Fanny Burney* (London, 1958).

——, ed., *The Journals and Letters of Fanny Burney* (4 vols, Oxford, 1973).

Hill, Constance, *Jane Austen: Her Homes and her Friends* (London, 1902).

Honan, Park, *Jane Austen: Her Life* (London, 1987).

Howe, Evelyn, 'Amateur Theatricals', Jane Austen Society, *Collected Reports, 1966–1975*, p. 121.

Hubback, J. H. and Edith C., *Jane Austen's Sailor Brothers* (London, 1906).

Jane Austen Society, 'George Austen's Crop Returns', *Report for 1994*, pp. 22–23.

——, 'Jane Austen's Christening Robe', *Collected Reports, 1966–1975*, pp. 36–37.

——, 'Jane Austen's Sampler', *Collected Reports, 1976–1985*, pp. 4–5.

Jarvis, William, 'Those Will Last us Some Time', Jane Austen Society, *Report for 1988*, pp. 19–23.

——, 'Who was John Lyford?', Jane Austen Society, *Collected Reports, 1949–1965*, pp. 216–18.

Jenkins, Elizabeth, 'The Marriage Registers at Steventon', Jane Austen Society, *Collected Reports, 1949–1965*, pp. 294–95.

——, 'Some Banking Accounts of the Austen Family', Jane Austen Society, *Collected Reports, 1949–1965*, pp. 58–61.

Johnson, Samuel, *Selected Writings*, ed. R. T. Davies (London, 1965).

Jones, Darryl, 'Frekes, Monsters and the Ladies: Attitudes to Female Sexuality in the 1790s', *Literature and History*, 3rd series, 4 (1995).

Jones, E. E. Duncan, 'Lydia Languish, Lydia Bennet and Dr Fordyce's Sermons', Jane Austen Society, *Collected Reports, 1949–65*, pp. 241–43.

Kent, Christopher A., 'The Imprudence of Being Prinny', *Persuasions*, 16 (1994), pp. 85–94.

Knox, Vicesimus (ed.), *Elegant Extracts: or Useful and Entertaining Passages in Prose* (2nd edn, London, 1785).

——, *Elegant Extracts: or Useful and Entertaining Pieces of Poetry Selected for the Improvement of Young Persons* (2 vols, London, 1801).

——, *Liberal Education* (London, 1781).

Koppel, Gene, *The Religious Dimension of Jane Austen's Novels* (Ann Arbor, MI, 1988).

Lane, Maggie, *A Charming Place: Bath in the Life and Novels of Jane Austen* (Bath, 1993).

——, *Jane Austen's England* (London, 1986).

——, *Jane Austen's Family, through Five Generations* (London, 1984).

——, *Jane Austen and Food* (London and Rio Grande, OH, 1995).

——, 'The Very Reverend Thomas Powys', Jane Austen Society, *Report for 1993*, pp. 8–12.

Lane, Margaret, 'The Insufferable Bad Manners of Mr Darcy', Jane Austen Society, *Collected Reports, 1976–85*, pp. 319–28.

Langford, Paul, 'British Politeness and the Progress of Western Manners: An Eighteenth-Century Enigma', *Transactions of the Royal Historical Society*, 6th series, 7 (1997), pp. 53–72.

Lascelles, Mary, *Jane Austen and her Art* (Oxford, 1939).

Lathom, Francis, *The Midnight Bell*, The Northanger Set of Horrid Novels (London, 1968).

Le Faye, Deirdre, 'Anna Lefroy's Original Memories of Jane Austen', *Review of English Studies*, new series, 39 (1988), pp. 417–21.

——, 'James Austen: Army Chaplain', Jane Austen Society, *Report for 1994*, pp. 8–11.

——, 'Jane Austen and her Hancock Relatives', *Review of English Studies*, new series, 30 (1979), pp. 12–27.

——, 'Jane Austen and William Hayley', *Notes and Queries*, 232, no. 1 (1987), pp. 25–26.

——, 'To Dwell Together in Unity', Jane Austen Society, *Report for 1989*, pp. 23–35.

——, 'Tom Lefroy and Jane Austen', Jane Austen Society, *Collected Reports, 1976–1985*, pp. 336–39.

——, ed., *Jane Austen: A Family Record* (London, 1989).

Lefroy, Anna, 'Anna Lefroy's Description of Steventon Rectory in the Rev. George Austen's Time', Jane Austen Society, *Collected Reports, 1966–1975*, pp. 245–48.

Lefroy, J. A. P., 'Jane Austen's Irish Friend: Rt Hon. Thomas Langlois Lefroy, 1776–1869', *Proceedings of the Huguenot Society of Great Britain and Ireland*, 23 (1979), pp. 148–65.

Lennox, Charlotte, *The Female Quixote: or The Adventures of Arabella* (London, 1752).

L'Estrange, A. G. (ed.), *A Life of Mary Russell Mitford: Related in a Selection from her Letters to her Friends* (London, 1870).

Lewis, Michael, *A Social History of the Navy, 1793–1815* (London, 1960).

Litz, A. Walton, 'The Loiterer: A Reflection of Jane Austen's Early Environment', *Review of English Studies*, new series, 12 (1961), pp. 251–61.

Lloyd, Christopher, and Anderson, R. C., *A Memoir of James Trevenen*, Navy Record Society, 101 (1959).

Locke, John, *Some Thoughts Concerning Education*, ed. J. L. Axtell (Cambridge, 1968).

Loudon, Irvine, *Death in Childbirth, 1800–1950* (Oxford, 1992).

MacKinnon, F. D., 'Topography and Travel in Jane Austen's Novels', *Cornhill Magazine*, 59 (1925), pp. 184–99.

Marcus, G. J., *Hearts of Oak: A Survey of British Sea Power in the Georgian Era* (Oxford, 1975).

Marshall, Dendy, *The British Post Office from its Beginnings to the End of 1925* (Oxford, 1926).

Martin, Joanna (ed.), *A Governess in the Age of Jane Austen: The Journals and Letters of Agnes Porter* (London and Rio Grande, OH, 1998).

Martin, Thomas Byam, *Letters and Papers of Admiral of the Fleet Sir Thomas Byam Martin* (ed. Sir Richard Vesey Hamilton), Navy Record Society, 1 (1903).

Mause, Lloyd de (ed.), *The History of Childhood* (London, 1974).

McKendrick, N., et al., *The Birth of a Consumer Society: The Commercialization of Eighteenth-Century England* (London, 1982).

Melville, Lewis, *Brighton: Its History, its Follies and its Fashions* (London, 1909).

Muir, Percy, *English Children's Books, 1600–1900* (London, 1954).

Murry, Ann, *Mentoria: or The Young Ladies Instructor* (3rd edn, London, 1782).

Namier, Sir Lewis, *The Structure of Politics at the Accession of George III* (2nd edn, London, 1957).

Newbery, John, 'ed.', *The History of Little Goody Two-Shoes* (London, 1765).

Nicolson, Nigel, *Godmersham Park, Kent* (Jane Austen Society, 1996).

——, *The World of Jane Austen* (London, 1991).

Nokes, David, *Jane Austen: A Life* (London, 1997).

Norris, W. B., *Jane Austen and Steventon* (Basingstoke, 1975).

O'Brien, 'Public Finance in the Wars with France, 1793–1815', in H. T. Dickinson (ed.), *Britain and the French Revolution, 1789–1815* (London, 1989), pp. 165–87.

Page, William (ed.), *The Victoria History of the Counties of England: Hampshire*, v (London, 1973).

Parkinson, C. N. *Trade in the Eastern Seas, 1793–1813* (London, 1937; reprint New York, 1969).

Pearson, Hesketh, *The Smith of Smiths* (London, 1984).

Peck, Louis F., *A Life of Matthew G. Lewis* (Cambridge, MA, 1961).

Percival, Thomas, *A Father's Instructions to his Children: Consisting of Moral Tales, Fables and Reflections Designed to Promote the Love of Virtue, a Taste for Knowledge, and an Early Acquaintance with the Works of Nature* (London, 1776).

Perry, Ruth, 'A Thinking Woman's Guide to British Imperialism', *Persuasions*, 16 (1994), pp. 95–106.

Pevsner, Nikolaus, 'The Architectural Setting of Jane Austen's Novels', *Warburg and Courtauld Institute Journal*, 31 (1968), pp. 404–22.

Piggott, Patrick, *The Innocent Diversion: A Study of Music in the Life and Writings of Jane Austen* (London, 1979).

Pitt, William, *The War Speeches of William Pitt the Younger*, (Oxford, 1940).

Porter, Roy, 'Sick People, Health and Doctors in Georgian England', *The Historian*, 21 (1988–89), pp. 3–6.

Pratt, H., *Eclectic Notes* (London, 1856).

Radcliffe, Ann, *The Mysteries of Udolpho* (London, 1794).

Reid-Walsh, Jacqueline, '"Entering the World" of Regency Society: The Ballroom Scenes in *Northanger Abbey*, "The Watsons" and *Mansfield Park*', *Persuasions*, 16 (1994), pp. 115–24.

Richards, R. D., 'The Lottery in the History of English Government Finance', *Economic History*, 3 (1934), pp. 57–76.

Richardson, Samuel, *The History of Sir Charles Grandison, in a Series of Letters* (6 vols, Oxford, 1931).

Rivers, Isabel, 'Shaftesburian Enthusiasm and the Evangelical Revival', in Jane Garnett and Colin Matthew, eds, *Revival and Religion since 1700: Essays for John Walsh* (London and Rio Grande, OH, 1993), pp. 21–39.

Roscoe, S., *Newbery – Carnan – Power: A Provisional Checklist of Books for Children and Young People, Issued under the Imprint of John Newbery and his Family, 1742–1802* (Harrow, Middlesex, 1966).

Rousseau, J.-J., *Emile* (Everyman Library, London, 1974).

——, *Lettre à d'Alembert sur les spectacles*, ed. M. Fuchs (Geneva, 1948).

Rupp, Gordon, *Religion in England, 1688–1791* (Oxford, 1968).

Sangster, Paul, *Pity My Simplicity: The Evangelical Revival and the Religious Education of Children, 1738–1800* (London, 1963).

Selwyn, David (ed.), *Jane Austen: Collected Poems and Verse of the Austen Family* (Manchester, 1996).

Shervington, Diana, 'Family Receipts', Jane Austen Society, *Collected Reports, 1976–85*, pp. 350–53.

——, 'Jane Austen's Music Books', Jane Austen Society, *Collected Reports, 1966–75*, 149–51.

Smyth, Charles, *The Art of Preaching: A Practical Survey of Preaching in the Church of England, 1747–1939* (London, 1940).

Southam, B. C. ed., *Jane Austen: The Critical Heritage*, i, *1811–70* (London, 1968).

Southam, Brian, 'A Source for Names?', Jane Austen Society, *News Letter*, 6 (1996).

——, '*Sir Charles Grandison* and Jane Austen's Men', *Persuasions*, 18 (1996), pp. 74–87.

Spencer, Jane, *The Rise of the Woman Novelist from Aphra Behn to Jane Austen* (Oxford, 1986).

Stafford, William, 'Religion and the Doctrine of Nationalism in England at the Time of the Revolutionary and Napoleonic Wars', in S. Mews, ed., *Religion and the National Identity* (Oxford, 1982), pp. 381–95.

Steeves, Harrison, *Before Jane Austen: The Shaping of the English Novel in the Eighteenth Century* (London, 1966).

Sterne, Laurence, *The Life and Opinions of Tristram Shandy, Gentleman*, ed. Graham Petrie (Harmondsworth, 1967).

Stovel, Bruce, 'A Nation Improving in Religion: Jane Austen's Prayers and their Place in her Life and Art', *Persuasions*, 16 (1994), pp. 185–96.

Sullivan, F. B., 'The Royal Naval Academy at Portsmouth', *Mariner's Mirror*, 63 (1977) pp. 311–26.

Summerfield, Geoffrey, *Fantasy and Reason: Children's Literature in the Eighteenth Century* (London, 1984).

Taylor, Norman and Hankinson, Alan, *Twelve Miles from a Lemon: Selected Writings and Sayings of Sydney Smith* (Cambridge, 1996).

Terry, Stephen, *The Diaries of Dummer: Reminiscences of an Old Sportsman, Stephen Terry of Dummer* (London, 1934).

The Spectator: Complete in One Volume (London, 1850).

Thomson, James, *The Works of James Thomson* (4 vols, London, 1773).

Thorne, R. G., ed., *History of Parliament: The House of Commons, 1790–1820* (5 vols, London, 1986).

Tomalin, Claire, *Jane Austen: A Life* (London, 1997).

Tomkins, J. M. S., *The Popular Novel in England, 1770–1800* (London, 1932).

Tucker, George Holbert, *A Goodly Heritage: A History of Jane Austen's Family* (Manchester, 1983).

——, *Jane Austen the Woman* (London, 1994).

——, 'Jane Austen's Topaz Cross', Jane Austen Society, *Collected Reports, 1976–1985*, pp. 76–77.

Valenze, Deborah, 'Charity, Custom and Humanity: Changing Attitudes towards the Poor in Eighteenth-Century England', in Jane Garnett and Colin Matthew (eds), *Revival and Religion since 1700: Essays for John Walsh* (London and Rio Grande, OH, 1993).

Vick, Robin, 'The Basingstoke Assemblies', Jane Austen Society, *Report for 1993*, pp. 22–25.

——, 'Court House at Overton', Jane Austen Society, *News Letter*, 8 (1997), p. 5.

——, 'The Royal Naval Academy at Portsmouth', Jane Austen Society, *Report for 1993*, pp. 24–28.

——, 'The Sale at Steventon Parsonage', Jane Austen Society, *Report for 1993*, pp. 13–16.

Vickers, William, *A Companion to the Altar* (Edinburgh, 1776).

Vincent-Buffault, Anne, *The History of Tears* (London, 1991).

Virgin, Peter, *The Church of England in an Age of Negligence, 1700–1840* (Cambridge, 1989).

Viveash, Chris, 'Jane Austen's First Royal Admirer', Jane Austen Society, *Report for 1994*, pp. 19–21.

——, 'Jane Austen and Kotzebue', Jane Austen Society, *Report for 1996*, pp. 29–31.

Wallace, Robert K., 'Jane Austen's Neglected Song Book', Jane Austen Society, *Collected Reports, 1976–1985*, pp. 121–25.

Walsh, J, Taylor, S. and Hayden, C., *The Church of England, c. 1689–c.1833: From Toleration to Tractarianism* (Cambridge, 1993).

Watson, J. Steven, *The Reign of George III* (Oxford, 1960).

Watts, Isaac, *Divine Songs: Attempted in Easy Language for the Use of Children* (London, 1715).

Wilberforce, William, *The Correspondence of William Wilberforce: Edited by his Sons* (2 vols, London, 1840).

Wiltshire, John, *Jane Austen and the Body* (Cambridge, 1992).

Wise, T. J. and Symington, J. A., eds, *The Brontës: Their Lives, Friendships and Correspondence* (4 vols, Oxford, 1932).

Woodforde, James, *The Diary of a Country Parson*, ed. John Beresford (5 vols, Oxford, 1981).

Young, B. W., 'Knock-Kneed Giants: Victorian Representations of Eighteenth-Century Thought', in Jane Garnett and Colin Matthew (eds), *Revival and Religion since 1700: Essays for John Walsh* (London and Rio Grande, OH, 1993), pp. 79–93.

Index

Illustrations are shown in bold